A Critical View

Carlos Fuentes

Edited by Robert Brody and Charles Rossman

 University of Texas Press, Austin

Requests for permission to reproduce material from this work
should be sent to Permissions, University of Texas Press,
Box 7819, Austin, Texas 78712.

LIBRARY OF CONGRESS CATALOGING IN PUBLICATION DATA

Main entry under title.
Carlos Fuentes, a critical view.
   (Texas Pan American Series)
   1. Fuentes, Carlos—Criticism and interpretation—Addresses,
essays, lectures. I. Brody, Robert. II. Rossman, Charles.
III. Series.
PQ7297.F793Z618   1982   863   82-10851
ISBN 0-292-71077-1

The Texas Pan American Series is published with the assistance
of a revolving publication fund established by the Pan American
Sulphur Company.

Carlos Fuentes

The Texas Pan American Series

Contents

Editors' Introduction   vii

Luis Leal
History and Myth in the Narrative of Carlos Fuentes   3

John S. Brushwood
Los días enmascarados and *Cantar de ciegos*: Reading the Stories
and Reading the Books   18

Richard M. Reeve
The Making of *La región más transparente*: 1949–1974   34

Lanin A. Gyurko
La muerte de Artemio Cruz and *Citizen Kane*: A Comparative
Analysis   64

Jaime Alazraki
Theme and System in Carlos Fuentes' *Aura*   95

Frank Dauster
The Wounded Vision: *Aura, Zona sagrada*, and *Cumpleaños*   106

Malva E. Filer
A Change of Skin and the Shaping of a Mexican Time   121

Roberto González Echevarría
Terra Nostra: Theory and Practice   132

Mary E. Davis
On Becoming Velázquez: Carlos Fuentes' *The Hydra Head*   146

Margaret Sayers Peden
Forking Paths, Infinite Novels, Ultimate Narrators   156

Gloria Durán
Dolls and Puppets as Wish-Fulfillment Symbols in Carlos
Fuentes   173

Merlin H. Forster
Carlos Fuentes as Dramatist   184

Manuel Durán
Carlos Fuentes as an Art Critic   193

George Gordon Wing
Some Remarks on the Literary Criticism of Carlos Fuentes   200

Chronology   217

Notes on Contributors   219

Editors' Introduction

Carlos Fuentes' renown as a writer in the Hispanic world has been firmly established for quite some time. He is truly a modern master. Each new novel stimulates a spate of critical reviews in newspapers and magazines from Mexico to Buenos Aires to Barcelona, as well as more considered reactions in scholarly journals and academic seminars. In the past quarter-century his steadily increasing reputation has transcended the boundaries of Mexican and even Hispanic literature at large. His growing prestige in the English-speaking world is what prompts us to offer this critical symposium, the first of its kind in English, on the work of Carlos Fuentes. All the essays are the result of original research; they have never before appeared elsewhere in print, and most have been prepared especially for this volume.

Luis Leal's opening essay presents its incisive analysis in a comprehensive manner which makes it perfect to introduce the rest. The reader not thoroughly familiar with Fuentes' work will be able to follow his literary trajectory under Professor Leal's critical guidance. We thought it best to present the next ten essays according to a pattern that roughly corresponds to the chronology of Fuentes' narratives themselves. Some of these articles afford fresh studies or new perspectives on single works, such as Richard Reeve's piece on *La región más transparente*, Jaime Alazraki's on *Aura*, Roberto González Echevarría's on *Terra Nostra*, Mary Davis' on *La cabeza de la hidra* and Margaret Sayers Peden's on *Una familia lejana*. Others present comparative studies of two or more narrative works of Fuentes, such as John Brushwood's essay on the collections of stories, *Los días enmascarados* and *Cantar de ciegos*, and Frank Dauster's on *Aura*, *Zona sagrada*, and *Cumpleaños*. Lanin Gyurko reaches outside Fuentes' canon for his comparative study of the influence of Orson Welles' film classic, *Citizen Kane*, on *La muerte de Artemio Cruz*. Malva Filer holds up two different genres for examination in her study of the interrelationships between *Cambio de piel* and the collection *Tiempo mexicano*. Gloria Durán traces the doll motif through several of Fuentes' works. The last three essays deal with aspects of Fuentes' work other than the narrative. Merlin Forster examines Fuentes' plays, while Manuel Durán and George Wing concern themselves with two different sides of Fuentes the critic.

These fourteen essays offer an extraordinarily wide range of topics and of methodological approaches. We believe this critical range and diversity reflect similar characteristics in the creative work of Carlos Fuentes, a man of formidable intellectual energy and curiosity who also happens to be one of Latin America's best writers.

This collection has been prepared with the reader of English especially in mind. Accordingly, we have asked our authors to quote from standard, readily available English translations of Carlos Fuentes' works whenever possible. In all other cases, whether of quotations from Fuentes or of quotations from other Spanish texts, the authors have prepared English translations of their references. These English translations are then cited by page number to the *original Spanish versions* in footnotes accompanying each article. We have not, however, asked the authors to avoid using Spanish. Hence, a given work is sometimes referred to by its Spanish title, and sometimes by its English title. Other Spanish words and phrases appear throughout these essays, particularly during analyses of Fuentes' style, when translation would rob the discussions of their point.

All quotations from the English translations of Fuentes' major novels are cited in the text by page number to the following editions, which are published in New York by Farrar, Straus, and Giroux:

Where the Air Is Clear, translated by Sam Hileman, 1960;
The Death of Artemio Cruz, translated by Sam Hileman, 1964;
Aura, bilingual edition translated by Lysander Kemp, 1975;
A Change of Skin, translated by Sam Hileman, 1968;
Terra Nostra, translated by Margaret Sayers Peden, 1976; and
The Hydra Head, translated by Margaret Sayers Peden, 1978.

Readers seeking fuller bibliographical information about the works of Carlos Fuentes, or about commentators on those works, should consult "An Annotated Bibliography on Carlos Fuentes: 1949–1969," by Richard M. Reeve (*Hispania*, 53 [October 1970]: 595–652), or Professor Reeve's forthcoming book-length bibliography of Fuentes, to be published by Scarecrow Press, which will cover the period 1949–80.

Finally, the editors would like to thank Ms. Bettie Cook, of the Plan II office at the University of Texas, for her frequent assistance, often at very short notice, in preparing the manuscript.

Carlos Fuentes

Luis Leal

History and Myth in the Narrative of Carlos Fuentes

I believe profoundly in societies that do not kill the past.
—Fuentes

Carlos Fuentes has stated that fiction can be useful in looking at history from new perspectives, and this is precisely what he has done in most of his novels, wherein he has presented a vision of history that cannot be gathered from the reading of history books. And, even more, he has reinterpreted history to present a new version of its development, a version reflected by a mind keenly conscious of the significance of past events in the shaping of the contemporary course of human events. In most of his novels he has gone one step further, to the recreation of history by the combination of realistic and mythical structures. The purpose of this essay is to trace the intrusion of history and myth upon Fuentes' narrative, and to observe how he has solved the technical problems involved and yet has managed to produce novels that are aesthetically satisfying.

The interaction between history and myth is a topic that has aroused the interest of the philosopher, the historian, and the literary critic since ancient times. Among contemporary historians Arnold Toynbee has stated, "History, like the drama and the novel, grew out of mythology, a primitive form of apprehension and expression in which . . . the line between fact and fiction is left undrawn." And if it is true, as he says, that "history cannot entirely dispense with the fictional elements," it is also true that fiction cannot entirely dispense with the historical elements and technique. "Lastly," says Toynbee, "the drama and the novel do not present fictions, complete fictions and nothing but fictions regarding personal relationships. If they did, the product, instead of deserving Aristotle's commendation that it was 'truer and more philosophical than history,' would consist of nonsensical and intolerable fantasies."[1]

One of the characteristics of the writers of the new Spanish

American novel, however, is the tendency to create pure fiction. One of the leaders of this trend has been Carlos Fuentes. He, like other new novelists (García Márquez, Cortázar, Rulfo, etc.), has moved in this direction by combining two narrative modes, the realistic (historical) and the mythical. Northrop Frye has discussed these two modes at length, and he differentiates between them by saying that realism is the art of verisimilitude, the art of implied similarity, and myth the art of implied metaphorical identity. However, he says that the presence of a mythical structure in realistic fiction "poses certain technical problems for making it plausible, and the devices used in solving these problems may be given the general name of *displacement*."[2]

The realistic-naturalistic fiction of the late nineteenth century degenerated into a documentary narrative in which the emphasis fell more upon historical documentation than on aesthetic elements. Novelists were more interested in giving historical facts than in creating reliable characters through whom they could present an artistic view of society. Carlos Fuentes, among others, acidly criticized the Spanish American realistic novel for the reliance it placed upon documenting the social life and describing the physical environment rather than presenting an integrated vision of that society. "Closer to geography than to literature," Fuentes said of those novels.[3]

In the novel of the Mexican Revolution Fuentes finds a change but not yet a complete break with the earlier fiction. He praises its authors for having introduced ambiguity in characterization, but deplores their dependence on historical fact, on documentation: "*Los de abajo, La sombra del caudillo*, and *Si me han de matar mañana*, over and above their possible defects in technique, and in spite of their documentary ballast, introduce an original note in the Spanish American novel: they introduce ambiguity. Because in the dynamics of the Revolution the heroes can be villains, and the villains can be heroes" (p. 15).

More important than the introduction of ambiguity is the introduction of myth. This innovation Fuentes finds in Juan Rulfo's novel, *Pedro Páramo*:

> There is in the Mexican novel of the Revolution, nevertheless, a forced lack of perspective. The subject matter found at close range burned the novelists' hands and forced them to use a documentary technique which, to a large extent, prevented them from penetrating into their own discoveries. It was necessary to wait until 1947 for Agustín Yáñez to write the first modern vision of Mexico's immediate past, in *Al filo del agua*,

and finally, in 1953 [1955], for Juan Rulfo to proceed, in *Pedro Páramo*, with the mythification of the situations, the characters, and the language of the Mexican countryside, thus ending forever the tendency, in the fiction of the Revolution, of using documentary materials. (pp. 15–16)

In *Pedro Páramo* Fuentes finds the thread that leads to the new Spanish American novel and, of course, to his own novels, which for the first time in Mexican letters mark the creation of a fiction that gives a mythified vision of history without sacrificing the aesthetic elements so essential in the new novel, and utilizing the most recent techniques of fiction writing. This he has done without abandoning realistic themes, for, aside from some fantastic elements in some of his works ("Chac Mool," *Aura, Cumpleaños*), his fiction is essentially realistic. He has, however, abandoned traditional realism, a realism that was expressed by psychological introspection or by the illustration of class relations, and has embraced the new realism based on the utilization of mythical structures and themes.

This change has not been abrupt. The title of his first book, *Los días enmascarados*, already referred to the Aztec myth of the five days at the end of the year when time stopped in readiness for the new life, the rebirth, the eternal return.[4] One of the stories, "Chac Mool," was inspired by a historical event, the 1952 Mexican exhibit in Europe which included the pre-Hispanic god of rain, the god whose mere presence brought on the rains, according to the Mexican newspaper account read by Fuentes: "The data from the sensational, journalistic account of the art exhibit focused my attention on a fact evident to all Mexicans: the living presence of old cosmological forms from a Mexico lost forever but which, nevertheless, refuses to die and manifests itself from time to time through a mystery, an apparition, a reflection."[5]

In "Chac Mool" Fuentes solves the problems of displacement by the use of realistic motifs: the action takes place in Mexico City and Acapulco; the two characters are clerks in a government office; and Filiberto, the protagonist, purchases a statue in a well-known market. To introduce historical fact, the technique of the diary, in which conversations are recorded, is used. The fictitious Filiberto writes about historical events in his diary, such as the introduction of Christianity after the Conquest and the effect it had on the conquered people. In the other aspect of the story Fuentes recreates the myth of the eternal return by the illusory transformation of the statue of the god which Filiberto had placed in the basement of his home. Chac Mool comes back to life with the coming of the rains and takes control of Filiberto's life, finally driving him to suicide. Thus Fuentes skillfully blends the historical and the mythical into a continuous narrative form which derives its structure from the tension created by the interaction between two different cultures, that of ancient Mexico, represented by Chac Mool, and the contemporary, represented by Filiberto.[6]

The technique used in this early story was soon perfected and expanded in the novel, and it has become the distinguishing mark of Fuentes' fiction. The models that he followed for this mode of fiction he found principally in William Faulkner, Malcolm Lowry, and Miguel Angel Asturias. From them he learned the art of utilizing myth, either as form or theme, in the context of the realistic novel. "In Faulkner, by means of the tragic search of everything left unsaid (of impossible writing) the myth of man unconquered in defeat, violence, and pain is born. In Lowry, it is not the class relations between Yvonne and the Consul that are important, but the myth of paradise lost and its tragic and fleeting representation in love" (*La nueva novela*, p. 19). The fiction of Asturias is important to Fuentes because it did not stop "with insignificant documentation, but found significance in myth and language. His method of giving a personality to the anonymous Guatemalan men was by endowing them with their myths and magic language, a language substantially related to that of the surrealists" (p. 24).

The novels of Fuentes, with some exceptions, can be considered as mythical approaches to history, or creative history. The success of his novels is due in great part to this use of myth to interpret history; for history, as Ernst Cassirer has observed, is determined by the mythology of a people. "In the relation between myth and history myth proves to be the primary, history the secondary and derived, factor. It is not by its history that the mythology of a nation is determined but, conversely, its history is determined by its mythology—or rather, the mythology of a people does not *determine* but *is* its fate, its destiny as decreed from the very beginning."[7] In his first major work, *Where the Air Is Clear*, Fuentes presents a mythical history of Mexico City and its four million (1958) inhabitants. The characters who represent the historical aspects of the novel are products of the Mexican Revolution and, at the same time, representative of Mexican society during the 1950s: Robles, the revolutionary turned into a conservative banker; his wife Norma, the social climber who marries for money; Zamacona, the brooding intellectual who becomes one of the sacrificial victims; the decadent Bobó, from the new upper middle class; Gabriel and Beto, the displaced *braceros* back from California; and the Ovando family, the impoverished representatives of the dethroned porfiristas.

In the novel, the representatives of its mythological counterpart are found in the old lady Teódula Moctezuma and Ixca Cienfuegos. They symbolize Mexico's past, a mythical Mexico that still survives and believes in ritual, in sacrifice as the only way for man to redeem himself. The Mexican people have been chosen by the gods to feed the sun and keep it moving so that mankind can survive. Without sacrifices this would be impossible. Displacement in the novel takes the form of parallel action in the fictional world representing history. Both Norma and Zamacona are sacrificed to modern gods. This revelation of the mythical nature of Mexican history is accomplished by the use of image and metaphor. The characters, the description of the city, the action, and the plot are all expressed by uniting two worlds, that of the remote past and that of the present. The interaction between the characters representing both cultures becomes the central technique of displacement. Mythical episodes are used by Fuentes to give his work a pure, literary quality. History and myth balance each other to give the novel equilibrium. The introduction, spoken by Ixca, offers the key to the structure of the novel. Mexico City, as the modern version of ancient Tenochtitlán, is the center of the world, "el ombligo del mundo," the umbilical cord of the world, a sacred city. "The center, then," states Mircea Eliade, "is pre-eminently the zone of the sacred, the zone of absolute reality" (p. 17). In his introductory speech Ixca says, in reference to Mexico City, "City of the three umbilical cords. . . . Incandescent prickly-pear. Eagle without wings. Serpent of star. . . ."[8] The image of the eagle and the serpent, related to the myth of the founding of the city, is repeated in the first chapter. Ixca also tells about the myth of the creation of the sun, which can be found in Sahagún. The god that became the sun was a humble god, a leprous god, "a leper, yes, the one who threw himself into the furnace of original creation to feed it. He reappeared transformed into a star. A motionless star. A single sacrifice, even if exemplary, was not enough. It was necessary to have a daily sacrifice, a daily feeding of the god, in order for him to shine, to keep moving, to feed others" (p. 254). This passage prepares the reader for the sacrifices in the historical world that are to follow.

Ixca Cienfuegos also questions whether the historical present is better than the mythical past. In a confrontation between Ixca and Zamacona, who represent the past and the present/future, Ixca asks the latter, "Is this cheap, petty power, bereft of greatness, better than that power which had, at least, the imagination of allying itself with the sun and the real, permanent, and inviolable cosmic powers?" (p. 361). Like Tolstoy's *War and Peace,* the novel ends with an essay (one of many in the book) in which Fuentes recapitulates the history of Mexico City from its foundation to the present, neatly balancing the mythical introduction. The technique of opposing two antagonistic elements (historical fact and myth), similar to that used in "Chac Mool," gives the novel tension. Irony, of course, cannot be ruled out. Fuentes himself has stated that the novel reflects "the excessive and somewhat mythical preoccupation [of the members of the 'Mexicanist' movement] over nationality, ancestry, and patrimony rampant at the time in Mexico."[9]

The Death of Artemio Cruz and *Aura* were published the same year, 1962. While in the latter work the mythical predominates, the historical elements surface in *The Death of Artemio Cruz,* but even here mythical aspects are evident in the structure of the subject matter and the characterization of the hero.[10] After writing the social history of Mexico City in *Where the Air Is Clear,* Fuentes continued and recreated the history of modern Mexico in *La muerte de Artemio Cruz,* approximately from the era of Santa Anna to the 1950s, with the period of the Revolution receiving the most attention. Historical personages are freely mentioned, as are historical facts and events. However, this is not a novel of the Revolution, as are those by Azuela or Guzmán. On the contrary, it is a mythified novel similar to Rulfo's *Pedro Páramo* or García Márquez's *Cien años de soledad.* It is also a history, as seen through the eyes of Artemio Cruz, an unreliable character. The mythical structure is found in the use of the myth of the descent into hell to depict the career of the hero who recreates in his mind, just before he dies in the hospital, the twelve most important moments of his life. These twelve days represent the twelve circles of Dante's Inferno, as well as the twelve months of the year. This mythical motif is repeated in the temporal structure of the novel, in which the narrative time covers the last twelve days in the life of Artemio. Comparing *Pedro Páramo* and *La muerte de Artemio Cruz,* Djelal Kadir has said, "Insofar as these works transcend to ritual and oracular image, they synchronize rhythm and pattern, thus becoming *myth* and archetype. The archetype re-enacted by these works is Mexican history become myth."[11]

In the novels published after *The Death of Artemio Cruz—Aura* (1962), *Zona sagrada* (1967), *Cambio de piel* (1967), *Cumpleaños* (1969), *Terra Nostra* (1975), *La cabeza de la hidra* (1978), and *Una familia lejana* (1980), Fuentes has given more emphasis to the mythical than to the historical, but never forgets history or the social condition, which underlies all his fiction.

In *Aura* he gives expression to the historical and the mythical by creating characters symbolic of both forms of thought. Two male characters—Llorente, a general of the period of Maximilian's Empire, and Felipe Montero, a young contemporary historian who later turns out to be the general's double—represent the historical component in the novelette. For balance, there are two additional archetypes, both female—Consuelo (Llorente's wife and a sorceress), who conquers time by recovering her youth, and Aura, her counterpart as a young girl. Consuelo accomplishes her transformation by performing an ancient rite, the sacrifice of a goat. "Through the paradox of rite, profane time and duration are suspended" (Eliade, p. 35). The creation of the mythical character(s) sprang from history. Fuentes has said that the inspiration for this novelette came to him in the Chapultepec Castle Museum where he saw a picture of Carlota, the young and beautiful wife of Maximilian. Later he found another picture of her in her coffin, "wearing the nightcap of a little girl: the Carlota who died insane, in a castle the same year that I was born, the two Carlotas: Aura and Consuelo."[12] As in an earlier story, "Tlactocatzine, del Jardín de Flandes" (in *Los días enmascarados*), the sacred place in *Aura* is reduced to a mansion in Mexico City. In the short story the mansion, dating from the time of Maximilian, was located on Puente de Alvarado, a street associated with the conquest of Mexico. In *Aura* the mansion is on Doncelas Street, in the old part of town which dates from the colonial period.

If the myth of the city or mansion as a sacred center is presented unconsciously in *Where the Air Is Clear* and *Aura* (the author has never mentioned this myth in referring to these novels), it is indeed intentional in *Zona sagrada* beginning with the obvious title. To leave no doubt in the mind of the critic, Fuentes has said regarding this novel, "I am very much interested in the mythical zone, and when I speak about a sacred zone, of course, I am establishing a territory, an enclosure. It is the very old idea of the temple, the temple as a defense against epidemics, against sieges . . . it is the place that is all places and in which myth has its seat." More significantly, he adds:

> *Zona sagrada* interests me a great deal as an experiment.
> The point of departure of the novel lies in the relations of a
> great movie star, a charmer who is at the same time a mother,
> with her son. The importance of living myths . . . is that they

really never end. . . . I found an equivalent in Apollodorus, for example, in the *Greek Myths* of Robert Graves: the true conclusion of the myth of Ulysses, the one that Homer does not relate.[13]

The mythical elements are to be found not only in the external structure, but also in the thematic content, the relation between Claudia Nervo, the mother, and Guillermo (Guillermito, Mito), the son. The first chapter, entitled "Happily Ever After," narrates the myth of the sirens in the story of Ulysses, but in a present-day context—a football game which is played in a sacred zone, the staked field. In the last chapter, "Zona sagrada," Mito is transformed into a dog. While in *Where the Air Is Clear*, the beginning and the ending of the novel are in opposition (mythical introduction, historical epilogue), in *Zona sagrada* they are parallel. The novel ends with the episode of Circe, the sorceress who changes men into animals. Since Claudia Nervo is associated with Circe, the transformation of Mito into a dog becomes a part of the myth.[14] As a theme, the myth of Ulysses has also been recreated, for the characters represent Penelope and her son Telemachus. Even Telegonus, the son of Ulysses and Circe, is there, under the name of Giancarlo. The historical part of the novel is based on the life story of a famous Mexican movie star.

Cambio de piel (*A Change of Skin*) signals a change of attitude in Fuentes as a novelist. Here for the first time he builds a purely fictional construct. He has said, "The only way to understand this novel is to accept its absolute fictitiousness. . . . It is a total fiction. It never pretends to reflect reality. It pretends to be a radical fiction, up to its last consequences" (*Homenaje*, p. 38). By radical fiction Fuentes means that some of the action is not realistic, that is, carried out by the fictitious personages, but rather invented or imagined by them and presented as if they had actually lived through the experiences. Also, the narrator could be a character imagined by one of the personages, such as Javier. Displacement is achieved by introducing numerous realistic motifs, starting with the date when the events in the novel begin—Palm Sunday, April 11, 1965. On that precise, historical day two couples leave Mexico City in a Volkswagen on their way to Veracruz, taking the old road and stopping at Cholula, where the rest of the action takes place, at a second-rate hotel and inside the great pyramid. This, however, is preceded by a prologue with a displacement function and in which the destruction of Cholula by Cortés and his men is recreated. Fuentes has said that in the novel there is an intention to fictionalize: "Therefore, the scenes in Prague or in New York, which in appearance are presented in a realistic manner, are some of the fictitious scenes of the novel. In the same way the narration about events in the past, which I also include, convert the history [story] into fiction, into pure imaginative narration" (*Homenaje*, p. 40).

Regarding his intention to present the empirical facts as fiction and the imaginative elements as real, Fuentes adds, "I believe that this is what gives unity to the novel, a novel that at times appears to have no unity . . . : History [*la historia*] is fiction, reality is apocryphal, the New Testament was written by Jules Verne" (*Homenaje*, p. 40). Therefore, the theme of the novel is the mythification of history. In history there is no progress, time has been abolished, as in myth. This explains why the violent acts occurring at the end of the novel—the death of Franz and Elizabeth in the center of the pyramid, the killing of Isabel by Javier in the hotel—are structured in parallel trajectories with some of the most violent events in history: the destruction of Cholula by Cortés, the massacre of the Jewish people. "There is," Fuentes has said, "a paralyzed history [in the novel]. There is a history converted into a Statue of History referring to itself, returned to itself. There is no historical progress, that is what the novel is trying to say: there is no eschatology, there is only pure perpetual present" (*Homenaje*, p. 41). History, therefore, becomes myth when its events are repeated and become a rite. "The gesture acquires meaning, reality, solely to the extent to which it repeats a primordial act" (Eliade, p. 5). In the novel, a number of ceremonial acts are repeated.

The myth of the sacrifice to feed the gods found in *La región más transparente* appears in *A Change of Skin* also. Two of the four principal characters, Franz and Elizabeth (the two foreigners) are sacrificed to the gods at Cholula by being buried alive as a result of an earth tremor. This sacrifice occurs inside the old pyramid, precisely in the "center of the pyramid, the navel, the cord from which the labyrinthic beehive of the *Gran Cu* [Great Temple] of Cholula is born."[15] The importance of the use of the pyramid as a motif has been pointed out by Fernando Benítez, who wrote, "Outside of Octavio Paz, no other writer has meditated about the fact that the pyramid is the geographical form of our country, from the coast to the volcanoes; that it has been the highest expression of the sacred for the last two thousand years."[16] In spite of its mythical nature, the novel has a social message. Fuentes himself has said, "The creative process of *Cambio de piel* was born with the intention of documenting all the vulgarity, the excesses, and the impurity of our world" (*Homenaje*, p. 47).

Cumpleaños (1969) is the first novel by Carlos Fuentes in which the action takes place outside of Mexico. It is also the first that transcends his preoccupation with Mexican history and myth, being based, instead, on European history and myth. However, there are, as in his first novels, both historical and fictitious personages. Also, in *Cumpleaños*, as in previous novels, there is a sacred place, where the theologian, accused of heresy, takes refuge to escape his enemies. This place becomes a bedroom in a contemporary London house where the old man, Nuncia, and the boy live. Both places merge into one labyrinthian residence symbolic of the universe. In the bedroom the old man remembers his past life which extends back to the thirteenth century, since he is the reincarnation of Siger de Brabant, a theologian from the University of Paris persecuted for his ideas by Etienne Tempier and Thomas Aquinas. In the present he is George, an architect in London, husband of Emily and father of Georgie, whose tenth birthday they are celebrating that day. This novel is the least realistic of those written by Carlos Fuentes; yet, even here, there are historical elements in the plot, in the artistic motifs, and in the description of the milieu: books read by the boy (*Treasure Island, Black Beauty*, etc.); realistic descriptions of London; the life story of Siger de Brabant (1235–1281/84), the French philosopher who came into conflict with his colleagues at the University of Paris, was accused of heresy and fled to Italy where he built a refuge at Orvieto but was, nevertheless, killed by an insane servant or secretary. He had accepted Averroism in its entirety, which drew the opposition of Albertus Magnus and Aquinas, and the condemnation of Bishop Tempier of Paris in 1270 and 1277. His ideas, especially his rejection of the real distinction between essence and existence, form the theme of *Cumpleaños*, although, here again, irony could very well play a part. The myth of immortality in the novel takes place through ceremony. The pact carried out between successors, from Siger to George, is sealed in blood. The distinguishing mark is a wound on the arm. This ceremony, like all mythical ceremonies, is repeated each time that the reincarnation takes place. The idea of a center or lack of a center as symbolic of order and chaos is also present:

> I never imagined that the dinner was to be served in the garden without a roof,[17] in the center of that hexagon that could be an imitation of the patio of the great romanesque castle of Capodimonte. But Emperor Frederick conceived it as an absolute center; it could be possible to lose oneself in the circular chambers, but finally one would end up in that pivot of the building. Here, on the other hand, nothing can persuade me

that the garden, like the whole building, is not eccentric: no one could find the point of its formal equilibrium.[18]

In this passage ceremony and sacred place come together, giving the novel a mythical tone. As Eliade has said, "Just as profane space is abolished by the symbolism of the Center, which projects any temple, palace, or building into the same central point of mythical space, so any meaningful act performed by archaic man, any real act, i.e., any repetition of an archetypal gesture, suspends duration, abolishes profane time, and participates in mythical time" (p. 36).

In *Cumpleaños* all traces of Mexican history have disappeared, but the same is not true of *Terra Nostra, The Hydra Head*, and *Una familia lejana*. *Terra Nostra* deals with the history of Spain during the Renaissance period, but in the second of its three parts, "The New World," the subject is pre-Hispanic Mexican myth and the conquest of the land.[19] By the use of history and myth Fuentes attempts to apprehend the meaning of the age of Philip II and, therefore, the destiny of the Hispanic people, both in the Old World and in the New World, and even in "The Other World," the title of the last part of the novel. As a technique he superimposes several historical periods, going back to the age of Tiberius and pre-Hispanic Mexico, and forward to the end of the century. By this means he creates a new historical reality which, although it is purely fictional, is based on empirical fact and real historical personages. The figure of Philip II, however, becomes an archetype, since it is a composite of several Spanish rulers who have exercised absolute power, and it is this obsession with power on the part of Philip II that gives universality to the novel.[20]

Terra Nostra opens with a scene in Paris on a precise day, July 14, 1999, and ends there on the last day of the same year, the end of the millennium. Thus, the entire narrative partakes of the apocalyptic myth. In the second part, Fuentes creates a space in the New World where historical, fictional, and mythical characters act their roles in a purely mythical time. But even here are found the ever-present historical references, presented with the techniques of fiction. "In *Terra Nostra* Hispanic culture is thereby viewed in terms of universal myth and history, for which it becomes the exemplary case" (Kerr, p. 92). Fuentes, himself, in his long essay *Cervantes o la crítica de la lectura*, has given the key to the historical background that structures the novel. "Surely," he says, "the present essay is a branch of the novel, *Terra Nostra*, that has kept me busy during the last six years. The three dates that constitute the temporal references in the novel can very well serve to establish the historical background of Cervantes and *Don Quijote*: 1492, 1521, 1598."[21] These dates, which appear in the novel's last chapter (Spanish ed., p. 779) are related to both the New World and Philip II. Since the mythical elements are just as important as the historical, the novel becomes a *summa* that attempts to give the reader a total view of Hispanic culture,[22] a view that only a novel can convey, for as Fuentes has said recently, "Many things history does not see, or reason, logic, science do not see, are perhaps seen by novelists. There are things only Dostoevski sees. You do not find it in the history books."[23]

In his last two novels, *The Hydra Head* and *Una familia lejana*, history plays a secondary role to fiction. A current event, the struggle for the control of Mexican oil deposits, is the subject of the first, a detective novel. The protagonist, Félix Maldonado, is patterned after a present-day mythical archetype, James Bond.[24] In *Una familia lejana* Fuentes tries to establish, in a minor way, the cultural relations between Mexico and France, as he had done with Spain in *Terra Nostra*, but in a more personal way. The protagonist, Mexican archeologist Hugo Heredia, husband of a French girl, Lucie, and father of two sons, Víctor and Antonio, delivers a long, historical essay in the first part of chapter 20. At the same time, the author identifies himself with the protagonist, thus becoming the hero of his own novel. Branly, fictitious friend of the narrator, tells him, "Tomorrow is November 11, Fuentes. It is your birthday."[25] (Fuentes *was* born on that day.) Then, on the last page of the novel, the reader discovers what he had already suspected. The narrator says to himself, "Heredia. You are Heredia" (p. 214).

Mythical elements in this novel, which predominate, are given expression by means of several devices: the association of the characters with the mythical past of Mexico (Lucie as La Llorona); the use of the double (Heredia and "Heredia"); the use of motifs related to the "Día de Muertos" (November 2); and, especially, the use of fiction itself as myth. Mexico is a country, says the narrator, "which has not resigned itself to banish death from the realm of the living" (p. 157). Above all, there is the myth of the cycle life-death-life. The action takes place in November, symbolic of the autumnal period of life when there is a brief pause before death; the title of the last chapter is "Verano de San Martín" (Indian Summer). Branly says, "For your other life, Fuentes, for your adjacent life. Think what it could have been and celebrate with me your anniversary and the arrival of Indian Summer with a wine that postpones death and offers us a second vintage" (p. 205). In this novel Fuentes also treats a topic at the center of his thinking: the past, history, must be preserved, for it is only by knowing the past that the present and the future can be understood. Hugo Heredia has chosen the profession of archeologist in order to preserve the past. "You had a past and you can't remember it. Try to identify it in the little time you have left or you shall lose your future" (p. 187). In a recent interview Fuentes said that "man is responsible for his history, including the past. He's also responsible for his past. It was not made by God, it was made by him. He must understand it. And I think that you can only have a present and a future if you have a past, if you remember your past, if you understand your past. Historical amnesia, I think, leads society to the greatest blunders of not understanding itself and not understanding others."[26]

In general, then, it can be said that the narrative of Carlos Fuentes swerved strongly at the beginning toward the historical, and strongly after 1969 toward the mythical, but never in a pure form. His idea of history, however, is not that of the empirical historian, but goes beyond fact to a reality that includes myth and legend, so important in the shaping of the Mexican mind. Quite often he fills the lacuna of the historical record with oral history, legend, or myth. His fiction reveals that history itself often becomes myth; and although it is based on a collection of facts, the mythical consciousness of the author is ever present before the facts are verbalized. Certainly, in Mexico the most famous historians have been myth makers; their works are composed of fact and fiction, as are novels. This is true from the early chronicles of Bernal Díaz del Castillo which, in spite of their title, are a combination of fact and myth. The same can be said of works by Fray Servando Teresa de Mier, Vicente Riva Palacio, and José Vasconcelos. Their authors are, more than true historians, true verbal artists, as is Carlos Fuentes, who said to Bill Moyers, "Beyond the knowledge of science, of logic and politics, there is the knowledge we call imagination. And it is only achieved through a verbal structure we call a poem or a novel. This is an important thing to keep alive in order to compensate for many of the voids of history" (p. 4). "The knowledge we call imagination" is greatly nurtured by myth. And although the employment of myth and history in the same work of fiction, as pointed out by Frye, poses a problem for the novelist, that problem has been solved by Fuentes by the use of displacement, that is, the balancing of history with myth to prevent the novel from becoming a social document, as is common with some of the novels of the Revolution, or, on the other hand, from losing verisimilitude. By fusing history and myth in his novels (and the same can be said of his play, *Todos los gatos son pardos*), Fuentes has been able not only to reveal important aspects of the mind and character of the Mexican people, but also to project his own hopes and aspirations, one of which is not to kill the past.

Notes

I wish to thank my wife, Gladys, for her help in the preparation of this paper.

1. Arnold J. Toynbee, *A Study of History* (New York: Oxford University Press, 1947), pp. 44, 45.
2. Northrop Frye, *Anatomy of Criticism* (Princeton: Princeton University Press, 1957), p. 136.
3. Carlos Fuentes, *La nueva novela hispanoamericana* (Mexico: Joaquín Mortiz, 1969), p. 9. My translation, as are all quotations from this work.
4. See Mircea Eliade, *The Myth of the Eternal Return or, Cosmos and History* (Princeton: Princeton University Press, 1971).
5. Fuentes interview in Emmanuel Carballo, "Carlos Fuentes (1928)," *Diecinueve protagonistas de la literatura mexicana del siglo XX* (Mexico: Empresas Editoriales, 1965), p. 428. My translation.
6. It is not our purpose here to deal with other aspects of the story, such as its symbolic meaning or fantastic nature.
7. Ernst Cassirer, *Mythical Thought*, vol. 2 of *The Philosophy of Symbolic Forms* (New Haven: Yale University Press, 1955), p. 5.
8. Carlos Fuentes, *La región más transparente* (Mexico: Fondo de Cultura Económica, 1958), p. 11. My translation, as are all quotations from this edition.
9. Luis Harss and Barbara Dohmann, *Into the Mainstream* (New York: Harper and Row, 1967), p. 292.
10. René Jara C., however, sees the novel as falling entirely within the mythical tradition. See his study, "El mito y la nueva novela hispanoamericana. A propósito de *La muerte de Artemio Cruz*," in *Homenaje a Carlos Fuentes*, ed. Helmy F. Giacomán (New York: Las Américas, 1971), p. 170; hereafter cited as *Homenaje*.
11. Djelal Kadir, "Same Voices, Other Tombs: Structures of Mexican Gothic," *Studies in Twentieth Century Literature*, 1 (Fall 1976): 52.
12. See Gloria Durán, "La bruja de Carlos Fuentes," in *Homenaje*, p. 249. There seems to be an inconsistency in Fuentes' statement. Carlota died January 19, 1927, and he was born November 11, 1928.
13. Fuentes interview in Emir Rodríguez Monegal, "Carlos Fuentes," in *Homenaje*, pp. 48, 49. My translation, as are all those from this interview.
14. For an interpretation of this metamorphosis as a symbolic death see Suzanne Jill Levine, "*Zona sagrada*: una lectura mítica," *Revista Iberoamericana*, 40 (1974): 622. See also Andrés O. Avellaneda, "Mito y negación de la historia en *Zona sagrada*," *Cuadernos Americanos*, 30, no. 175 (1971): 239–248; also, in *Homenaje*: Severo Sarduy, "Un fetiche de cachemira," pp. 261–273; A. Brehil Luna, "Despliegue de mundos en

Zona sagrada," pp. 355–363; Jaime López-Sanz, "Carlos Fuentes: *Zona sagrada,"* pp. 377–383.

15. Carlos Fuentes, *Cambio de piel* (Mexico: Joaquín Mortiz, 1967), p. 369. My translation.

16. Fernando Benítez, Prólogo to *Novelas,* by Carlos Fuentes, vol. 1 of *Obras completas* (Mexico: Aguilar, 1974), p. 36. My translation.

17. In Spanish the word *cielo* (*jardín sin cielo*) means not only sky and heaven but also roof.

18. Carlos Fuentes, *Cumpleaños* (Mexico: Joaquín Mortiz, 1969), p. 49. My translation.

19. Carlos Fuentes, *Terra Nostra* (Mexico: Joaquín Mortiz, 1975). Translated by Margaret S. Peden with the same title (New York: Farrar, 1976).

20. See Lucille Kerr, "The Paradox of Power and Mystery: Carlos Fuentes' *Terra Nostra,"* *PMLA,* 95 (January 1980): 91–102.

21. Carlos Fuentes, *Cervantes o la crítica de la lectura* (Mexico: Joaquín Mortiz, 1976), p. 36. My translation.

22. See José Miguel Oviedo, "Fuentes: Sinfonía del Nuevo Mundo," *Hispamérica,* 6, no. 16 (April 1977): 19–32, and Margaret S. Peden, *"Terra Nostra:* Fact and Fiction," *The American Hispanist* 1, no. 1 (September 1975): 4–6.

23. "The Many Worlds of Carlos Fuentes," *Bill Moyers' Journal* (transcript of PBS program aired June 19, 1980), p. 4.

24 Carlos Fuentes, *La cabeza de la hidra* (Mexico: Joaquín Mortiz, 1978). Translated by Margaret S. Peden, *The Hydra Head* (New York: Farrar, 1978).

25. Carlos Fuentes, *Una familia lejana* (Mexico: Ediciones Era, 1980), p. 204. My translation, as are other quotations from this work. Forthcoming is Margaret Sayers Peden's translation, under the title *Distant Relations.*

26. "The Many Worlds of Carlos Fuentes," p. 4.

John S. Brushwood

Los días enmascarados and *Cantar de ciegos*: Reading the Stories and Reading the Books

Several characteristics of Carlos Fuentes' fiction vie for attention in any analytical consideration of his work. Stylistic virtuosity, the joining of past and present, what it means to be Mexican, his commentary on the human estate, all readily come to mind. On the other hand, if one thinks in terms of what actually happens to a reader during the experience of a Fuentes narrative, the desire to know how the story turns out is as important as any other facet of the act of reading. Most of Fuentes' short stories, individually analyzed, show how skillfully he uses the enigma code.[1] However, it is possible to reveal certain details of the narrative process, in separate stories, and still not describe adequately the experience of reading either *Los días enmascarados* or *Cantar de ciegos* as a total work, leaving the stories in the order of presentation.[2] In other words, the experience of reading a volume of stories is different from reading the stories separately. It seems possible that, by combining analysis of individual stories with analysis of each volume as an entity in itself, one may illuminate some aspects of Fuentes' narrative technique and gain some insight into the success or failure of volumes of stories.

Fuentes' short fictions show him to be rather traditional in his penchant for resolution, even though the resolution may sometimes take for granted an element of unreality. Very often his stories end with an ironic twist reminiscent of de Maupassant or O. Henry. This resemblance is largely confined to the denouement, of course, since Fuentes' narration (the act of transforming the story material into the narrative we read) is highly original, complicated, and variable from story to story with regard to details of technique.[3] Manipulation of focus is probably the most important technical phenomenon in Fuentes' narration. The relationship of focus to denouement may be an important key to understanding how his fictions work or, one might say, how his narratives ensnare the reader and turn him around at the end. Four of the six stories in *Los días enmascarados* and five of the seven in *Cantar de ciegos* depend in some fashion on a first-person narrating voice; however, these voices function in very different ways, and they also relate to the denouement in different ways. In stories not dependent on a first-person voice, the focus of narration is still related, in important ways, to the resolutions of the narratives.[4]

"Chac Mool," the first story in *Los días enmascarados*, has become a kind of Fuentes showcase because it combines the author's predilection for fantasy and his interest in joining two periods of time—or better, showing how the past continues to be a vital factor in the present.[5] Another characteristic—the recurrence of first-person narration—may be added to this complex of typical attributes. The framing narration is by a first-person voice who reads the diary of a deceased friend, thereby conceding the focus of narration to the friend. However, the framing device acquires uncommon importance at the end of the story, when the first, apparently external, narrator reasserts his role and discovers (reveals) that his friend, who died by drowning, has been replaced in his own house, by a vitalized idol—Chac Mool, a pre-Hispanic deity associated with rain.

Unquestionably, readers who know something about Acapulco and the pre-Hispanic pantheon approach "Chac Mool" with a richer "repertory" (Wolfgang Iser's term—see n. 3) than those who do not. However, Fuentes employs several strategies (also Iser's term) that compensate for the possible deficiency in shared information; the most effective is identification with the first narrator, with whom the reader may experience the second narrator's diary account. By sharing the first narrator's experience, one may feel himself a participant in the narration, and is puzzled by the circumstance just as the first narrator is puzzled.

The story early poses the question of why Filiberto drowned. Once within the diary, a reader may expect to discover the explanation. In fact, the basic narrator takes an important step toward satisfying reader curiosity when, halfway through the story, Narrator One observes that, at a certain point in the diary, Filiberto's handwriting shows signs of nervousness or instability, although it has been normal up to this point. This advice is an essential communication between Narrator One and the text reader (really coreader of the diary, along with Narrator One), since the printed text cannot reflect such a change. Reader anticipation is heightened, but the diary itself never answers the question. It is the first narrator, to whom the reader is attached from the beginning, who resolves the enigma. Narrator One is no longer just the reader of a diary, no longer a simple carrier of the enigma; he becomes an essential actor in the narrative. When he arrives at his friend's house with the body of the deceased, he is greeted by a Chac Mool who has displaced his owner as master of the house. The resolution incorporates fantasy, but it is no less a resolution. According to Tzvetan Todorov's exposition, the fantastic changes into the marvelous at the end of this narrative.[6] At this point, the reader shares knowledge with Narrator One, but not experience.

It is commonplace—one might even say it is fashionable—to comment on Fuentes' theme of *mexicanidad* (Mexicanness). This theme is certainly apparent in "Chac Mool," since the story refers to both Mexican myth and contemporary Mexican life. Dauster makes an even more specific observation with reference to the appearance of Chac Mool at the end of the story. The former idol now seems not only to be a living person in charge of the house, he also uses some of the most vulgar symbols of contemporary society (lipstick, cheap lotion, etc.). Dauster takes this awkward contrast to be a commentary on modern Mexico.[7] A similar concern for *mexicanidad* characterizes two of the remaining five stories in *Los días enmascarados*, "Tlactocatzine, del Jardín de Flandes" and "Por boca de los dioses." Genevieve Mary Ramírez discusses the book as if it were divided into two parts, one consisting of three stories clearly referring to Mexico, and another of the remaining three stories that, for different reasons, seem almost generically distinct from the first group.[8] Ramírez comments on the latter set and points out all the possible ways they may refer to Mexico. She also notes that the basically "Mexican" stories are the first, third, and fifth. In other words, the two sets are intercalated, not separated. As a result, the experience of reading *Los días enmascarados* as a total, logically arranged literary work is quite different from reading individual stories or one of the two sets.

"En defensa de la Trigolibia" comes as something of a shock, in sequence following "Chac Mool." It is a political allegory on the values cultivated and defended by two superpowers, presumably the United States and the Soviet Union. It has few characteristics of fiction or even of narrative. Its tone is that of commentary on world politics, with humor afforded by clever wordplay that satirizes bureaucratese but tends to negate its own effect by becoming tiresome before the end of the piece.[9] Generically, it is more like satirical political journalism than a story. Ramírez says it is "written almost in an essay style."[10] It has neither characterization nor story line; phenomena such as focus of narration or story-time versus narrative-time are not relevant to this allegorical sketch. Its final sentence-paragraph, "This is the defense of Trigolibia," actually constitutes a summary of what has gone before. It does signify, of course, that what has gone before is the writer's interpretation of the defense of Trigolibia; it is the way he sees the situation.

This disembodied voice confronts the reader at the outset: "Trigolibia is the supreme value of the Nusitanians" (p. 30). A reader just finishing "Chac Mool" has already been removed from the intimate association with Narrator One, in the first story. However, the exterior commentator of "En defensa de la Trigolibia" most likely jars one into a different mood altogether. In the first few moments of reading, the play on terminology may suggest the possibility of some kind of fantasy, but the allegory becomes apparent shortly thereafter. The repertory activated in the experience of this essay is totally different from that of "Chac Mool." "En defensa de la Trigolibia" calls for no knowledge at all of Mexico or of mythology; its referent is global politics. Furthermore, the commenting voice need make no effort to compensate for the lack of information on the part of the reader; he assumes the referent is familiar to all. His strategy, therefore, is to satirize by inventing a system of terms, and oversimplifying a complex situation. The reader must change his own strategy completely. Instead of using the procedures necessary for participation in a joining of reality and fantasy, he must now adapt to an interpretation of allegory, in a manner that is more intellectual than emotional. In the process, one becomes aware of Fuentes' commitment to political awareness, and this fact relates back to "Chac Mool" by emphasizing the aspects of the first story that suggest social commentary. The end of the second piece—that is, the final sentence quoted above—emphasizes its expository nature, for it is in no way a denouement. In one sense, it is typical of the author, an excellent essayist who frequently becomes discursive in his fiction. However, it is certainly not typical of Fuentes to terminate narratives on an anticlimactic note.

The nonfiction character of "En defensa de la Trigolibia" initiates the seesaw experience created by intercalating two sets of stories in *Los días enmascarados*. The third story, "Tlactocatzine, del Jardín de Flandes" belongs to the same group as "Chac Mool." Indeed, once the reader has adjusted to the second story, the third will be just as great a shock in its turn. A diary account is the form of the narration; however, unlike "Chac Mool," this story does not use a narrator intervening between the diary and the reader. Consequently, the effect is different; narrator and reader both conform to different strategies. To a considerable degree, the reader of "Tlactocatzine" is in a position corresponding to that of Narrator One in

"Chac Mool." The difference between the two stories is especially important in the denouement because the story of the diarist is left incomplete (we do not know what happens to him). As a result, full emphasis falls upon the unusual circumstance that he narrates.

The narrator is given the opportunity to live in an old house in Mexico City. Within the house, closed off from the hubbub of contemporary city life, the diarist finds himself confronting a fantastic situation involving the presence of a ghostly woman. The denouement reveals that she is the Empress Carlota. A number of clues precede this revelation, but the practiced reader of Fuentes cannot be certain at what point he knows her identity, because the study naturally reminds one of *Aura* and of Fuentes' interest in the period of the French Intervention. What is absolutely certain is that the repertory makes requirements of the reader similar to those in the experience of "Chac Mool." Interestingly enough, the intercalation of "En defensa de la Trigolibia" may well add a dimension to the reading of "Tlactocatzine." Since the political satire tends to point out the author's interest in the state of society—even with the reflective reference to "Chac Mool"—one is now tempted to look for similar significations in "Tlactocatzine." They are far from plentiful. It is possible to read the total situation as referring to the struggle between the persistence of the past and the willful destruction of it by modern Mexico, because the diarist speculates that the owner of the house may have bought it with demolition in mind. The strategies used in the narration do not encourage the search for such meanings. The focus of narration leaves one confronting the event that established the identity of the mysterious woman and, at the same time, asking if there is a rational explanation of her presence. The empress' name is apparent over a coat of arms; as for the rest of it, one must choose between the uncanny and the marvelous, as Todorov defines the alternatives. The diarist makes no choice; he just states the case. Obviously, this experience of fiction alters a reader's set of procedures for understanding, as contrasted with the political satire that immediately precedes.

The seesaw swings again with the reading of "Letanía de la orquídea," though the change is not as abrupt. This fourth story begins with an unidentified voice speaking to an unidentified hearer: "Mira, vé: ya empezó el invierno" ("Hey, look: winter has already begun") (p. 51). One surmises, on the basis of the language, that the speaker is not Mexican. The next sentence reveals that the scene is Panama. For the rest of the story, a voice outside the narrative relates events from the viewpoint of Muriel, a character based on the tropical prototype. Fuentes' prose style is mildly disconcerting because of its heavily rich imagery. No one would deny the author's lyricism, of course, but the richness in "Letanía" seems unusual: "Visceral light, yellow as rain when it mixes with dust. . . . The windows shook until sounding a reticent dactyl" (p. 51). Readers may well not know how to react to this stylistic procedure—could it be some kind of parody on intensely poetic prose? The portrait of Muriel develops schematically as he does typically tropical things. An allegory is taking shape, though one may not be immediately aware that such is the case. The stylization of Muriel crosses into fantasy when his coccyx sprouts an orchid. The clincher of the allegory comes when he decides to grow orchids for sale and the plant itself causes his death. So Muriel is Panama; the highly figurative language which may have been disconcerting early in the experience of "Letanía" now becomes part of the façade that disguises the Panamanian tragedy. As one finishes this story, a return to the beginning of it is almost inevitable because the interpretation comes to fruition only at the end, and one needs to reconsider the process of development. The referent is in fact not so much life in Panama as it is the Panamanian circumstance. The reader participates not by understanding Muriel as a human individual, but as the symbol of a political situation. Fuentes has avoided an essay, but the narrative clearly indicates the importance of social commentary in his work.

The element of fantasy is the most important similarity between "Letanía de la orquídea" and the story preceding it, as well as the one following it. For the reader of the volume *Los días enmascarados*, fantasy probably establishes itself, by the time these four stories are read, as the primary characteristic in common. Only "En defensa de la Trigolibia" requires accepting an entirely different referent and an equally different set of strategies. The fifth story, "Por boca de los dioses," reaffirms the importance of fantasy and returns to the referential complex of "Chac Mool" and "Tlactocatzine." It involves awareness of contemporary Mexico, of modern art as contrasted with the art of the colonial period, and the present-day influence of the pre-Hispanic past, in the person of Tlazol, a goddess who is associated with filth and also—in a way very important to this short story—with cleaning up and forgiveness or expiation.[11] Suggestions of allegory abound—modern impatience with tradition; modern Mexico assassinates its colonial self and the pre-Hispanic component persists, even dominates the present; the protagonist descends into the nether regions. The actual experience of reading "Por boca de los dioses," however, does not exact quite so systematic an interpretation.

The narration is by a first-person voice who is the main character in the story but who tells it retrospectively. This time of narration is important because he appears to recount his own demise as the denouement: "Tlazol embraced me in a spasm devoid of sighs. The knife remained there, in my guts, like a pivot out of control, turning by itself while she was opening the door to the caravan of minute sounds of wings and snakes that were gathering in the hall, and twisted guitars and internal voices were singing" (p. 82). If one assumes the factual existence of the I-narrator, he must have survived this incident. Therefore, our strategy must be capable of dealing with fantasy on more than one level.

The narrator describes himself in a nightmarish situation at the beginning of the story—an introduction in parentheses. Then the narration appears to turn to real events occurring in a real world, related in the first person by Oliverio. However, this apparently real-life situation requires an adjustment on the reader's part when Oliverio removes a pair of lips from a Tamayo painting. They accompany him and speak; the narration becomes almost as if Oliverio were narrating the story of the lips. This phenomenon must be appreciated along with the intervention of Tlazol who, in the final scene, functions in an apparently definitive way; however, the scene ends in a kind of surrealistic suggestiveness that recalls the opening scene, which was parenthetical. Among other considerations, one must keep in mind the possibility of a Tamayo painting brought to life. "Por boca de los dioses" is the least resolved of all the stories in this volume, except insofar as resolution may take the form of dissolution.

The final story, "El que inventó la pólvora," returns to social commentary of the direct kind. It is a satire on consumerism—a society in which products are less and less durable and the motto is "use everything," until the cataclysm occurs. The narration is in first person by the only character, the survivor, who relates the process of deterioration retrospectively, then shifts to present tense as he tells how he sits on the shore of a newly made sea and starts a fire by friction. The impact of this denouement must have been considerably greater in 1954, when the volume was published, than it is today, since the possibility of such a return to primitivism has now become a commonplace. The commentary on consumerism, on the other hand, seems even more vital now.

As a work of fiction, "El que inventó la pólvora" is of little consequence. It is more of a satirical essay, lightly fictionalized—or one might better say "narrationized." Its referent is a widely recognized social phenomenon that requires no special strategy to compensate for a difference in repertory between author and reader. In this respect, it is probably the most effective communication, over a wide range of readership, of all the stories in this first volume. It certainly is not a typical Fuentes story, however, and it ends the book on a rather strange note. (One might, of course, note the intensification of destruction, followed by a new beginning, and so make an association with *Terra Nostra*.)

Any one of the stories in *Los días enmascarados* is noteworthy for the steadily increasing intensity that the narrators manage to achieve—even in those pieces that belong only marginally to the short story genre. The volume, experienced as a single work, does not share this characteristic with its six separate parts. Quite to the contrary, the volume destroys the possibility of increasing intensity by persistently changing the functions the reader has to perform, so creating a seesaw effect of reading two kinds of texts and moving back and forth from one kind of experience to another.

Since the effect of increasing intensity—concluding, in five of the six selections, with an ironic denouement—depends largely on the manipulation of narrating voice and focusing eye, it is interesting to speculate on how else the stories might have been arranged. If one were to take into account the active role of the reader (the extent to which the reader becomes an accomplice of the narrative strategy), "Chac Mool" would undoubtedly be the opening story if one wished to begin with the highest degree of involvement. "Por boca de los dioses" would follow, the "Tlactocatzine" would be third. This ordering would have the disadvantage of running counter to the increasing intensity of each individual story, since the reader of this proposed sequence would feel less and less involved. However, it would have the advantage of preparing the reader to go on to the other stories which might be arranged with "Letanía" first, followed by "El que inventó la pólvora" and then by "En defensa de la Trigolibia," so continuing to move toward less reader involvement by increasing the intensity of author commentary. There is a strong argument for omitting the last three stories in the above scheme—that is, for publishing them separately or for identifying them as a separate unit in the volume with the other three. In such a case, the three stories in the first group might be placed in the reverse order to allow reader involvement to increase during the experience of reading the unit of three. Placed in whatever order, in a separate section, the satirical pieces would still retain much of the chief effect of their presence: to emphasize certain social concerns and to needle reader consciousness with respect to the author's social awareness as communicated in the other three stories.

When Richard Reeve characterized *Cantar de ciegos* as "the

mosaic world of modern Mexico," he clarified this allusion to the book's "Mexicanness" by saying that Fuentes had earlier dealt with the question of "what is Mexico?" and, in the new volume of short stories, turned to a consideration of "who are the Mexicans?"[12] This explanation sheds some light on the tendency to think of this book as a kind of turning point in Fuentes' work, even though his narratives from the first to the latest have much in common with each other.[13] There does appear to be a shifting emphasis—a change somewhat less radical than a transition—in Fuentes' work, with regard to the extratextual reality that constitutes the referent. One might say that the persistence of the pre-Hispanic past in the present becomes a less important factor than it was in *Los días enmascarados* and *La región más transparente;* on the other hand, *Cambio de piel* alone is enough to prove that he has not totally given up his concern for "what is Mexico?" in spite of the obvious universality of that novel. The sense of difference between the first volume of short stories and *Cantar de ciegos* is created partially, of course, by some shift in emphasis; however, the difference is even more clearly the result of greater consistency in the author's act of communication, manifested especially in the intricate manipulation of narrating voice and focusing eye. While these strategies do vary in some ways from story to story, *Cantar de ciegos* does not challenge the reader, with respect to "accepted procedures," as frequently as *Los días enmascarados* does.[14]

"Las dos Elenas," the first story in *Cantar de ciegos*, takes its title from the names of two women, mother and daughter, whose contrasting characters affect the actions of the first-person narrator.[15] Elena Senior is an attractive, middle-aged, society matron. Her daughter, the wife of the narrator (Victor), is a caricature of "modern" woman, in her dress, her interest in art and her advanced ideas. She even proposes that she needs to live with two men in order to feel fulfilled. She insists on discussing this possibility when she and Victor have Sunday dinner with her parents.

The narrative actually begins with a commentary by Elena Senior on this particular point. Addressing herself to Victor, she lists her daughter's manias and pronounces all of them at least minimally acceptable up to, but not including, her explaining to her father that she wishes to live with two men. Although Victor is the first-person narrator, this fact does not become apparent until after his mother-in-law has stated her case. The procedure is a very important aspect of the narration because the negative attitude toward Elena Junior is established by her mother, not by Victor. The story develops then in the words of Victor, and it is mainly a characterization of Elena Junior through his reporting of what she said and did. The narration is in the past tense until the last paragraph when Victor, having taken leave of Elena Junior, who is going to spend the entire day painting, turns his MG toward Lomas de Chapultepec, where he knows Elena Senior and his own fulfillment are awaiting him. The irony of the denouement is greatly intensified by the fact that Victor never criticizes his wife. His mother-in-law's exposition, at the beginning of the narrative, establishes the base of Elena Junior's characterization and, incidentally, of her own. One may not notice immediately that her initial statement reveals her as very permissive, though there is a point beyond which she will not allow the façade to be further destroyed.

"La muñeca reina," the story that follows, is quite different in theme, but the strategies are largely the same. A first-person narrator tells the story and also sees what happens. A change of tense is important because it moves the narrative voice from a retrospective position outside the narrative to an actually present time within the narrative. Such a change has an important effect in the last paragraph of "Las dos Elenas," so it is hardly surprising in "La muñeca reina," except possibly because it is even more important.

The story tells of the narrator's wish to relive the time of a cherished memory—the friendship of a young girl. Taking advantage of a clue, he finds her (now after many years), but the discovery is grotesque. The change of tense makes the idealized memory a past reality; the actual discovery is in the present: "I ring the bell. The shower becomes heavier and insistent" (p. 47). The sense of actuality created by the use of present tense comes close to making the narrator a dual personage. In the years intervening between the memory and the present, he has become the seeker rather than the sought. "La muñeca reina" has some of the spectral quality that characterizes three of the stories in *Los días enmascarados*; however, the denouement does not depend in any way on fantasy. It is rather a case of irony created by reality asserting itself.

The exterior reality to which "Fortuna lo que ha querido" refers is notably similar to that of "Las dos Elenas." An artist successful in both painting and sexual conquest is characterized by inconstancy in both fields of endeavor. The subtlety of the narration is extremely attractive. The narrator does not refer to himself in a first-person form until the last paragraph of the narrative; however, his involvement with the protagonist may be felt earlier. The position of the narrator is outside the narrative, and the voice speaks in third person, but a tense change suggests a relationship that is not wholly omniscient. After providing the reader with a good deal of information about the painter—all in simple past tense—the narrator suggests a closer relationship with the artist by inserting a present perfect: "He left the hotel after the '63 exhibit. *Alejandro has always suffered feverish collapses* after presenting a new collection of paintings . . ." (p. 54, my emphasis). Given this relationship between narrator and protagonist, it is appropriate that readers not know the reason for all of the latter's actions. At the end of the narrative, he turns away from a meeting with a possible conquest. The narrator does not explain why he makes this decision. It may be that he esteems this particular woman too highly to settle for just another affair; it may be that he fears rejection. Presumably the narrator does not know. He reaffirms the relationship already suggested by saying at the end of the narrative: "A while ago I reminded him that he was already thirty-three and that he should think of marrying someday. Alejandro just looked at me sadly" (p. 68).

With the exception of some place names, there is little to identify the first three stories in *Cantar de ciegos* as Mexican. The first and third have as their referents two internationally recognizable aspects of modern society; "La muñeca reina" may appear less familiar because of its grotesque denouement, but it could happen in many other countries as well as in Mexico. "Vieja moralidad," the story that follows "Fortuna lo que ha querido," is slightly more specific in its cultural reference, though not enough to require special preparation or compensation through particular strategies. The protagonist's grandfather is a *republicano juarista*, a clergy-baiter. The old man's heterodoxy allows him to maintain a female companion in his rural home. He is also the guardian of Alberto, his adolescent grandson, who narrates the story. A covey of sanctimonious aunts rescue Alberto from this morally reprehensible environment. They take him to the city (Morelia) and install him in the home of one of the good ladies, where he may be properly educated, both formally and informally. In the course of events, he becomes his aunt's youthful lover, with a second aunt somewhat less than figuratively waiting on the sidelines.

The first-person narrator functions in this story very nearly as he does in "Las dos Elenas." The narrative begins with the grandfather speaking, actually berating the seminarians who pass by his house. He reveals his anticlericalism and then the narrating role of Alberto becomes apparent. The boy tells what happened up to and including the amorous overtures of the second aunt. By this time, one is already appreciating the irony of the switch in moral rectitude. But still another irony is to come. Alberto reports that he wrote a letter to his grandfather, asking him to come to get him becai se Alberto thinks there is probably more morality in the country. Then switching to present tense—just as Victor does, in another intrafamily moral irony, at the end of "Las dos Elenas"—Alberto says, referring to the letter, "Pero todavía no me decido a mandarla" (p. 91). The ironic situation, therefore, is left intact—in progress, one might say—even though it functions as a resolution in the narration.

"El costo de la vida," the fifth story, presents the first real problem regarding the aesthetic consistency—or equanimity—of *Cantar de ciegos*. Both repertory and strategies are different from those of the preceding selections. The protagonist, a member of the lower middle class, economically speaking, has more problems than he has means of coping with them. A series of unpredictable circumstances leads to his death. The narrative offers no problem of credibility if one is reasonably aware of circumstances in contemporary Mexico; less informed readers may find much that seems strange (e.g., the deplorable economic condition of a school teacher), and may become so involved with this novel-of-customs aspect of the story that they may lose contact with its more general significance. The narrating voice uses third person, and though large parts of the story are focused from the point of view of Salvador, the protagonist, the effect is very different from the ironies produced by the first-person narrator position. In "El costo de la vida," the irony is created by outside reporting of contingent circumstance.

Analysts of Fuentes' short stories are generally not very kind to "El costo de la vida." Reeve says "being a chapter of the unpublished novel *La patria de nadie*, this story never achieves an identity or unity of its own"; Dauster considers it "the least successful story in the volume"; Ramírez calls it "the weakest story in the collection."[16] When removed from the context of the volume in which it appears, "El costo de la vida" seems not to deserve such negative regard. The extratextual reality to which it refers recalls the author's *La región más transparente*. The narration accomplishes all that is normally required of a successful short story. The narrative begins at a point in the basic story where the character and circumstance of Salvador may be rapidly glimpsed. A basic conflict is established early—between the depressing demands of his struggle to survive and his desire to live with some degree of joy. The events that take place subsequently all intensify this conflict. He asks for assistance from his father; he brings back memories of his Golden Age, in conversation with his old buddies. He picks up a girl and goes with her to Chapultepec (a clear evasion of obligation to his sick wife); he gets a job as a taxi driver in order to meet his financial obligations.

This careful intensification of the basic conflict adds impact to the denouement when, in an act of friendship, Salvador meets death unexpectedly. In the words of a less skillful writer, this story might indeed have become too diffuse. Fuentes employs several strategies that avoid this result. The principal one is unabashed control of the narration, even to the point of summarizing scene—in addition, of course, to the expected balancing of scene and summary. For example, a paragraph from the episode of reminiscing with friends takes this form:

> And Alfred remembered that when he graduated the family gave him the old car and everyone went out to celebrate in a big way by club-hopping all over the city. They were very drunk and Raimundo said that Alfredo didn't know how to drive and he began to struggle with Alfredo to let him take the wheel and the car almost turned over at a traffic circle on the Reforma and Raimundo said that he wanted to throw up and the door opened and Raimundo fell out onto the street and broke his neck. (p. 103)

Given the impact of "El costo de la vida" when it is read and analyzed outside the context of *Cantar de ciegos*, one may reasonably conclude that the adverse reaction it creates when read as part of the volume is probably caused by the eccentricity of its strategies (as compared with the preceding stories).

The sixth story, "Una alma pura," recovers the equilibrium and appears to be universally admired. The narrating voice belongs to the protagonist's sister. He was a Mexican expatriate who went to Europe because the cultural ambience of his native country was not to his liking. The past tenses in the preceding sentence indicate the time situation in the narrative. The sister addresses her brother, now deceased. The present time of the story is the hours immediately preceding her departure by plane to accompany his remains on the return trip to Mexico. Her reminiscence, addressed to him, narrates the story of his chaotic and ultimately unsatisfying life abroad. Naturally, it happens in the past, and is so differentiated in her narration. She tells his story and characterizes herself. Leaving the reminiscence and focusing on the present, just before departing, she is granted the opportunity to know—via a letter handed her—the last words of her brother. Ironically, in spite of the relationship she claims, she destroys the letter without reading it. The narration again is resolved but, in a sense, unfinished.

The final work in *Cantar de ciegos*, "A la víbora de la mar," is really best thought of as an addendum to the volume. Its length sets it apart because it runs to seventy-three pages; the other six pieces average about twenty pages each. The repertory is somewhat different from the short stories, although its referent is a cosmopolitan society. The shipboard scene (a vacation cruise) suggests the ship-of-fools motif, and the dedication to Julio Cortázar recalls his *Los premios*. Fuentes' story is focused on the innocence of a Mexican woman tourist and the confidence men who deceive her and take her money. The story, carefully worked out by an external narrator using third person, is a tragicomedy. Riotously funny at times, the narrative ends with the woman's tragic realization that she has been exploited not only in terms of her money but, even worse, in terms of her affection. The fact that "A la víbora de la mar" functions as an addendum to the volume does not mean it is inferior to the rest. It stands separately, might well have been published separately; it is fortunate for the aesthetic consistency of *Cantar de ciegos* that it appears last.

Considering *Cantar de ciegos* as a total experience, one might argue reasonably that "El costo de la vida" is poorly placed. Using the same rationale that suggested the rearrangement of stories in *Los días enmascarados*, a preferable ordering of the later volume might be "Las dos Elenas," "Vieja moralidad," "Fortuna lo que ha querido," "Una alma pura," "La muñeca reina," "El costo de la vida," and "A la víbora de la mar" still in the place appropriate to a separate work. This ordering gives maximum importance to similarities among the first-person voice strategies. However, the rearrangement would not make as much difference as in *Los días enmascarados*, because the variations in repertory and in strategy are much less abrupt and less radical in *Cantar de ciegos*.

The suggested rearrangement of *Los días enmascarados* would make the book seem a mature work; the present ordering creates the impression of a series of exercises. By placing together the stories in which Fuentes' narrative ingenuity is most effective, the reader's aesthetic act in realizing the narratives is more complete. The remaining pieces could still establish the author's expository gift without distorting the experience of the first set. Since the stories depend on the author's use of first-person narration, ironic revelation, and a combination of the two, these strategies function most efficiently when the reader understands, throughout a series of stories, that he is expected to use the same procedures in appreciating the experience. To a very considerable extent, this purpose is accomplished in *Cantar de ciegos*. Indeed, the rearrangement of the second volume, suggested above, might be more beneficial to "El costo de la vida" as a separate unit than it would be to the volume as a whole (its merits would be freed from the restraints imposed by the use of strategies that are different from those in the selections preceding and following). The other selections (always excluding "A la víbora de la mar" because of its length as well as for the narrative procedures used) enjoy a common set of strategies, based on Fuentes' handling of the narrating voice and the focusing eye, that create consistency in the aesthetic experience. These stories are, for the same reasons, closely akin to the three selections in *Los días enmascarados* that can unquestionably be called short stories.

Notes

1. I refer to Roland Barthes' "hermeneutic code," as he uses the term in *S/Z* (New York: Hill and Wang, 1974).
2. Carlos Fuentes, *Los días enmascarados* (Mexico: Los Presentes, 1954), *Cantar de ciegos* (Mexico: Joaquín Mortiz, 1964). Page references made parenthetically within the text are to these editions.
3. The concepts and terminology used here with regard to narration are based upon—and for the most part borrowed from—Gérard Genette's "Discours du récit," now available in an English translation by Jane E. Lewin: Gérard Genette, *Narrative Discourse* (Ithaca, N.Y.: Cornell University Press, 1980). I have adopted the Lewin translation of Genette's terminology. Concepts and terminology of reader theory, as used here, are influenced mainly by Wolfgang Iser's *The Act of Reading* (Baltimore: Johns Hopkins University Press, 1978).
4. In this connection, it is interesting to note Richard Reeve's analysis of the manipulation of character in Fuentes' earliest published short story, "Pastel rancio." See Richard Reeve, "Un poco de luz sobre nueve años oscuros: los cuentos desconocidos de Carlos Fuentes," *Revista Iberoamericana*, 72 (July–September 1970): 475. Manipulation of characters in Fuentes' work is often affected by careful handling of who is telling and who is seeing in the act of narration.
5. Frank Dauster makes an interesting contrast between Fuentes and Cortázar on this point. He observes the same interest on the part of both writers, with metaphysical emphasis in Cortázar and social emphasis in Fuentes. See "La transposición de la realidad en las obras cortas de Carlos Fuentes," *Kentucky Romance Quarterly*, 19, no. 3 (1972): 301–315.
6. Grossly oversimplifying Todorov's ideas, one may say that the fantastic endures so long as one wavers between a natural explanation and a supernatural explanation of what appears to be outside the limits of reality. Beyond this point of uncertainty, the fantastic turns into the uncanny (if a natural explanation is accepted) or into the marvelous (if a

supernatural explanation is accepted). Tzvetan Todorov, *The Fantastic* (Ithaca, N.Y.: Cornell University Press, 1975).

7. Dauster, "La transposición," pp. 302–303.

8. Genevieve Mary Ramírez, "Evolution of Thought in the Prose Fiction of Carlos Fuentes" (Ph.D. diss., UCLA, 1977), p. 86.

9. Dauster ("La transposición," p. 305) points out that even if the piece is taken only as a verbal *tour de force*—without even considering the exaggeration of the allegory—it falls of its own weight.

10. Ramírez ("Evolution of Thought," p. 87) offers a full interpretation of the allegory.

11. C. A. Burland, *The Gods of Mexico* (New York: G. P. Putnam's Sons, 1967), pp. 134–135.

12. Richard Reeve, "El mundo mosaico del mexicano moderno: *Cantar de ciegos*, de Carlos Fuentes," *Nueva Narrativa Hispanoamericana*, 1, no. 2 (September 1971): 79–86. Specific definition of the transition is on p. 86.

13. Ramírez ("Evolution of Thought," p. 246) sees the volume as a transition from Mexican concerns to universality. It should be noted, however, that themes are not likely to become more universal than those of the three satirical stories in *Los días enmascarados*.

14. Wolfgang Iser's term "strategies" refers to J. L. Austin's three main conditions for the success of a performative utterance, the second of which is "procedures accepted by both" (author and reader, in the case of prose fiction). See Iser's *The Act of Reading*, especially p. 69. Although one could hardly accuse Fuentes of using procedures not accepted by his reader, in *Los días enmascarados* the ordering of the stories requires the reader always to shift from one set of procedures to another.

15. The "doubling" in this story is discussed by Joseph Chrzanowski in "The Double in 'Las dos Elenas' by Carlos Fuentes," *Romance Notes*, 18, no. 1 (1977): 1–5.

16. Reeve, "El mundo mosaico," p. 86; Dauster, "La transposición," p. 308; Ramírez, "Evolution of Thought," p. 237.

Richard M. Reeve

The Making of *La región más transparente*: 1949–1974

It is the practice of some authors, especially poets, to rework and polish their writings over a period of many years while continuing to make additions and corrections to future editions. Not so with Carlos Fuentes, who seems to produce a literary work and to leave it immediately in the hands of the reader and critic, while moving on to his next endeavor. Thus the case of the composition and reworking of *La región más transparente* over a period of a quarter of a century is an anomaly worthy of close examination. It is relatively easy to establish the concluding date of this process, 1974, which saw the publication of the novel in the Aguilar edition of his *Obras completas* with its apparent final revisions. But my choice of 1949 as the year when Fuentes began the novel is much more arbitrary.

The inspiration for a panoramic novel about life in the modern metropolis no doubt arose in Carlos Fuentes' mind with his experiences as a child moving from one large city to another: Washington, D.C.; Rio de Janeiro; Santiago, Chile; Buenos Aires; and finally to Mexico City. Also, by the age of fifteen he had read John Dos Passos' *Manhattan Transfer*, marveling at its style and structure.[1] The year 1949 is decisive, however, since it marks the beginning of Fuentes' active publishing career and includes among other key but little known writings a short story set in New York City and a series of articles about the cultural milieu of the Mexican capital. Finally, a later date in the mid-1950s might also be defended. With the publication of his collection of short stories, *Los días enmascarados* (1954) Fuentes could dedicate himself in earnest to his novel, and indeed fragments of the work began appearing in magazines and newspapers in the years 1955 and 1956. Beginning in the fall of 1956, Fuentes, as the fortunate recipient of a fellowship from the Rockefeller-sponsored Centro Mexicano de Escritores, was able to devote himself full time to *La región más transparente*. The novel itself, after much speculation and controversy, finally appeared in the spring of 1958.

Mexico in the 1950s

Carlos' father, Rafael Fuentes Boettiger, embarked upon a long and distinguished career as a diplomat in the 1920s and served with every president of Mexico from the Revolution to the 1950s. The main action of *La región más transparente* transpires in the years 1951 and 1953, during the presidency of Miguel Alemán, Mexico's 58th president and the first civilian since Juárez to hold the office for a full term. Mexico was passing through a period of unprecedented change and growth. Alemán, who was known as the businessman's president, remains to this day the center of impassioned controversy, but during the fifties his dynamic personality and colossal enterprises seemed to bedazzle the multitude. Skyscrapers began dotting the skyline, the magnificent new campus of the National University rose up on a former lava bed, and North American tourists arrived in increasing numbers. Mexico was becoming more international with the influx of Spanish refugees in the late thirties and other European nationals in the forties.

During the decade of the fifties the country was governed in the main by two presidents named Adolfo: Ruiz Cortines and López Mateos. Fuentes has characterized them as belonging to the faceless center; neither radical like Cárdenas nor rightist like Alemán.[2] *La región más transparente* was published in 1958, an election year. The 6th of July elections were characterized as the quietest in history; women voted for a president for the first time. López Mateos received 6,767,754 votes; Luis Alvarez, his PAN opponent, obtained 705,303, while Miguel Menéndez López, the presidential candidate for the Communist Party, received fewer write-in votes than comic actor Cantinflas.[3]

Mexico's population continued to spiral at the astonishing and alarming rate of 3 percent annually. The capital city was estimated to have 5,448,218 inhabitants. Classroom and teacher shortages were so severe that only 41 percent of school-age children could attend school. Illiteracy was estimated at 50 percent.

In cultural achievements, 1958 saw increasing literary activity. It was labeled the year of the novel and *La región más transparente* the novel of the year.[4] Poetry was less fortunate and only Octavio Paz's excellent *La estación violenta* mitigated a disastrous year for the genre. José Luis Martínez published the important but controversial *Antología del ensayo mexicano*. Critics lamented the decline of the theater in Mexico although attendance was higher than ever. Of the eighty plays presented during the year only twelve were written by Mexican playwrights. During 1958 Luis G. Basurto's *Cada quien su vida* would reach one thousand consecutive representations and actress Rita Macedo (Fuentes' fiancée) and Ernest Alonso combined to produce *Intermezzo* by Jean Giraudoux. Emmanuel Carballo counted forty-one books of fiction published in the country during 1958. He believed Fuentes to be the best of the new writers and Martín Luis Guzmán, who had just published *Muertes históricas*, to be the best of the veterans.[5] Luis Spota's *Casi el paraíso* remained the best seller of the year with its third and fourth printings and a total of 21,000 copies in three years, a very sizable figure for a Latin American novel in those days.

Foreshadowing of *La región más transparente* in Fuentes' Early Writings

In contrast to many Mexican writers of the early part of this century, Carlos Fuentes did not grow up nor spend any appreciable time in the rural countryside. Those authors, most of whom were eventually drawn to the city (Azuela, Yáñez, Rulfo), had rural experiences from their childhood and youth to draw upon. Others (Martín Luis Guzmán) would live in the interior during the emotion-filled years of the Revolution and would often return to this unique occurrence in their fiction.

   Not so with Fuentes, who in fact seldom resided in Mexico. By the time he was a teenager, he had spent more time in the United States than in any Latin country. At this crucial period of his life Fuentes was almost to the point of losing his native language, thus motivating his parents to send him to summer school in Mexico.[6] Consequently Fuentes was above all a man with a vision of the big city, or rather of many big cities. He also enjoyed the unique advantage of being able to compare his own Mexican metropolis with most of the major ones in this hemisphere. This fascination with cities would burgeon until, not surprisingly, his first published writings would focus on the novelty of Mexico City, eventually culminating in his masterful portrait of the Mexican capital in his first novel.

   Although Fuentes composed several unpublished works of fiction during his teenage years,[7] his first known published short story, "Pastel rancio," appeared in the November 1949 issue of *Mañana*. Surprisingly, the piece is set in New York City rather than the Distrito Federal de México. Fuentes had visited Manhattan on numerous occasions and had sailed to South America from there in 1941. The main events of the story revolve around the disembarking of transoceanic passengers and would thus disqualify the nonport cities of Washington, D.C., and Mexico City that Fuentes might logically have chosen as his setting. The description of New York is brief—the principal action is the arrival of a displaced person from war-torn Europe. The European refugee will become a popular character in *La región más transparente* and again is prominent in *Cambio de piel* (1967). Even the Jewish race of the main character foreshadows protagonists in later works. The Jew is much less numerous in Mexico City than other major Latin American metropolises and seldom appears in Mexican fiction.

Carlos Fuentes did not publish another piece of fiction for five years, but the numerous essays which were beginning to appear anticipate topics of importance which would surface in his novel, still almost a decade away from publication. During the fall of 1949 José Pagés Llergo invited him to collaborate in the Mexican weekly *Hoy*. Fuentes had not yet turned twenty-one. His first article, "Fue al infierno de visita pero lo vio tan mal que decidió regresar a México,"[8] was not of a caliber to make Fuentes immortal. It consisted of an interview with Leonardo Alcalá who claimed to be the third incarnation of God. Even so, the statements on reincarnation would show up in later writings, and the setting, an impoverished "barrio" of Mexico City, is not too distant from that of the "pelado" group in *La región más transparente*. Other articles by Fuentes published in *Hoy* during the following months treated "basfumismo," existentialism, and the Mexican cinema, most of which we will examine in more detail in later sections.

The most important of these articles carried the long but significant title, "Descubriendo al México de 1950: México es la única gran ciudad mestiza que existe en el mundo."[9] In spite of the piece's supreme importance in foreshadowing themes in Fuentes' first novel, it has surprisingly not yet been analyzed by the critics. The essay begins with the author labeling the Mexican capital a "metropolis and large village" (p. 32). Perhaps in his earlier residence in Argentina Fuentes recalled Lucio V. López using the term "la gran aldea" in a novel of the same title to refer to Buenos Aires. In any case it is a logical slogan for a city experiencing rapid growth and changing its character. Fuentes next focuses on the contrasts: "New and old city, beautiful and ugly owing to its decadence and newness" (p. 32). Another unique feature is the lack of ghettos. Next comes a comparison with other famous metropolitan centers in which

Fuentes had lived: "Río de Janeiro has what God has given her, New York what man gave her, and Mexico has God, man and tourists" (p. 32). The theme of the unrelenting past which resurfaces to haunt the present is later developed in many of Fuentes' short stories and novels, but is anticipated in these lines from the essay: "Upon the pyramids still stinking with thick and black blood are raised the elaborate walls of the Cathedral; upon the vestibules and moldy patios are built the 'Pepe Bars'; who knows what will be constructed tomorrow. No one knows and no one cares. Variety makes everything more interesting" (p. 32).

Fuentes next passes to "México Abajo" and begins by listing a number of cantinas and brothels. One announces "English Spoken" and another "paint me red and blue and call me Superman." The latter phrase is used word for word in a cocktail party scene in the first novel. Another fascinating facet of the lower depths of Mexico City, according to Fuentes, is the enormous number of witches and wizards. A few names are given including that of Leonardo Alcalá, the New Messiah of Canal de Norte about whom Fuentes had previously written.

Several paragraphs are subsequently devoted to "Mexico Arriba," a class Fuentes knew much more intimately, as we shall see a bit later. Among the city's aristocracy he lists: "New rich, the pseudopopoffs and other social climbers." Each will be pictured in detail in his novel. He then asks the question: "And the aristocracy of the day before yesterday? They're the only ones who don't count; they make up the bourgeoisie of today" (p. 32). The same phrase appears almost intact in the novel, where, to the identical question asked by Príncipe Vampa, Charlotte García responds: "They're the only ones who don't count, at least not in Mexico, they're the petite bourgeoisie of today" (Región, p. 32). A major percentage of the Mexican aristocracy is made up of foreigners: "A curious phenomenon on the Mexican social scene are the 'Internationals Incorporated'; false aristocratic titles, eccentric poses, people who don't do anything because it would take up too much of their time" (p. 32). The above-mentioned false-titled gentry are extremely important and Fuentes referred in not too oblique a fashion to a recent scandal in Mexico City which would serve as novelistic material for both Fuentes and Luis Spota.

Fuentes further pictures his capital, Mexico City, as the "one place on earth so pliable, eccentric, and uncivilized that 'snobbism' and 'esnobismo' embrace fraternally." After a lengthy quotation from Eça de Queiroz, Fuentes concludes with "enough of the new 'grandezas mexicanas,'" recalling the famous poem by Balbuena which also is cited at a cocktail party in *La región más transparente*.

Now let us look briefly at nine short stories published between the years 1954 and 1956 containing themes which surface in the novel. "Pantera en jazz" was printed in the short-lived and little-known magazine *Ideas de México*.[10] It is practically unknown to the public and Fuentes has never chosen to include it in any of his anthologies. The plot follows a student who fears that a panther has found its way into his bathroom. Never willing to look and unable to call the police, the protagonist eventually loses his mind. Only a few months later Fuentes treats the subject in almost identical fashion in his famous short story "Chac Mool." In the latter instance the presence from the past which destroys modern man is a statue of a Mayan rain god. In the same *Los días enmascarados* anthology, published in November of 1954, the author repeats the theme in "Por boca de los dioses" and "Tlactocatzine, del Jardín de Flandes." In the first an Aztec goddess kills a contemporary Mexican and in the second it is the ghost of nineteenth-century Carlota of Hapsburg who accomplishes the deed. In each case they anticipate the semi-mythical figures of Ixca Cienfuegos and Teódula Moctezuma in *La región más transparente*. The latter is constantly pleading for her disciple to provide a sacrifice. Ixca will defend his philosophy of returning to the past to save Mexico in a spirited debate with intellectual Manuel Zamacona (spokesman for the future) and banker Federico Robles (man of the present).

The conflict between the present and the past so prominent in the above-cited stories is treated in a more universal fashion in the science fiction story "El que inventó la pólvora," also found in *Los días enmascarados*. Here modern technology is the villain which brings about the end of civilization. Another story in the volume, "Letanía de la orquídea," takes place in Panama. The dual worlds of Panama and the Canal Zone, which Fuentes had just visited in September 1954, personify the Spanish-and-English-speaking "aristocracy" of the "International Set" pictured in *La región más transparente*, but to a broader degree mirror the dual background of Fuentes himself. The final story in the volume is "En defensa de la Trigolibia," an essay-like work which has been little studied. Perhaps more than any of his early publications this brief linguistic *tour de force* demonstrates Fuentes' remarkable ear for language which can be observed in all of his writings.

In March and September of 1956, just two years before the appearance of *La región más transparente*, Fuentes issued two more stories which have not been collected in anthologies. The first, "El muñeco," follows the madness of Empress Carlota on her return to Europe in a vain attempt to save Maximilian's crumbling empire. Whole passages from the story describing the execution of the emperor and the embalming of his body are quoted verbatim in the final sixteen-page monologue which concludes the novel.[11] "Trigo errante," the second story, has a setting in modern-day Israel and includes as protagonist Lazarus, who still remains alive after the miracle of his raising by Jesus. The themes of immortality and reincarnation so central to later novels such as *Cambio de piel* and *Cumpleaños* make a curious early appearance in *La región más transparente*. In a debate between Robles, Cienfuegos, and Zamacona, the role of Lazarus becomes pivotal in the latter's argument.

> "The only one who can never be saved is he who is resurrected, because he can neither commit crime nor feel guilt. He has known death and come back from it."
> "Lazarus?" said Cienfuegos.
> "Lazarus. In the unconscious background of his spirit palpitates the conviction that every time he dies, he will be brought back to life. He may be grasping and treacherous, he may commit all crimes with the certainty that on the day of death he will return to commit new crimes. No one may hold him to account. Lazarus cannot die on earth. But he is dead forever in heaven. The resurrected man may not save himself because he cannot renounce anything, because he isn't free, because he can't sin." (*Región*, pp. 296–297)

Before concluding we should mention that as a student at the National University Carlos Fuentes was on the staff of the school's journal, *Revista de la Universidad de México*. In this capacity he wrote more than a dozen book and motion picture reviews. The book reviews help us to understand Fuentes' contemporaneous reading habits, but have little use for the purposes of this essay. Such is not the case of the motion picture reviews, which will be discussed in another section.

Real Life Sources

Many events from Fuentes' personal life as a young man growing up in Mexico City at mid-century are no doubt reflected in *La región más transparente*. Some are known and a few can be deduced, but it is the broader panorama of the national intellectual, political and cultural scene which will now be our principal focus.

We have previously discussed the Alemán era in our introductory remarks and will not repeat these observations. Suffice it to say that the period represented a time of substantial change and growth which has seldom been duplicated in Mexican history. Carlos Fuentes' family belonged to the social and political elite. As a handsome, articulate, wealthy and extroverted organizer he was not simply a witness of the changing face of Mexico, but a participant in its inner circle. Two of his acquaintances, Pablo Palomino and Daniel Dueñas, have documented this period, and their articles plus occasional notices in the society pages furnish us with considerable information on these years. Carlos excelled in organizing parties, and his presence was particularly sought after at such gatherings where he was "a magnificent participant with his gaiety and facility for mimicry." Dueñas recalls: "We still recall him at Ricardo de Villar's house pretending to be an Uruguayan anarchist or interpreting oriental operas with a gong and showing only the whites of his eyes." His playful nature can be seen in other accounts of the time: "We all celebrated his success as a blind beggar wandering up and down Madero and San Juan de Letrán streets alongside Enrique Creel de la Barra."[12] And a brief note from the society page of June 1949: "Carlitos Fuentes related his most recent nocturnal adventures and combats with cabdrivers. Doña Berta, his mother, is somewhat disturbed over the turbulent life of her precocious offspring."[13] As a regular at the literary *tertulias* held at the home of Cristina Moya, Carlos played the role of the *enfant terrible* "reading short stories savoring of simultaneism, dadaism, and . . . snobbism" (Dueñas, p. 76).

Perhaps Fuentes' most controversial and sensational activity at the time was his participation in the founding of an exclusive social circle called "Vasfumistas." Attempts were made at that period and in later years to give Vasfumismo (also spelled Basfumismo and Vhazfumismo) the status of a philosophical orientation similar to the European vanguard groups of the twenties and thirties, but in reality it was more of a tight-knit social group. Pablo Palomino recalls that they had viewed some silent film classics and decided to try something similar: "Something which was totally new, without any precedents." They possessed the means among themselves to produce the film; one of their close friends had practical filming experience, and they would be the actors. Later it was decided that Fuentes and Creel de la Barra would write a play rather than a film script. Ernesto de la Peña put forth a name for the group, "Basfumismo," which suggested also their slogan: "por el humo, al ser" ("through smoke to being").[14]

Huge parties were held which were outstandingly successful; plans for the play and film were dropped for the time being. The society columns buzzed with rumors of their mysterious doings. Under the title of "Definición para el basfumismo" they were described as: "All geniuses, all frustrated, touched in the head but not locked up, harmless crazies (except Valentín Saldaña, Ruggiero Asta and Carlitos Fuentes) plus more than a little extraordinary."[15] Even Carlos published an article with the intriguing title of "¡Pero usted no sabe aún lo que es el basfumismo!" which instead of clarifying the issues only clouded them more.[16]

Because of the exclusive nature of the group, jealous outsiders began spreading rumors about the practice of nefarious rites and prohibited cults. A wealthy owner of a bakery even contributed funds to help eradicate this social evil. Certain politicians anxious to exploit the basfumista publicity sought discussions with its members.[17] But by the end of 1949 the movement had run its course; one of its members was married and Fuentes was on his way to Europe for graduate studies.

Although "Basfumismo" died a quiet death, its memory lingered on in later fiction. Many of the cocktail parties in *La región más transparente* would seem to be recreations of basfumista entertainments. Probably a good number of the fictional party goers were modeled on real people, and Bobo Gutiérrez, the irrepressible festivity organizer in the novel, is not too much different from Fuentes himself. Pablo Palomino, the previously mentioned chronicler of the movement and friend of Fuentes, has also left us a fictional view of the time in his little-known novel *Autopsia*.

Palomino's *Autopsia* precedes *La región más transparente* by almost three years, having been published in August of 1955. It had a small one-time printing of 1,000 copies and except for one known review the novel seems to have been (and continues to be) totally ignored. Although it is much briefer (164 pages) and less ambitious than Fuentes' novel, the two works share a number of characteristics. Both are urban novels set in contemporary Mexico City. One of Palomino's characters agonizes about having children in the Atomic Age. Another main character is a foreigner (Italian) living in Mexico and there is even a lesbian. Palomino presents several cocktail party scenes with snatches of conversation on a variety of political and cultural topics: those of Fuentes, however, are infinitely more dynamic and demonstrate a much greater artistic skill. The psychological insights in *Autopsia* are the traditional author-narrator interpretation while Fuentes makes greater use of the stream-of-consciousness technique. In one chapter Palomino has a character frequent the lower class night life of Mexico City anticipating in skeletal fashion Fuentes' more consummately drawn *pelado* sections. Both would appear to be based on basfumista nocturnal escapades of the two youthful authors.

On the intellectual-artistic scene only the writers-philosophers are in evidence in *La región más transparente*. Strangely enough, painters are missing as are actors and actresses. This is hard to explain since Fuentes' good friend and neighbor is none other than famed painter José Luis Cuevas, and his fiancée, Rita Macedo, had starred in Buñuel films. These fields of endeavor were certainly not unknown to Fuentes and would be used in later fiction.

Two groups of writers make their appearance in the novel, one led by Tomás Mediana and a looser grouping represented by, but not necessarily directed by, Manuel Zamacona. Mediana is not an active participant in *La región más transparente* but is recalled in a flashback by Rodrigo Pola. Mediana's group flourished in the decades of the twenties and thirties. They wished to renovate Mexican literature by producing a new journal which would translate innovative European writers. Tomás subscribes to the *Nouvelle Revue Française* and wants Mexico to become acquainted with Proust. In many ways this group seems to describe the "Contemporáneos" movement which became active shortly before Fuentes' birth but some of whose members he would probably know through his father's government service (Torres Bodet) or in the journalistic field (Novo).

It is the second grouping of writers, which flourished in the late forties and early fifties, precisely the exact time period of *La región más transparente*, which most interests us. Its principal representative, Manuel Zamacona, is primarily a poet, a profession which banker Federico Robles considers a luxury in an underdeveloped country. Although Zamacona first appears in the novel at a cocktail party, it is the following day as Zamacona is writing an essay on Mexico that we come to know him. Fuentes actually includes the entire nine-page text of the essay! Among Zamacona's reading materials are *El laberinto de la soledad* and volumes by Guardini, Alfonso Reyes and Nerval. In one scene he has just returned from a series of formal discussions.

A round-table discussion of Mexican literature. It is necessary to mention the serapes of Saltillo, was Franz Kafka the tool of Wall Street, is social literature anything more than the eternal triangle between two Stajanovitches and a tractor, if we are not the more universal the more Mexican we are, and vice versa, should we write like Marxists or like Buddhists. Many prescriptions, zero books. (*Región*, p. 292)

In an interview, Fuentes has described Zamacona as a "composite portrait of many Mexican intellectuals. Many recognized themselves in him. They protested, they attacked me in the street, they tried to set my house on fire. So there must be some truth to the portrait. Because at the bottom, in the whole 'Mexicanist' movement, there was that redemptorist attitude." [18]

To better comprehend the above statement it will be useful to review the intellectual climate in Mexico City during the early fifties. In the late forties there emerged the Grupo Filosófico Hiperión, headed by Leopoldo Zea and including in its membership Jorge Portilla, Joaquín Macgregor, Emilio Uranga, Luis Villoro, Ricardo Guerra, Salvador Reyes Nevares, and Fausto Vega. [19] "Hiperión" was the name selected because it symbolized the union between heaven and earth and was to demonstrate the group's preoccupation with both universal and national answers to the dilemmas facing their country. Round table discussions and a series of more than a dozen publications followed in the next few years. The series entitled "México y lo Mexicano" consisted of studies by philosophers, historians, economists, sociologists, scientists, psychologists, and literary figures. Foreigners who had visited Mexico or written about it also contributed: Mariano Picón Salas, José Gaos and José Moreno Villas. One name strangely missing is that of Octavio Paz, who was apparently in Europe most of this time although his famous *El laberinto de la soledad* was published in 1950. The following year *El perfil del hombre y la cultura en México* by Samuel Ramos, which first appeared in 1934, was reprinted in an inexpensive edition.

Another source of fictional material which Fuentes was to take from real life was the large foreign population which comprised both an important and a highly visible element of Mexican society, especially among the upper classes. They were labeled the "International Set," and as we have already seen, Fuentes alluded to them in his early essay on Mexico City. It seems somewhat strange that in spite of his long years of residence in the United States, Fuentes in interviews mentions no friends among this group and the only North Americans in his fiction tend to be caricatures of the simple-minded tourist or the money-grabbing businessman-investor.

The Spaniard, on the other hand, is viewed much differently. Mexico was profoundly affected by the Spanish Civil War, and its sympathies were so strongly in favor of the Republic that it has only recently renewed diplomatic relations with the post-Franco government. Refugees from the peninsula found a welcome home in Mexico, and Spanish intellectuals played significant roles in the university and the publishing world. Fuentes studied with one of these exiles, Manuel Martínez Pedroso, and paid homage to him in an article in the *Revista de la Universidad de México* in the summer of 1958. Pedroso, who translated *Das Kapital*, had been rector at the Universidad de Salamanca and *diputado* at the Cortes of 1936. Later he served the Republic in Warsaw and Moscow before coming to Mexico. Salvador Novo writes of the professor's fondness for Fuentes: "He also spoke to me about Carlos Fuentes of whom he is very fond, a paternal fondness. He is alarmed about the premature fervor of the Fondo publicists who are proclaiming him Mexico's best writer."[20]

In *La región más transparente* Fuentes includes a sympathetic episode in which Spanish exiles recall their escape from Fascist Spain; the incident is brief and does not form a part of the novel's plot. Four years later Fuentes would return to the subject in *La muerte de Artemio Cruz* and follow Lorenzo Cruz on his idealistic crusade to Spain to carry on what he felt were his father's revolutionary goals.

A considerably more negative view is offered in *La región más transparente* of the exiled European nobility who come to Mexican shores. Among them: Contessa Aspacuccoli, Conde Lemini, Natasha, the Serbian Prince "Pinky," and Príncipe Vampa. At least one has bought his title, and even worse, another turns out to be a fraud. In real life Fuentes would often mingle with the nobility at their parties. A note from a society page in 1950 states: "Carlitos Fuentes invited everyone present to Prince Bernard of Holland's ball."[21] Fuentes was not in the country in the fall of 1941 when King Carol, recently exiled from the throne of Romania, would arrive in Mexico with a female traveling companion and a reported $7,000,000 to "set up court." It was the social event of the year. Fuentes very definitely was in Mexico in 1949 for the much publicized Otto Wilhelm von Hohenzollern escapade. Otto, supposedly the little known son of the Kaiser by a second marriage, was feted by an adoring Mexican upper society, interviewed frequently and even invited to write a series of articles on the world situation for the weekly *Mañana*. The prince turned out to be the adventurer Rico David Tancous, wanted by several governments including the U.S. for bigamy, false impersonation, and robbery.[22]

Within a decade two best-selling novels in Mexico would treat the bogus prince theme—*La región más transparente* was one of them. The other was by journalist Luis Spota who authored many popular books based on current events. His novel, *Casi el paraíso*, used the imposter as the central character, and since the public saw it as a roman à clef, it was an immediate success, going through six editions in four years. Spota's prince turns out to be the illegitimate son of a poor Italian prostitute. Before he can wed the daughter of a Mexican millionaire he is discovered and arrested by Mexican immigration officials and the FBI.

For Fuentes the imposter prince becomes only a minor episode, who although discovered is not arrested. One character recalls the scandal:

> "And what news is there of the imposter Vampa?" Charlotte raised a hand to her heart. "Ay! Don't remind me of that fatal blow. I don't know how to breathe afterward. Just think how he fooled us!"
> Bobo's face wrinkled in pain. "His only title was to a pizza show in 'Frisco. He was a cook there."
> "And we treated him as a blue blood! Don't remind me Bobo, I die of anger . . . and imagine, Pierre Caseaux gave him a job in his kitchen. Every time I eat there, I have the feeling the macaroni knows all my secrets." (p. 351)

Since Spota had already beaten Fuentes to the punch by two years it is an interesting speculation as to whether the latter might not have planned to do more with the episode. Both novels also share other similar characters: the party organizer, Charlotte García in *La región más transparente* and Carmen Pérez Mendiola in *Casi el paraíso*. Others are the wealthy bankers who have risen from poverty to power through their participation in the Revolution. Spota's Alonso Ronia states: "Thirty years ago I was out in the provinces plowing behind a team of mules."[23] Fuentes' Federico Robles' father did the same on a plot of ground in Uruapan.

One final area of Mexican cultural life which Fuentes utilizes to create his fictional world is the Mexican motion picture industry. From his early youth Fuentes has been a fan of the cinema. Many of his characters talk about the movies and screen stars. His first wife, Rita Macedo, had worked in several Buñuel films, and *La región más transparente* is dedicated to her. Fuentes, himself, has written several admiring articles on Buñuel plus a review of the latter's *El ángel exterminador*. He is also the author of a number of film scripts, the most important being *Los caifanes*, which won a prize at Cannes, and *Pedro Páramo*, based on Juan Rulfo's famous novel. In 1953 and

1954 Fuentes regularly reviewed films, among them *Beat the Devil* with Humphrey Bogart and Marlon Brando's *The Wild One*, for the *Revista de la Universidad de México*.[24]

In *La región más transparente* Fuentes' vision of the Mexican motion picture industry is anything but favorable. In fact his presentation of the producers and script writers crosses the line to caricature. Rodrigo Pola, a frustrated poet, finally finds fame and fortune turning out potboiler scripts. What began as a daring treatment of social taboos is "adapted" by the producers to the public taste, to the actresses they already have in mind and to previously chosen sites —all combined with some religion and ranchero music! The delighted producers tell Pola to write up the script in the following week and two weeks later the film will be shot and completed. If all this seems too farcical we can only cite an article which appeared almost as if by coincidence in a Mexico City daily a few months after Fuentes' novel came out. In it Benito Alazraki, once the great hope of Mexico with prestigious films such as *Raices*, stated: "I prefer to make B movies and drive a Cadillac than artistic cinema and ride the city buses."[25]

Pre-Publication Fragments of *La región más transparente*

Some three years before *La región más transparente* would appear in the bookstores of Mexico City, fragments of the novel were beginning to be published in local newspapers and magazines. Some of the selections show only moderate stylistic changes from the 1958 version, but others contain major changes in characters and plots. These fragments furnish a most fascinating insight into the evolution of the novel before it reached its final form.

The earliest of the four known fragments was published in the March 28, 1955 issue of *Revista de la Universidad de México*. It is three pages long and carries the title "Los restos." The novel version in smaller format has a length of nine pages and is titled "Los de Ovando." Essentially they are of identical length with most of the changes consisting of stylistic polishing. All of the same characters appear and all carry the same names: Pimpinela de Ovando, Doña Lorenza, Juaquinito, Don Francisco, Fernanda, Benjamín, Norma Larragoiti, and Federico Robles. The selection follows the self-imposed exile of the wealthy de Ovando family with the fall of Porfirio Díaz and their subsequent return to Mexico City. Most of the changes are of the word substitution variety: for example: "tenía apuntados" becomes in the novel "estaban apuntados," "recámara" changes to "alcoba," "escenas pastoriles" later becomes "escenas bucólicas," "azotea alquilada" is modified to "azotea arrendada," and "¿no?" is replaced by "¿verdad?" Federico Robles' bank is called "Banco Internacional de Crédito Industrial S.A." in the 1955 version, but in the novel it is "Banco de Ahorro Mexicano S.A." Another change throughout the novel version is the italicizing of several French words. One phrase eliminated from the novel describes the infantile Benjamín: "Luego se sentaba en el suelo a jugar al águila o sol; dos águilas, perdía y entonces quedaba prohibido comer postre."[26]

Our next pre-novel fragment was published in the November–December 1955 issue of *Revista Mexicana de Literatura*, the second number of a journal Fuentes cofounded. Here the title is "La línea de la vida"; in the novel it is the name of the principal character in the chapter, "Gervasio Pola." Once more the majority of the changes are word substitutions: "supurando" becomes in the novel "supurantes," "yo y Pedro" is reversed to "Pedro y yo," the same with "ya acercándose" to "acercándose ya," "el pino" to "un pino," and "a las llamas" to "al fuego." There are two examples of "las plantas" clarified to "las plantas del pie." Another expansion is "la madrugada" to "el principio de la madrugada." Other stylistic changes seen in the novel will be the use of italics to call attention to the occurrence of stream of consciousness.

Some significant additions can be noted toward the end of the episode. Whereas the federal officer in charge of the execution is simply called "el capitán rubio," in the novel he is named and described more fully: "Captain Zamacona, blond and slender, with a carefully waxed mustache." He will appear several more times in the book and his sister, Mercedes Zamacona, is the center of one of the main episodes. All of which seems to indicate that while Fuentes may have had his main episodes already in mind or on paper by 1955, he still was working out relationships between characters and events. This is evident in another addition. In the fragment at the moment of Gervasio Pola's execution, he is thinking only of "mujeres" and "padres." In contrast, the novel includes the significant line: "to your wife, to your unknown son." This wife and unseen son also play major roles in the novel. One other new line in the final version is "¡Viva Madero!—gritó Froilán en el instante de la descarga." The 1955 fragment omits mention of the shot; only their falling to the ground is described.

The third novel fragment also appeared in Fuentes' journal *Revista Mexicana de Literatura*, this time in the sixth number dated July–August 1956. Both have the same title, "Maccualli," the Nahuatl word for commoners. The action follows a typical Sunday afternoon of several lower class "pelados" as they attend the bullfights and then visit some cantinas. The journal selection is shorter, omitting the first five and a half pages in which the pelados converse with Ixca Cienfuegos and the last five pages as one of them unexpectedly meets a former girlfriend in a brothel.

Of the four selections we are examining, this one is closest to the final 1958 rendering. "El domingo" changes to "El domingo siguiente," the cantina "Los amores de Cúpido" becomes Mexicanized to "Los amores de Cuauhtémoc," "tennis" is spelled "tenis," the same with "zipper" to "ziper," "¡Si quieres ver cogidas . . ." is finalized as "Si quieres cogidas . . . ," and "los expendios de libros pornográficos" is toned down to "puestos de revistas." Also the next-to-last line in the magazine version, which did not seem to make sense and was probably a typographical error, is removed from the novel.

"Calavera del quince" is the title of one of the chapters in *La región más transparente*; it is called the same in the final fragment we shall examine. Apparently it is the same selection which was printed in the June 26, 1955, Sunday supplement of *Novedades*, but I have been unable to examine it and have therefore used the version published by Emmanuel Carballo in his *Cuentos mexicanos modernos* (1956). Of all the four selections we have studied, this seems to differ the most from what eventually appeared in the novel. Each version contains about twenty scenes, but only half are duplicates. The anthology selection devotes considerable space to Tomás Mediana, who is dropped from the novel. The jailing of labor agitator, Feliciano Sánchez, also appears but in the novel is placed in the preceding chapter. A nameless Indian on a pilgrimage whose story is told in five short fragments receives but one paragraph in the novel version.

On the other hand, the novel account adds scenes of Robles working in his office, Zamacona taking leave of Cienfuegos, Bobo and the international set traveling to Cuernavaca, Zamacona's death, Robles recalling his childhood, Robles telling his wife that they are ruined, Teódula throwing her jewels into Robles' burning house, Ixca by Rosa Morales' side after the death of her son, and Teódula's statement to Ixca that his mission is completed. One final difference we will discuss in a moment is the changes of names given to three characters.

Perhaps the most striking alteration in the two accounts is the complete dropping of the character of Tomás Mediana. In the novel he never makes an appearance, but is part of Rodrigo Pola's past recalled in a conversation with Ixca. Mediana, as we have stated earlier, was head of a writer's group which wanted to introduce the innovative European movements to Mexican readers. In the 1955 selection we see a more personal side of his character, and told from his point of view. His father has returned unexpectedly and is working as a humble waiter in a café. Tomás had hardly known him, was not even sure his parents had ever married, since his father was such a carefree Don Juan. For years he had told everyone that his father had died in France in the battle of the Marne. In later scenes Mediana reflects upon his literary career. It would appear likely that Fuentes had originally intended to make Tomás one of his major characters but in the end reduced his importance since the novel already included two other writers, Rodrigo Pola and Manuel Zamacona.

The scene describing the death of Doña Zenaida's son also shows considerable reworking. In the novel Ixca Cienfuegos stands by her side comforting her. Fuentes gives her the more mundane name of Rosa Morales, possibly in order not to distract from the high priestess of the primitive religion whom he dubs with the exotic sobriquet of Teódula Moctezuma. Rosa Morales is probably more fitting as a name symbolizing her plebeian status; her husband, a taxi driver, is Juan Morales.

The most interesting metamorphosis to observe in these two versions is that of the pelados. The novel follows four, maybe five. In the fragment there are only two and their names are changed; Fifo is called Gabriel in the novel, but there will also be a pelado by the name of Fifo. Nacho will be converted to Beto. In the novel Gabriel has worked as a bracero and frequently includes English words in his speech. The early account has him say: "Ya tan temprano" while Fuentes changes this in the novel to "ya tan erly." On the same page a phrase with the word "suit" is added (meaning "dulce" not "traje"). Fuentes in the novel also seems more intent on capturing their authentic slang usage: "para" becomes "pa'," "tomen de la botella" changes to "empínense la botella," and "no juegues con la muerte" is "hoy me la pela la mera muerte calaca." "Si no fuera por los amigos" changes to "Si no fuera por los cuates" and "¡Se me hace lo que el aire a Juárez!" becomes "le viene más guango que el aire a Juárez, mano." Several songs are changed in the two accounts. The words from the famous corrido by José A. Jiménez, "no vale nada, la vida, la vida no vale nada," are not found in La región más transparente but curiously enough surface in 1962 on the title page of La muerte de Artemio Cruz.

Probably the most interesting modification is what Fuentes has done with the violent murder of one of the pelados. In the early version an unknown "gordo" comes up to Fifo in a cantina and after stabbing him says: "A mí nadie me mira así" ("Nobody looks at me like that"). The novel has Gabriel (previously called Fifo in the fragment) stabbed by a "thin man with a slouch hat" who runs into the pelado unexpectedly. The murderer's words this time are "I told you, buddy, you wouldn't catch me twice . . . you can't treat me like this. . . ." However, the words "Nobody looks at me like that" are not forgotten but utilized earlier by Fuentes in the novel's chapter by a "marble-eyed man" when he unexpectedly stabs Manuel Zamacona, who has stopped in a small town for gasoline.

First Reactions to the Novel

La región más transparente appeared in the stores of Mexico City on Monday, April 7, 1958. The previous day Elena Poniatowska had published a lengthy interview with Fuentes in the Sunday cultural supplement of the newspaper *Novedades*. Apparently, she had read a pre-publication copy of the novel. Emmanuel Carballo writing eleven years later states that the book was published on the 29th of March.[27] Most likely he was consulting the printing information on the last page of the novel. These are always estimates and may vary by several weeks or more. The date given by Poniatowska at the time of the event seems much more likely. Numerous reviews were printed in various Mexico City newspapers during the months of April, May, and June. Opinions vary on how quickly the novel sold out; some reports say a week, others suggest several months. A second printing is dated November 18, 1958. The April printing was 4,000 copies and the one in November numbered 5,000; both respectable amounts for the time. The November edition remained available for several years and was purchased by the author of this study in Mexico City in the summer of 1960. Of the Mexican novels of that period it seems likely that only *Casi el paraíso* had sold in greater numbers over a short span.

The title of the novel dates all the way back to 1917, coming from Alfonso Reyes' famous epigraph introducing a chapter of *Visión de Anáhuac*: "Viajero: has llegado a la región más transparente del aire." It is probable that at first Fuentes intended to use the whole phrase since that is the one given with the fragments published in 1955 and 1956. In the end, however, he dropped the last part, "del aire." No one would accuse Fuentes of plagiarizing his title; it had long since become a popular designation for the Valley of Mexico. The choice was a fortuitous one; it was easily identified with Mexico City, but offered intriguing possibilities for irony since the novel pictured the capital city as anything but clear and beautiful. Some confusion has arisen about the originality of the phrase with Alfonso Reyes. It seems that Rodolfo, his brother, had been quoted that it came from Alexander Humbolt's description of New Spain. Alfonso says that this is not the case; he had thought up the phrase himself.[28]

The controversy surrounding *La región más transparente* did not begin in 1958, but actually several years earlier with the publication of the novel fragments. An anonymous note commenting on the "de Ovando" chapter suggested "if the whole resembles the sample, Carlos Fuentes without doubt will be recognized as one of Mexico's outstanding novelists."[29] The "Línea de la vida" episode in *Revista Mexicana de Literatura* produced four very favorable reviews.[30] On the other hand, Fernando Benítez, director of the "México en la Cultura" supplement of *Novedades* was called on the carpet for printing some of the controversial material of the young novelist. One thing about Fuentes' writings, they were never ignored!

In the spring of 1958 there were complaints that *La región más transparente* was launched on the market as if it were a new laundry detergent, a comment almost identical to what had been said in 1954 about *Los días enmascarados*. As a matter of fact, there may have been considerable truth in the allegation. An anonymous note about this time is typical of the abundance of publicity given the book: "They say that Emmanuel Carballo doesn't begin his television program anymore by greeting the public from the 'región más transparente del aire,' but rather from the 'región más Carlosfuentes.'"[31]

Most of the earlier reviewers were personally acquainted with Fuentes, and thus their prejudices either for or against him naturally come to the surface. Of approximately two dozen reviews published in the first few months, five were openly hostile, another dozen extremely laudatory and the rest fairly neutral. In somewhat of an understatement J. M. García Ascot portrayed *La región más transparente* as "a book which has produced some controversy." Enrique González Rojo observed, "This novel inaugurates, in our opinion, a new cycle in the twentieth century Mexican novel." José Emilio Pacheco commented enthusiastically: "Many of the pages of *La región más transparente* will go down in history as some of the finest prose writing ever produced in Mexico." Rafael Solana, an important author in his own right, believed that Fuentes may have been overly ambitious, "but the presence of a great writer can be detected in each page." For Luis Cardoza y Aragón it was "one of the most significant books published in Mexico in recent years."[32]

On the other side of the coin, Arturo Martínez Cáceres was less than generous:

The first impression that the novel produces is of a torpid, almost unnecessary, complexity. The influence of Faulkner, undigested let alone assimilated, can be detected, amen to some pseudomodernist techniques whose origin even the novice reader will immediately recognize as Proustian, Woolfian, Joycean and Huxlean; all of which give the book a respectable size which certainly is not the least of its defects.[33]

Journalist Rubén Salazar Mallén, whose own novels in the forties were considered forerunners for their experimental techniques, called *La región más transparente* "nothing but a pastiche." This word would be widely repeated by future reviewers. He goes on to say: "Carlos Fuentes has made an ingenious transplant of James Joyce's *Ulysses*, but he is thirty-five years late."[34] He nevertheless felt that Fuentes had talent if he would close his ears to the blind adulation of friends. Salazar Mallén's review of *Las buenas conciencias* the following year was very positive.

One surprising source of negative criticism came from playwright and novelist Elena Garro, wife of Fuentes' good friend Octavio Paz. She had her doubts even about the book's genre:

> It is true that Fuentes piles on one apparent novelistic element after another; piling on words, names, actions; loading more images on top of the already inundated ones. Fuentes gets carried away: carried away with the sound of his portable Remington. He beats on it so loud that the reader can't escape from the deafening noise of keys pounded on for hours on end. One must put the book aside, rest from the noise and the confusion which grow by the minute.

She concludes: "The evaluation of this book, in spite of the good laugh that it gave us, is tragic. It is a book by someone who has only partially found himself and who is struggling desperately to find others."[35] As a result of her ferocious utterances she would be nicknamed "the claw" by the local writing community.

The most vicious attack on the novel did not surface until three years later and appeared in the letters to the editor of the Mexico City newspaper, *Excélsior*. Apparently it began as a protest against Fuentes and his colleagues who were accused of using the National University facilities, in particular the radio station, to disseminate Communist propaganda. Licenciado Eulogio Cervantes (the name is suspect!) accuses Fuentes of blatant plagiarism: "*La región más transparente* is the product of a series of 'expropriations' as ferocious as those realized in Cuba by Castro." He calls the novel a "pastiche" using the techniques of Joyce, Dos Passos, Baroja and Cela, and adds, "We shouldn't condemn him for imitating Cela or Joice [sic], only for doing it so badly." Señor Cervantes then lists some sixty pages of the novel which are taken from Paz's *El laberinto de la soledad*, several major characters from Michael Valbeck's *Caídos del cielo* (*Headlong from Heaven* in its original English version), parts from Jorge Portillas' *Fenomenología del relajo* and Eunice Odio's long poem, *El tránsito del fuego.*[36]

We have already discussed the portrayal of, but certainly not the plagiarism of, the Hiperión group—Octavio Paz and other intellectuals of the early fifties who were concerned with defining Mexico's past, present, and future. Perhaps a few words are in order regarding Valbeck's *Headlong from Heaven*. This South African novel was translated into Spanish in the late 1950s and José Vázquez Amaral, reviewing *La región más transparente* for *Saturday Review*, first called attention to what he felt was a similarity between the two books.[37] In reality the kinship is very superficial. Valbeck tells of a wealthy but ugly businessman married to a beautiful woman, a plot which has occurred hundreds of times in fiction and probably millions of times in real life. The rest of the novel develops along the lines of a "who done it." Finally, I have examined with considerable care Odio's long poem, *El tránsito del fuego*, and can find absolutely no points of comparison.

As might be expected, the reaction of fellow novelists, especially those outside of Mexico, tended to be very favorable. On September 7, 1958, Julio Cortázar sent congratulations from Paris and enclosed a lengthy and perceptive analysis of *La región más transparente* which is published in the Aguilar edition of Fuentes' *Obras completas*. While well aware that many of the allusions to Mexican customs and history passed over his head, he nonetheless saw many typical character types (Rodrigo Pola, Norma, Gabriel) which "are very similar to certain Argentine types which appear in Europe with considerable modification."[38] On the negative side he found the introductory chapters slow moving and confused; also the characterization of the motion picture people as too "stereotyped and caricatured at the same time." The chapters on Gervasio Pola and Rodrigo he believed to be particularly well done as were those on Robles and the pelados: "Your dialogues are real dialogues, not that strange product that so many novelists invent (I'm thinking of Mallea, for example); as if they had never spoken to their lover or even their banker."

The Cuban novelist and poet, José Lezama Lima, was equally laudatory: "I have read your novel *La región más transparente* and have found it powerful and desirable, vibrating in its symbols and masks." He admonishes Fuentes not to worry about those who try to find influences in every paragraph: "They found influences in Proust and Joyce; and they invented many others. But if we are found to have them . . . we must be beheaded." He concludes by observing: "I don't believe there have been written in Mexico, or in any other part of America, very many novels better than yours."[39]

Writing from Uruguay Mario Benedetti concluded that *La región más transparente* offered an honest portrait of many Latin American problems. Upon the first reading of several of Fuentes' novels he had made critical notes in the margins, but: "the second time I decided to just enjoy each novel."[40] Peruvian Mario Vargas Llosa saw the novel as "a seething crowded mural of Mexico City, an attempt to capture in fiction all the layers of that pyramid from the indigenous base with its ceremonial rites to its pinnacle made up of a cosmopolitan and snobbish oligarchy whose appetites, fashions and impudences are borrowed from New York and Paris."[41]

Of particular interest are Carlos Fuentes' own observations given in a variety of interviews over the years in which he has proffered his own analysis of the strengths and weaknesses of *La región más transparente*. In speaking to Luis Harss he called it, "A biography of a city . . . a synthesis of present day Mexico." To a French reporter he commented, "In my first novel I tried, among other things, to write a personal biography about that species of whale anchored in our high valley, Mexico City: its silhouettes, its secrets, a city which I love and hate at the same time because in it are presented with the greatest brutality the miseries and hopes of all my country. I tried to produce a synthesis of present-day Mexico: conflicts, aspirations, rancors."[42]

Fuentes also answered Emmanuel Carballo in much the same vein: "It began as an elementary observation of Mexico City and the necessity of being a witness to what was happening to it. I wanted to offer a testimony of its life, rediscovered by the imagination." In a letter to the *Saturday Review* Carlos suggested: "*Where the Air Is Clear* is the first of a series of novels designed to give an extensive and interwoven panorama of Mexican life. It depicts the black part of Mexico, a Mexico that is now dying and being swept away by a vigorous younger generation."[43]

In December 1958 during an interview with Elena Poniatowska, Fuentes was anxious to talk about his next novel, but agreed to comment a bit further on his first. Among the defects which he now perceived in *La región más transparente* were: "The incapacity of reducing to a unity an excess of material. Symbols piled upon characters without letting them evolve more naturally. Too many contortions, a continuous verbal exaltation which detracts from the rest of the novel, a lack of love, superficialities." In response to Poniatowska's assessment of the characters as almost caricatures, he answers: "But they really are caricatures! It would have been a lie to give them human dimension. All these puppets of the cocktail parties, the Jockey Club, the International Set, showers and bankers conventions are cardboard paper-dolls. How can a newly arrived bourgeoisie be human?" Asked what he feels are the strengths of the novel, Fuentes answers: "Objectively, one thing. I swear that I wrote it from beginning to end with all the honesty I was capable of at that time. In any case, when I wrote *La región más transparente* I promised myself never to lie. I lived inside that world."[44]

Translations and Critical Reaction from Abroad

The first reactions to *La región más transparente* from abroad came not from journalists, but from professors of Spanish literature who were working with the Spanish edition. In the fall of 1958 the first two reviews of the novel were published in the United States. George Wing, then a young professor at the University of California at Berkeley, wrote a short review in the fall issue of *Books Abroad*. He saw Fuentes as an angry young man who felt deeply "the betrayal of the ideals of the Revolution." Wing made comparisons with Dos Passos' writings and concluded by calling *La región más transparente* the best Mexican novel since *Al filo del agua*. In November of 1958 Jefferson Rea Spell, a long-time observer of the Latin American novel and professor at the University of Texas, published a brief review in *The Hispanic American Historical Review* in which he observed: "This novel, which reveals acquaintance with and sympathy for certain new techniques in fiction writing, will repay the effort expended in its reading."[45]

The following year, Luis Andrés Murrillo produced for *Revista Iberoamericana* the most extensive review of the novel printed in the United States up to that time. He labeled the work "panorámico-histórico" and "realista-simbólico." After some perceptive comments on characterization and structure he concluded with these remarks on the style: "Many lines of the book are genuine prose poems. The final section in which the symbol-city comes together contains pages composed with extraordinary virtuosity." In the winter of 1964 University of Connecticut professor Robert G. Mead, Jr., a keen student of Latin American literature who follows the literary movements but also monitors the publishing industry and social environment, brought out the first of his two major studies on Carlos Fuentes. The earlier one in *Books Abroad* (1964) examined Fuentes as part of the contemporary Mexican scene. Mead had the advantage of five years of perspective and was thoroughly acquainted with the criticism on *La región más transparente* previously published in Mexico City. He saw the three types of reactions that the novel produced as a mirror of current Mexican literary criticism.[46]

By the time Mead's article was in circulation the English translation of *La región más transparente* was out and many newspaper and magazine reviews had appeared in the U.S.A. No exact publication date of this version is known although the first review was printed in September 1960 with most of the others appearing in November and December of that year; a few followed in the early months of 1961.

The English title chosen was *Where the Air Is Clear*, the publisher was Ivan Obolensky in New York, and the translator was Sam Hileman. Hileman had first met Fuentes in Mexico City during the mid-1950s when the two enjoyed fellowships at the Centro Mexicano de Escritores. Hileman, himself a writer, lived in later years in Los Angeles where he did graduate work in English at U.C.L.A. During the next decade he subsequently translated three other novels by Fuentes: *Las buenas conciencias, La muerte de Artemio Cruz* and *Cambio de piel. Where the Air Is Clear* sold quite well in the bookstores. A second printing of the novel was made that same year and in 1971 Obolensky brought out a paperback edition under the Noonday label which is still available.

Where the Air Is Clear was reviewed by a variety of publications in the United States and Great Britain. Major newspapers in all sections of the country recognized it: in New York the *Times*, the *Herald Tribune*, and the *World Telegram and Sun*; in the Midwest the *Chicago Tribune*, the *Columbus Dispatch*, and the *Kansas City Star*; and elsewhere papers in San Francisco, St. Petersburg, Raleigh, Abilene, El Paso, and New Orleans. Magazines which reviewed the novel ranged from religious (*Catholic World*) to Marxist (*People's World, Mainstream*) in addition to such prestigious publications as the *New Yorker*, *Commonweal*, the *National Guardian*, and the *Saturday Review*.

Anthony West in the *New Yorker* and Selden Rodman in the *New York Times* were the most enthusiastic. Rodman had met Fuentes several years earlier in Mexico, although he did not mention the fact in his review. He saw the work as "the most ambitious and skillful novel to come out of Mexico in a long time, and by all odds the most 'modern.'" [47] West also lauded the work while recognizing the "many errors of taste and simple beginner's mistakes." Speaking of Fuentes he observed: "he creates his people wholesale and marches them off by battalions, lavishly equipped with life stories, to take their place in his full-scale social panorama." He concluded: "If Señor Fuentes is not the most polished and assured writer, and if some of his episodes are coarsely imagined and hasty, he is at any rate endowed with the courage and the power to attempt and to achieve a really big thing." [48]

On the more negative side are the observations of Richard Gilman in *Commonweal* and José Vázquez Amaral in the *Saturday Review*. While admiring some parts of the novel, Gilman observed: "But it doesn't really come off. The form and experience don't quite hold together. . . . It steps into a solipsistic world of manifestos, occult reveries, private myth-making and over-literary hymns to life that never attain the verbal originality and imaginative coherence that might justify them." Vázquez Amaral pointed out many possible influences and borrowings and saw the work as a roman à clef. (His attempts to identify the characters brought an angry letter from Fuentes which was published in a later number of the magazine.) His conclusion is that *Where the Air Is Clear* is an ambitious "pastiche," but does not give credit to Salazar Mallén who had used the word two years earlier. Vázquez Amaral is one of the few critics to mention the language of the translation which he feels is much too free. "It is not fair to quarrel with the translator's difficulties with slang. But it is hard to justify inaccurate interpretations of standard Spanish." [49]

Perhaps a few words would be appropriate regarding the translation, especially since we have a unique situation in a contemporary work of the existence of two translations into English. Almost a year before the novel was published Lysander Kemp included an English version of a chapter in *Evergreen Review*. [50] Interestingly enough, Kemp translated Fuentes' novelette, *Aura*, six years later.

Both translations are quite free; perhaps Kemp's reads a bit smoother, but Hileman may capture Fuentes' unique style better. Both take liberties in translating and both make mistakes. In the first paragraph of the "Gervasio Pola" chapter Hileman erroneously translates "botines de cuero" as "leather buttons," while Kemp omits to mention that Islas is "calvo." A page later the "puertas" of a garbage cart is called "cover" by Hileman. He also expands "cúmulo de basura" to read, "rotted vegetables and excrement," while Kemp keeps it as "load of garbage." For "Gervasio, al pie de la sierra, aflojó los muslos," Hileman reads: "At the foot of the mountain, Gervasio dropped," and Kemp: "Gervasio slackened his pace at the foot of the sierra."

Through the years additional translations have been made of *La región más transparente;* into French (1964), Czech (1966), Polish (1972) and German (1973).[51] The French edition done by Robert Marrast includes a prologue by Miguel Angel Asturias. Marrast also translated the French version of *La muerte de Artemio Cruz.* Also noteworthy in the French edition of *La región más transparente* is the inclusion of a chronology of Mexican history combined with events from the lives of characters in the novel. For example, under the date of 1909 we read in the first column that Federico Robles goes to live in Morelia with a priest; the second column states that Francisco I. Madero declares himself a candidate for president of Mexico. Another first is a list of characters in the novel. Some eight members of the de Ovando family are cataloged, seven Zamaconas, and three Polas. Other listings are: the Bourgeoisie, Foreigners, Intellectuals, Lower Class, and Revolutionaries. These listings and descriptions make reading the novel much less confusing, especially in the initial chapters when so many characters are introduced. Occasionally we are given background information that does not appear in the novel. Dardo Morratto is an Argentine writer, but we now discover (perhaps in jest) that he has been secretary to Victoria Ocampo and a proofreader for Jorge Luis Borges. Also for the first time we discover that Tomás Mediana, about whom we have spoken several times, dies tragically in 1950.

La región más transparente Today

In spite of the almost universal recognition of *La muerte de Artemio Cruz* as Fuentes' masterpiece and the publicity surrounding each new publication, *La región más transparente* continues to reach a substantial body of new and appreciative readers each year. At most recent count it had gone through more than a dozen Spanish printings and has been continually available in English.

Perhaps the most significant publishing event of the seventies regarding the book was its inclusion in the 1,414 page *Obras completas,* volume I, done by Aguilar in 1974. The pages have been reset in a slightly larger format which is easier to read, although each continues to contain thirty-six lines. The newer version also includes the useful "Cuadro Cronológico" and the list of "personajes" which had first appeared in the French edition.

There seems to be only a very slight revision of the text. A few typographical errors are corrected and most foreign words are now in italics ("blue-jeans," "Handicap," "claxon," "Jockey," "kaputt," "pedigree," "very fain"). A few words change: "hilos de gomina" (Fondo version, p. 22) becomes "Hilo de gomina" (Aguilar version, p. 166). A period does not end a paragraph of stream of consciousness in the Fondo edition (p. 43), "profesa" (Fondo, p. 454) is capitalized by Aguilar (p. 624). The incorrect date, 1857, for the execution of Maximilian (Fondo, p. 454) is printed in long form and corrected by Aguilar: "mil ochocientos sesenta y siete" (p. 624).

With the passage of time *La región más transparente* has grown in stature among the Mexican critics. The occasion of its fourth printing, exactly a decade after the first, produced an uncommonly large number of reviews, apparently by younger critics. The shock of technique and exposé had worn off and the book's style no longer seemed out of place in Latin American fiction. Several reviewers commented upon the volume's historical importance as a "novel which breaks barriers." Rigoberto Lasso Tizareño observed: "This novel in our opinion opens a new cycle in the Mexican novel of our century." Vilma Fuentes (no relation) stated: ". . . for a new generation different and far removed, *La región más transparente* is enlightening in its chaos, while it appears fantastic and unbelievable in its historical background. Fuentes' book has grown but not aged."[52]

Perhaps Emmanuel Carballo, who collaborated with Fuentes in a number of literary activities in the fifties, has best summed up the novel's importance: "For me the most important event of that year (1958) was the publication of *La región más transparente*, a work which closes the cycle of the rural-provincial novel and opens that of the post-revolutionary and metropolitan novel, fiercely critical. With this book Carlos Fuentes is converted into the style dictator of Mexican prose."[53]

Notes

1. Most of the biographical portion of this study is taken from the introductory section of Fuentes' *Obras completas*, vol. I (Mexico: Aguilar, 1974) and Emmanuel Carballo's "Conversación con Carlos Fuentes," *Siempre*, May 23, 1962, pp. v–viii, "La Cultura en México."
2. Carlos Fuentes, *Tiempo mexicano* (Mexico: Joaquín Mortiz, 1971), p. 66.
3. Statistics about Mexico during the decade of the 1950s come mainly from the annual supplements of the *Encyclopaedia Britannica*.
4. Emmanuel Carballo, "El año de la novela," *Novedades*, December 28, 1958, p. 1 of "México en la Cultura."
5. Ibid.

6. Carballo, "Conversación con Carlos Fuentes," pp. v, vi.
7. See *Obras completas,* vol. I, and Carballo's "Conversación con Carlos Fuentes" for Fuentes' comments on these pieces.
8. *Hoy,* August 20, 1949, pp. 30–35.
9. *Hoy,* December 10, 1949, pp. 32–33, 82. Subsequent citations to this article are made parenthetically in the text.
10. *Ideas de México,* 1, no. 3 (January–February 1954): 119–124.
11. "El muñeco," *Revista de la Universidad de México,* 10, no. 7 (March 1956): 7–8. For examples of Maximilian references in *La región* see pp. 453–454.
12. Daniel Dueñas, "Carlos Fuentes: de 'niño bien' a novelista de los habitantes de D.F.," *Hoy,* May 17, 1958, pp. 76–77.
13. María Palomino (signed Alba Montejo), "Impertinentes," *Hoy,* June 18, 1949, p. 60.
14. Pablo Palomino, "Sueño y mentira del 'vasfumismo,'" *Mañana,* 26, no. 325 (November 26, 1949): 18.
15. María Palomino, "Impertinentes: Definición para el basfumismo," *Hoy,* July 2, 1949, p. 62.
16. *Hoy,* October 29, 1949, pp. 24, 66.
17. Pablo Palomino, "Sueño y mentira," p. 20.
18. Luis Harss, "Carlos Fuentes, Mexico's Metropolitan Eye," *New Mexico Quarterly,* 36, no. 1 (Spring 1966): 40.
19. See my article: "Octavio Paz and Hiperión in *La región más transparente*: Plagiarism, Caricature or . . . ?" *Chasqui,* 2, no. 3 (May 1974): 13–25.
20. Salvador Novo, "Cartas a un amigo," *Hoy,* May 3, 1958, p. 28.
21. María Palomino, "Impertinentes: Restos basfumistas," *Hoy,* February 25, 1950, p. 64.
22. "¿Príncipe o aventurero?" *Hispanoamericano,* January 6, 1950, pp. 3–4.
23. Luis Spota, *Casi el paraíso* (Mexico: Fondo de Cultura Económica, 1956), p. 36.
24. See my bibliography for all of Fuentes' motion picture reviews: Richard Reeve, "An Annotated Bibliography on Carlos Fuentes: 1949–1969," *Hispania,* 53 (October 1970): 595–652.
25. Benito Alazraki, "Prefiero hacer churros y andar en Cadillac, que películas de cine-club y andar en camión," *Novedades,* December 28, 1958, p. 4 of "México en la Cultura."
26. "Los restos," *Revista de la Universidad de México,* 9 (March 1955): 9.
27. Emmanuel Carballo, "La política y el cuento mexicano de hoy," *Siempre,* October 29, 1969, p. viii, "La Cultura en México."
28. "Una carta de Alfonso Reyes," *El Libro y el Pueblo,* 42 (July 1968): 21–22.
29. "Autores y Libros," *Novedades,* November 13, 1955, p. 2 of "México en la Cultura."
30. See my bibliography in *Hispania,* 53 (October 1970).
31. "Autores y Libros," *Novedades,* May 25, 1958, p. 4 of "México en la Cultura."

32. J. M. García Ascot, "*La región más transparente*, un libro de gran importancia que crece con la ferocidad de ciertas oposiciones," *Novedades*, May 11, 1958, pp. 2, 10 of "México en la Cultura"; Enrique González Rojo, *Letras Nuevas*, 4 (July–August 1958): 47; José Emilio Pacheco, *Estaciones*, 3, no. 10 (Summer 1958): 195; Rafael Solana, "Novelas y no novelas," *El Universal*, September 14, 1958, p. 3 of "Revista de la Semana"; Luis Cardoza y Aragón, "El pro y el contra de una escandalosa novela," *Novedades*, May 11, 1958, p. 1 of "México en la Cultura."

33. "Escándalo y literatura," *El Nacional*, October 5, 1958, p. 2 of "Suplemento Semanario."

34. "James Joyce vernáculo," *Mañana*, 762 (April 19, 1958): 58.

35. Elena Garro, "El pro y el contra de una escandalosa novela," *Novedades*, May 11, 1958, p. 1 of "México en la Cultura."

36. More easily accessible is the same version published in the journal *Imagen*, 25 (September–October 1961): 56–58. Quotation on p. 57.

37. José Vázquez Amaral, "Mexico's Melting Pot," *Saturday Review*, 43 (November 19, 1960): 29.

38. Julio Cortázar, in Fuentes, *Obras completas*, vol. I, p. 136.

39. José Lezama Lima, in Fuentes, *Obras completas*, pp. 133, 134.

40. Mario Benedetti, "Carlos Fuentes: Una dramática conciencia americana," *Tiempos Modernos*, 1 (December 1964): 12.

41. Mario Vargas Llosa, "Novela primitiva y novela de creación en América," *Revista de la Universidad de México*, 23, no. 10 (June 1969): 32.

42. Harss, "Metropolitan Eye," p. 35; Claude Couffon, "Carlos Fuentes nos habla de la nueva novela mexicana," *Cuadernos* (Paris), 42 (May–June 1960): 67.

43. Carballo, "Conversación con Carlos Fuentes," p. vi; Fuentes, "South of the Border," *Saturday Review*, 43 (December 17, 1960): 27.

44. Poniatowska, "Entrevista con Carlos Fuentes," *Novedades*, December 28, 1958, p. 6 of "México en la Cultura."

45. George Wing, *Books Abroad*, 32, no. 4 (Autumn 1958): 386; Jefferson Rea Spell, *Hispanic American Historical Review*, 39, no. 4 (November 1958): 676.

46. Luis Andrés Murrillo, *Revista Iberoamericana*, 24, no. 47 (1959): 196; Robert G. Mead, Jr., "Carlos Fuentes, Mexico's Angry Novelist," *Books Abroad*, 38, no. 4 (Autumn 1964): 380–382. See also his expanded version in *Hispania*, 50, no. 2 (May 1967): 229–235.

47. Selden Rodman, "Heroes Must Fail," *New York Times*, November 13, 1960, section 8, p. 44.

48. Anthony West, "The Whole Life," *New Yorker*, March 4, 1961, p. 123.

49. Richard Gilman, "Self-Conscious Culture of Modern Mexico," *Commonweal*, 73, no. 510 (February 10, 1961): 511; Fuentes, "South of the Border," p. 27; Vázquez Amaral, "Mexico's Melting Pot," p. 29.

50. Lysander Kemp, "The Life Line," *Evergreen Review*, 2, no. 7 (Winter 1959): 75–84.

51. For further details on the translations see my bibliography in *Hispania*.

52. Rigoberto Lasso Tizareño, "Nueva edición de *La región más trans-*

parente," *Boletín Bibliográfico de Hacienda,* 404 (December 1, 1968): 23; Vilma Fuentes, "¿Qué es hoy *La región más transparente?" Excélsior,* June 23, 1968, p. 6, "Diorama de la Cultura."

53. Emmanuel Carballo, "La prosa hoy y hace diez años," *Excélsior,* April 28, 1968, p. 5, "Diorama de la Cultura."

Lanin A. Gyurko

La muerte de Artemio Cruz and *Citizen Kane*: A Comparative Analysis

In several interviews, Fuentes has commented on the enormous impact exerted on him by *Citizen Kane*—a film that he first saw at the age of ten and most certainly has viewed many times since. According to Fuentes: "When I came with my father to the World's Fair in 1940, *Citizen Kane* was being shown in New York. I saw it and that was the beginning of the world for me. It is probably the single most influential aesthetic thrill I've had in my life. . . . That movie left a very, very profound mark on my spirit."[1] The question that this essay addresses is, "what specific influence has Orson Welles' brilliant film had on Fuentes' art?" One novel in particular demonstrates how Carlos Fuentes, who throughout his work is a very visual writer, who has collaborated in the making of several films, and who originally wrote one of his major novels, *Zona sagrada*, as a filmscript, has been inspired by Welles—*La muerte de Artemio Cruz*. The protagonist of this novel is a composite figure, one whose role as revolutionary fighter turned opportunist and plutocrat corresponds to actual historical figures, to the careers of many of the revolutionary generals who later exploited their privileged positions to construct lavish mansions for themselves, aping the Porfirian aristocrats whom they had overthrown and betraying the ideals of land, labor, and educational reform for which the Revolution had been fought. Yet a significant part of the genesis of Artemio Cruz, as we shall see, is found in fantasy, namely in Welles' Charles Foster Kane—like Cruz a poor boy suddenly wrenched away from a childhood realm of innocence, launched on a career of social idealism that finally degenerates into demagoguery and self-aggrandizement. Both men amass huge fortunes and control vast conglomerate empires but fail to achieve what they most desire. And the influence of *Citizen Kane* on *La muerte de Artemio Cruz* does not stop with character creation; it is found in the structure of Fuentes' novel, with its multiple and constantly shifting points of view on the protagonist, its evocation of Cruz's life not as a chronological progression from birth to death but as a series of fragments that shift rapidly in time, from Cruz's early career to his old age and back to his childhood in response to the associational flux of his stricken consciousness, and in its style—its dramatic intensity, its mannered delivery, and its baroque pyramiding of images. This is not to detract from the uniqueness and the profundity of Fuentes' creation, a novel that has already become a modern classic of Latin American literature, but rather to demonstrate how the influences on Fuentes by leading artists such as Welles have brought about the opening up of Mexican literature, resulting in its emergence as a truly universal art form.

The fact that Fuentes chose to create a symbol of modern Mexico in the form of a dying plutocrat itself owes much to Welles' film, which begins at the end—by focusing on its protagonist as he lies on his deathbed. Both novel and film concentrate on the development of a single, titanic individual who is given the awesomeness and the complexity necessary to stand as a symbol of an entire nation. The bold, brash, irreverent spirit of Kane is symbolic of a young country rapidly moving away from its nineteenth-century rural traditions toward massive industrialization, resulting in the consolidation of gigantic trusts that Kane both invests in and fights to break up. Kane's vitality—his enormous enthusiasm, his boundless energy, his obsessive emphasis on bigness ("If the headlines are big enough, it makes the news big"), his single-handed transformation of a small, staid newspaper into a farflung journalistic empire—is symbolic of a young nation flexing its economic and military might and for the first time in its history assuming a commanding role in world affairs. Kane defines himself first and foremost as an American, and it is significant that the script for the film was originally entitled *The American*. Naremore, in his extensive analysis of *Citizen Kane*, interprets the protagonist as "a man designed to embody all the strengths and failings of capitalist democracy" and comments on the relationship between the development of the individual and that of the nation: "America moves from the age of the Tycoon, through the period of populist muckraking, and into the era of 'mass communications,' with turn-of-the-century types like Kane being destroyed by the very process they have set into motion."[2] Several of the characters in *Citizen Kane* are both individuals and national symbols. Significantly, Susan Alexander, Kane's second wife, is referred to as "a cross-section of the American public." Kane's brutal manipulation of her and his virtual imprisonment of her at Xanadu even while professing his love and need for her are symbolic of his basic ambivalence toward the American people—his deep desire to be loved by them but his feelings of superiority and his marked contempt for the masses and his incessant exploitation of them in order to rise to power.

Like Welles, Fuentes is a master at creating characters who function not only as individuals but as national symbols. In *La región más transparente* and in *La muerte de Artemio Cruz*, primary and secondary characters become symbols of both ancient and modern Mexico. Artemio Cruz is developed in terms of both Hernán Cortés, to indicate the continuing influence that the archetype of the *conquistador* wields in Mexican society, and an Aztec emperor—a modern version of Moctezuma or even of the Aztec god Huitzilopochtli, as Cruz relentlessly demands blood sacrifice in order to renew himself. Cruz's self-betrayal is symbolic of Mexico's failure to actualize the ideals of the Revolution of 1910; Cruz's desperate struggle for rebirth and for self-transcendence symbolizes the nation that time and again throughout its sanguinary history has struggled to re-create itself—after the conquest, after its independence from Spain, after the liberal reforms of the Juárez era, after the Revolution of 1910, after the nationalization of its petroleum resources under Cárdenas. Yet Cruz's final and irrevocable incarceration in self, his inability to reconstitute the shattered remnants of both his moral and his physical self, constitutes Fuentes' warning to his countrymen about the extreme dangers to the national integrity and autonomy that could result from Mexico's failure to unify the fragments of the national self—its diverse social classes, the poverty and disease-stricken masses on the one side and its economic and social elite on the other, its Indian and its *criollo* identities, its pre-Columbian heritage and its commercial and technological present.

The paradoxical nature of Cruz and Kane is evident from the very beginning of both works. At the outset of the film, in the *March of Time* newsreel, headlines from newspapers across the world convey the markedly ambivalent nature of Kane, and serve to adumbrate the entire structure of the film—the multiple and contradictory points of view concerning the protagonist: "Entire Nation Mourns Great Publisher as Outstanding American"; "Death of Publisher Finds Few Who Will Mourn for Him"; "Stormy Career Ends for 'U.S. Fascist No. 1'"; "Kane, Sponsor of Democracy, Dies."[3] Kane's guardian, the financial tycoon Thatcher, denounces the iconoclastic trust-buster as a communist, yet one of the workers whose devotion Kane has attempted to gain excoriates him as a fascist. Welles himself has commented on the deliberate inconsistencies in Kane's nature. The result of these paradoxes is to leave the viewer with an unsolvable mystery concerning Kane's true identity—as unsolvable as that of Howard Hughes, another multimillionaire who, like Kane, died in seclusion, and, ironically, who also had an island retreat, aptly called the *Hotel Xanadu*: "Kane, we are told, loved only his mother—only his newspaper—only his second wife—only himself. Maybe he loved all of these, or none. It is for the audience to judge. Kane was selfish and selfless, an idealist, a scoundrel, a very big man and a very little one. It depends on who's talking about him. He is never judged with the objectivity of an author, and the point of the picture is not so much the solution of the problem as its presentation."[4]

Ambivalence toward the protagonist is found not only among the various people—the once idealistic and now cynical Leland, the embittered Susan Alexander, the servile Bernstein, the greedy and sinister Raymond, but even within the same account. For example, from the perspective of Susan Alexander Kane, the person whose career and whose life Kane has almost destroyed, the protagonist is evoked as both ruthless and pitiable.

A similar ambivalence characterizes Artemio Cruz, who not only on his deathbed but throughout his life is portrayed as a congeries of warring selves that are given bold structural form through the use of a triadic perspective—first, second, and third person accounts of the life of Cruz, each person widely varying in its assessment of the protagonist. The self-exalting I-narrative of Cruz the potentate contrasts markedly with the self-evaluating and self-condemning second-person voice of conscience. Just as the problematic Kane represents a significant departure from the unidimensional protagonists of so many Hollywood films made before and after *Citizen Kane*, so too does Artemio Cruz break through the Manichean mold into which so many characters in Latin American literature are cast—either ruthless, despotic *cacique* or submissive *peón*, corrupt foreign exploiter or self-sacrificing, heroic *criollo*. The multiverse of Cruz's self, his dual nature as both national defender and *malinchista*, as both unscrupulous *hacendado* and extremely sensitive and guilt-ridden victim desperately reaching out for love—and fearing rejection—is conveyed through the *tú* narrative. This second-person narrative in itself is an awesome paradox, both superego and representative of Cruz's physiological self, both individual and collective, both condemning Cruz and yet seeking to penetrate his motives. Obsessed with the recapitulation of Cruz's past and scrutiny of his moral failings, this voice addresses him in the future tense: "Ayer volarás," as if self-renewal and salvation were still possible for him: "Confess that always, even when it has seemed otherwise, you have found in black the germ of its opposite; your own cruelty, when you have been cruel, has it not been tinged with a certain tenderness? . . . Your bravery will be the brother of your cowardice and even its twin; your hatred will be born of your love. . . . You will not have been either good or evil, generous or selfish, faithful or traitorous" (pp. 28–29). Both Kane and Cruz are extraordinarily complex characters. According to Fowler, "The Welles film . . . gave the most searching and complete analysis ever made on film of an individual, imaginary or real."[5] And certainly Artemio Cruz is one of the most three-dimensional characters in all of Latin American fiction.

The theme of the fall from paradise—and the desperate, often pathetic attempts by both protagonists throughout their lives to regain that lost paradise—is a key one in both film and novel. The following remark by Welles applies equally to both works: "Almost all serious stories in the world are stories of a failure with a death in it. . . . But there is more lost paradise in them than defeat. To me that's the central theme in Western culture, the lost paradise."[6]

Early in his life Cruz suffers the warping of his idealism and of his capacity to love. He is expelled from the natural paradise that is the world of his youth at Cocuya, Veracruz, from the romantic paradise within the hellworld of war that he shares but briefly with Regina before her brutal death, and from the illusion of redemptive unity that he seeks with Catalina. His primary response in protecting his fragile, inner self against the threat of further frustration and hurt is to retreat into a self-made and self-sustained world in which he can feel secure. For the spiritual paradise of love that he has been denied, Cruz substitutes a material paradise that seems to proclaim his invincibility—the old monastery at Coyoacán that he transforms into a palace. His actions parallel the retreat by Kane from the external world into a self-made and self-contained universe—the world of Xanadu. Both protagonists fashion themselves to be demigods, creating the universe anew. Kane transforms marshland into mountain; he imports his own scenery—entire forests; he constructs Xanadu as a world in which he can reign supreme. Both protagonists rise up as satanic figures. Artemio Cruz, exulting in his power as a terrestrial god, even attempts to bargain with God for his salvation, promising to believe in Him in exchange for being granted perpetual life on earth: "And the heaven that is power over uncounted men with hidden faces and forgotten names, named by the thousand on the payrolls of my mines, my factories, my newspaper. . . . This is to be God, eh? [To be feared and hated and all the rest, this is to be God, truly, eh?] (p. 155).[7]

An essential part of the structuring of both film and novel is the incorporation of leitmotivs. In works that shift so rapidly and often abruptly in point of view, that reverse so often the temporal sequence, the use of these leitmotivs accomplishes two goals: it grants continuity to the many truncated scenes and episodes and injects a deep sense of mystery and suspense that in a more traditional novel or film would be provided by the development of the plot. In *Citizen Kane* there are two major leitmotivs, one explicit and the other more subtly developed but just as significant: Rosebud and the glass ball. Similarly, in *La muerte de Artemio Cruz* there are two major leitmotivs—the *convolvulus* or moonflower, and the enigmatic phrase that appears in twelve of the thirteen sections of Cruz's first-person monologue: "Cruzamos el río a caballo." The leitmotivs in both film and novel represent the remote past of the protagonists; they also symbolize the spiritual center that is lacking in their lives.

Like almost every aspect of *Citizen Kane*, the motif of Rosebud is complex and ambiguous. The reporter Thompson is instructed to solve the mystery of this single word, uttered by Kane at the moment of his death. Yet, although Thompson delves methodically into Kane's past, his investigation is ultimately futile. Although the viewer of *Citizen Kane* is seemingly privileged by being allowed to witness what Thompson will never discover—the word "Rosebud" emblazoned on the sled that is tossed like a piece of rubbish into the furnace at Xanadu—the revelation of "Rosebud" only heightens the mystery of Kane. The sled has a multiple significance. First of all, it is a symbol of Kane's past—of past innocence and also of past trauma, because it represents the childhood of which he was deprived. It symbolizes the exuberance and joy of Kane's childhood in Colorado and it also becomes the weapon—an ineffectual one—that Kane utilizes to defend his childhood world against the intruder Thatcher. Similarly, the boy Cruz with equal bewilderment and desperation will take a rifle blindly to keep his world from being shattered by the agent of the new *hacendado*, who has come to take Cruz's guardian and surrogate father Lunero away.

The second major visual leitmotiv—one that appears briefly at the beginning of the film, is later reduced almost to inconspicuousness as it is glimpsed among Susan's possessions in her apartment, and then reemerges to the explicit level at the climax of the film, as the demented Kane rampages through Susan's room at Xanadu and is halted in his destructive fury only by the encountering of the object—is the glass ball, which contains a snow scene. In a sense, this glass ball, a dimestore object of trivial material value, constitutes a spiritual response to the vast and treasure-laden but mausoleum-like Xanadu. As Naremore states, "It symbolizes an ideal—a self-enclosed realm, immune from change, where Kane can feel he has control over his life."[8] And, like Rosebud, it symbolizes the irrecoverable past—the halcyon boyhood in the snow, the family home in Colorado, the maternal love from which Kane was permanently severed by his mother's decision to send him away.

Welles expertly uses the technique of suspended coherence, as he keeps returning to the theme of Rosebud without clarifying it until the very end. Fuentes too utilizes the device of suspended coherence in the sense that Humphrey defines the term, as a "method of suspending sense impressions and ideas in the memory for so long that they reappear at unexpected and seemingly unreasonable places."[9] Through his use of this technique, Fuentes, like Welles, underscores the enigmatic nature of the protagonist. The deaths of the protagonists, evident from the outset of both film and novel, remove all possible suspense concerning the outcome. Suspense comes instead as a result of the layer by layer revelation of the extraordinary characters of both protagonists.

Fuentes interpolates into the sections of Cruz's subjective, anguished, first-person monologue two leitmotivs that are clarified—and then only partially—only at the very end. The first mystery is that of the *convolvulus* flower, symbolic of immortality. It is startling that this very delicate, poetic image should appear in the monologue of Artemio Cruz, replete with images of brutality and obscenity, with memories of power plays and acts of oppression of those attempting to claim the rights they ostensibly had won as a result of the revolution. The image of the moonflower is originally triggered involuntarily within Cruz's moribund psyche, as a response to the sudden darkening of his room—symbolic of the shadow of death. Desperately, heroically struggling to raise up barriers against death, to obtain terrestrial immortality, Cruz recalls—and identifies with—the image of the flower that comes to life in the darkness: "They closed the curtains, right? It is night, right? And there are plants that must have the light of darkness in order to flower, they wait until darkness comes out, the moonflower, it opens its petals in the evening. The moonflower. There was a moonflower vine on that hut near the river. It opened its flowers in the evening" (p. 135). It is significant that this image is the only one now left to Cruz of his boyhood realm at Cocuya, an idyllic life that he once believed to be eternal—a childhood paradise that he had returned to over and over again, even to the extent of restoring the burned-out mansion of his ancestors. The thrust toward the past that is characteristic of much of Cruz's life is very similar to the absorption into the past of Kane, who first encounters Susan Alexander as he is on his way to the Western Manhattan Warehouse to inspect the family belongings that he has had shipped East from Colorado. It is ironic that Kane, who for much of his life has traveled incessantly, should finally prefer to remain a recluse at Xanadu, which thus becomes an enormous protective womb. Similarly, Cruz toward the end of his life retreats into Coyoacán in a futile attempt to conquer time and death. The observation that Leland makes concerning Kane, "He was disappointed in the world, so he built one of his own," applies equally well to Artemio Cruz, who like the arrogant but essentially childish Kane, attempts to live life totally on his own terms:

> He preferred these old walls with their two centuries of sandstone and tezontle. In a strange way they took him back into their own past and reflected a land that did not want everything to be transient. Yes, he was quite aware that there had been a process of substitution, the waving of a magic wand. And there was also no doubt that the old timbers and stone, the ironwork and mouldings, the refectory tables, the cabinets, the grainwork, the inlays, that these conspired to bring back to him, with a faint perfume of nostalgia, the scenes, the smells, the tactile sensations of his own youth. (p. 244)

Both protagonists, who publicly appear so dedicated to the future, to the building of new worlds, are privately obsessed with recovering the security, comfort, and love that the past represents.

The theme of idealism—and of the repeated betrayal of those ideals—is an important one in both of these works. Kane's very name constitutes an allusion to the biblical Cain; the slaying of Abel is paralleled by Kane's destruction of the career of his soulmate, Jed Leland, and his impelling of Susan Kane, whom he purportedly loves, to an attempt to commit suicide. First the rustication then the firing of Leland represent Kane's gradual suppression of the idealistic part of himself. An ominous revelation of Kane's unprincipled nature behind his idealistic façade is evident from the start of his journalistic career. The impetuous Kane takes over a staid and musty but highly reputable newspaper, the *Inquirer*, and although mouthing reformist phrases on the one hand, immediately concocts a story that blows up a routine missing person case into a murder mystery—viciously accusing an innocent man of the merely purported crime. Both Kane and Cruz ceaselessly inflate, distort, and sensationalize the news, slandering their enemies while at the same time pandering to the lowest denominator of public taste—the demand for the lurid—Kane in order to gain power and fame, Cruz in order to destroy his enemies and to divert the attention of the public away from his own acts of brutal oppression.

Initially Kane is a crusader—he attacks monopolies, rails against the corruption of machine politics, and becomes an impassioned advocate of the common man. Yet although professing his unstinting dedication to the public service and the public good, the reckless Kane really has little understanding and no genuine concern for the needs of the people. At best Kane's paternalism is a type of *noblesse oblige*, at worst it is rampant opportunism. The demagoguery of Kane is matched by that of Cruz. Like Kane, Cruz is extremely skillful at manipulating the media, at creating an elaborate public façade as champion of the people. It is significant that Cruz too owns his own newspaper, one that even after his death will promulgate the false image of him as revolutionary hero and national architect, just as the *Inquirer* trumpets the monumental deeds of Charles Foster Kane. Kane and Cruz have accrued tremendous wealth and power that they could utilize to actualize their ideals and to construct new, progressive societies. As the head of a publishing empire, Kane has an unparalleled opportunity to enlighten public opinion, to unify a vast nation in its development of a collective conscience and in its pursuit of a common good. Instead Kane squanders his immense talent and energy, dedicating much of his career to the stirring up of jingoistic fever, even manufacturing a war through his headlines. At the close of the military phase of the Mexican Revolution, Cruz too has the opportunity—even greater, relatively speaking, than that of Kane—to reshape the whole of his society to benefit his countrymen, all of *los de abajo* who had fought for social equality. Cruz has the position and the authority to break the stranglehold of cyclic time that throughout the centuries—from the epoch of the Aztec conquerors—has acted as a curse on his country, repeatedly demolishing an old set of exploiters and oppressors only to raise up a new set in their place. Yet the insecure and exceedingly ambitious Cruz, like Kane, forfeits his initial idealism and plunges into a career of self-aggrandizement. Both become transfixed, and, finally, enslaved by their drive for power.

Shortly after assuming control of the *Inquirer*, Kane feels compelled to make a public declaration of his idealism, as he prints on the front page his *Declaration of Principles*:

> I. I will provide the people of this city with a daily newspaper that will tell all the news honestly.

II. I will also provide them with a fighting and tireless champion of their rights as human beings.

But Kane's principles are undercut, right from the start, by the mocking words of Leland, who acts as Kane's conscience. Leland ends his assessment of Kane's intentions on a note of ironic deflation: "I'd like to keep that particular piece of paper myself. I have a hunch it might turn out to be something pretty important, a document . . . like the Declaration of Independence, or the Constitution . . . and my first report card at school" (CC, p. 352). The plummeting from the mentioning of historical documents of universal significance to the mundane level of elementary school achievement is an indication that Leland from the very start suspects the worthlessness of Kane's declaration. Kane will betray the people's trust and betray too his best friend, as he fires Leland for daring to write a negative review of Susan's singing performance. But most of all Kane will betray himself, as he becomes obsessively dedicated to a massive and futile campaign to prove to the voting public that they were wrong in rejecting him.

Kane's pseudoidealism is also mocked by the very structure of the film. An example of visual undercutting, accomplished through a rapid alteration in point of view, is analyzed by McBride: "Welles undercuts the spirit of Kane's high-minded speech by cutting to the dandyish Leland on the words 'the workingman and the slum child' and to Bernstein and his unsavory associates applauding after the words 'the underprivileged, the underpaid and the underfed.'"[10]

The spectre of Cain pollutes the lives of both Kane and Cruz. In Fuentes' novel, *cainismo* falls as a generational curse over the Menchaca line, from which Cruz descends, and, symbolically, as a seemingly indelible curse over the whole of Mexican history, which is evoked by Fuentes in this and other works as a series of betrayals, beginning with that of Moctezuma and ending with those of Porfirio Díaz, Victoriano Huerta, and the revolutionaries themselves. On the individual level, Cruz's father is ambushed and killed after he is betrayed by his own brother, Pedro, who carries a loaded gun and who could have defended him. Pedro's desertion of his brother adumbrates a whole series of betrayals by Artemio. The double who functions as a conscience figure is important in both *Citizen Kane* and *La muerte de Artemio Cruz*. Paralleling Kane's many encounters with Leland are the episodes in which Cruz is forced to confront a figure who both resembles him physically and who incarnates the moral qualities—courage, strength of convictions, honor, capacity to love—that Cruz has betrayed. The unknown soldier on the battlefield who strangely resembles him and who dies in his place, Gonzalo Bernal, Laura, Lorenzo, all are spiritual doubles of Cruz, and all are sacrificed by the protagonist just as Kane sacrifices Leland for daring to challenge him and for tearing down the carefully elaborated façade of social benefactor that Kane has erected. The death of these idealists symbolizes Cruz's lifelong suppression of his own idealistic potential, which he replaces by a rhetorical façade of revolutionary commitment merely to curry the favor of the *campesinos*, while secretly selling their land to purchase building lots for himself in Mexico City. Cruz's behavior becomes a perfect example of what Mariano Azuela has referred to as *el complejo de la Malinche*—the surrendering of his identity by the Mexican to foreigners before whom he remains awed—repeating the pattern of La Malinche and the other Indian women who voluntarily gave themselves to the Spaniards, whom they perceived as gods. The constant undermining of the idealistic pretentiousness of Cruz is done both thematically—through key confrontations between Cruz with the genuine idealists, and structurally, through the continual antagonism between the first-person and the second-person narratives, as the second person voice challenges and probes and squelches the vaunted ego. The second person voice of conscience castigates Cruz for his sellout of his *mexicanidad*, as he apes the values and lifestyle and even the dress of those who have exploited his country: "You will not be Artemio Cruz . . . you will not . . . wear Italian silk shirts, collect cufflinks, order your neckties from New York, wear three-button blue suits, prefer Irish cashmere, drink gin and tonic, own a Volvo, a Cadillac, and a Rambler Wagon" (pp. 238–239).

Yet both men have the capacity for self-awareness and for self-criticism. When Jed Leland writes an honest review of Susan's disastrous performance at the Chicago Opera House, Kane's markedly ambivalent nature is manifested by his first completing the review for Leland—in exactly the same negative manner as it had begun—and then summarily firing the drama critic for failing to perform the self-abasing role that Kane expects all of those around him to play. Cruz too finally achieves self-awareness and even rejects that aspect of himself affirmed in the first-person narrative—Cruz the power broker, demagogue, and robber baron. Yet, ironically, Cruz's self-critique and self-rejection occur when it is too late for him to alter his life. Suddenly forced into confrontation with the Cruz of the past, the aggressive, rapacious Cruz projected by the voice on the tape recorder, the dying Cruz is brought to an admission of the hollowness of the role that he has so thoroughly mastered. On his deathbed, he seeks first sensual then spiritual consolation—and, in what appears to be the operating of poetic justice, finds neither:

> *Tell him to establish a clear contrast between an anarchic, bloody movement that is destructive of private property and human rights alike, and an ordered revolution, peaceful and legal, such as the Mexican Revolution, which was directed by a middle class inspired by Jefferson. The people have short memories. . . .*
> Oh, what a barrage of meanings, implications, words. Oh, what fatigue. They won't understand my gesture, my fingers can hardly move: but let it be shut off now, I'm bored with it, it means nothing, just crap, crap. . . . (p. 197. Italics in English edition.)

Kane has been described as a kind of "Barnum who conceals his private self behind a dazzling set of public images."[11] Similarly, Artemio Cruz is a master of masquerade, hiding his fragile, sensitive inner self behind an assortment of masks. The inner world of Cruz and his other selves that will remain mere potentialities are penetratingly revealed and explored in the second-person narrative that breaks through the elaborate façade of *machista* and *conquistador* that Cruz has constructed. Similarly, Kane alludes to the other self, the truly great self that will never be actualized:

> KANE: Well, I always gagged on that silver spoon. You know, Mr. Bernstein, if I hadn't been very rich, I might have been a really great man.
> THATCHER: What would you like to have been?
> KANE: Everything you hate. (CC, p. 340)

In addition to leitmotivs, mirror imagery is utilized extensively in both film and novel. In *Citizen Kane* there is an eery incident in which the aging Kane, immediately after Susan walks out on him, is seen reflected endlessly in a hall of mirrors at Xanadu. This incessant duplication suggests several aspects of Kane's character—his multiplicity of selves and also his failure to integrate them. The myriad reflections symbolize Kane's enormous ego but also the futility of his actions—his permanent entrapment in the self. It is ironic that the newspaper magnate, who has dedicated his career to the creation of images, should now himself be reduced to but a series of images. Bernstein too is evoked as both self and image as he is shown reflected in a glass desk top. Dominated by the portrait of

Kane above his desk just as he was dominated by Kane while the magnate was alive, Bernstein's reflected image—the image of Kane's will—seems to acquire more life than the man himself.

As in *Citizen Kane*, mirror imagery is utilized throughout *La muerte de Artemio Cruz*—to emphasize the disjointed nature of Cruz, the permanent split in his identity, as his conscience is suppressed, isolated into a form, the *tú* narrative, that always remains structurally independent of the first-person monologue. Mirrors emphasize the tremendous discrepancy between the actual and the potential Cruz. At the very beginning of the narrative, the dying Cruz is forced to see himself reflected grotesquely in the facets of Teresa's purse, which present him with a cubist portrait of himself. The subsequent structuring of the novel into mere fragments of identity that will never be recomposed is adumbrated by this bizarre mirroring.

It is ironic that the socially responsible self, the true revolutionary that Cruz could have been, appears to him as but a reflected image, as he enters a revolving glass door. This simulacrum that seems to act independently of Cruz is a projection of his conscience that is struggling to assert itself. Cruz the corporate magnate has remained oblivious to the poverty and suffering all around him—the adverse social conditions that men like himself, *los de abajo*, had fought and died in an attempt to eradicate:

> Vendors of lottery tickets, bootblacks, women in rebozos, children with their upper lips smeared with mucous swarmed around him as he moved toward the revolving door and passed into the vestibule and adjusted his necktie in front of the glass and through it, in the second glass, which looked out on Madero, saw a man identical to himself, wearing the same double-breasted suit, but colorless, tightening the knot of the same tie with the same nicotine fingers, a man surrounded by beggars, who let his hand drop at the same instant he in the vestibule did, and turned and walked down the block, while he, for the moment a little disoriented, looked for the elevator. (p. 17)

Time and again when Cruz confronts his mirrored image, he refuses to acknowledge it. The last of these reflections is that of the aged and decrepit Cruz as he falls against his glass desktop, shattering it, and ironically merging his two selves. Only on his deathbed does the *alter ego*, the second-person voice, claim its victory—"te venzo"— by forcing Cruz to confront his past and his past failings.

Both Fuentes and Welles expertly fuse theme and structure. The severe alienation that characterizes the lives of their protagonists—estrangement not only from those around them but also from self, from their origins, from the selves they had the potential to become—is not merely described, it is given structural form, and its impact is thus intensified. In *The Magic World of Orson Welles*, Naremore shows how carefully constructed the scenes are to emphasize visually the extreme social alienation of the characters:

> . . . the actors often took unnatural positions, their figures arranged in a slanting line that ran out in front of the camera, so that characters in the extreme foreground or in the distance became subjects for the director's visual commentary. Actors seldom confronted one another face to face, as they do in the shot/reverse shot editing of the ordinary film. The communications scientists would say that the positions of figures on the screen were "sociofugal," or not conducive to direct human interaction, and this slight physical suggestion of an inability to communicate is fully appropriate to the theme of social alienation which is implicit in the film.[12]

The increasing estrangement between Kane and Emily is brilliantly telescoped—and intensified—by a montage in which the same scene—husband and wife at the breakfast table—is shown repeatedly as the years pass. The first time the scene is shot, the newlyweds are seated close together at one end of a small table, but each time the scene is repeated, they are farther and farther apart, until finally each is seen at the opposite end of a huge table, each engrossed in a different newspaper. Like Welles, Fuentes uses many techniques to depict the crippling isolation of his characters, many of whom—Cruz, Catalina, Ludivinia, Pedro, Don Gamaliel—remained locked within their pride, delusions of grandeur, guilt, or fear. At several points in the narrative, in particular in episodes that depict confrontations between Cruz and Catalina, Ludivinia and Pedro, Fuentes shows two people who are desperately seeking to reach out toward one another but cannot find any basis of communication. Fuentes develops these scenes in terms of a dialogue—to indicate the need to communicate—but significantly, remits that dialogue to the level of soliloquy. Thus the intense, conflictive drama of the encounter is emphasized and also, by the technique of recording words that are never uttered, the unbridgeable chasm between mother and son, or husband and wife, is stressed. The disdain that Ludivinia evinces toward her pusillanimous son Pedro, the one who could not uphold the *macho* code of the Menchaca line, and the withdrawing of her affection from one of her children while she glorifies the stronger, adumbrates the social relationships in the next generation. Within this closed, fatalistic familial structuring, the exclusivity demonstrated by Ludivinia will be repeated by Cruz's contempt for his daughter Teresa and his favoring of the *macho* figure Lorenzo:

> They looked at each other, mother and son, with a wall of a resurrection between them.
> *Are you here*, she said to him silently, *to tell me that we no longer have land or greatness? That others have taken from us what we took from others? Have you come to tell me what I have always known since my first night as a wife?*
> *I came with a pretext*, he replied with his eyes. *I didn't want to be alone any more.*
> *I would like to remember what you were like as a child*, she went on. *I loved you then. When a mother is young, she loves all her children. As old women, we know better. No one has a right to be loved without a reason. Blood ties are not reason enough. The right reason is blood loved without reason.*
> *I have wanted to be strong like my brother. For example, I have treated that mulatto and the boy with an iron hand. I have forbidden them ever to set foot in the house.*
> (pp. 287–288)

Both Cruz and Kane suffer from an inability to love. Cruz loves genuinely only once—in his relationship with Regina, which is severed by death. So great is the loss of Regina that Cruz will never again risk exposing his inner self to even the possibility of hurt, humiliation or defeat in love. Thus, although he wants to love Catalina, he will never confess to her his guilt over her brother's death, fearing that his wife will interpret any show of humility on his part as a sign of weakness that will arouse only her contempt. Similarly, Cruz refuses to sever his relationship with Catalina in order to marry Laura, again because he fears that by giving himself totally to her as he had to Regina, he will once more expose himself to the possibility of losing that love. Thus, at the end of his life, Cruz prefers the loveless relationship with Lilia to the genuine love he could have shared with Laura—because he need only command and Lilia, although resentful, will obey him.

Love and the irremediable loss of love plays an important part in Kane's life as well. The lifelong effect that the loss of Regina has upon Artemio Cruz is paralleled by the indelible mark that Kane's separation from his mother leaves upon him. Much of his life is spent in a futile attempt symbolically to regain that love. It is significant that the voting public is perceived by him as a source of love that is greater than that offered to him by his wife and child. When Emily attempts to convince Kane to withdraw from the election in order to save their marriage, Kane is stung by her words and demonstrates the extent to which he is emotionally committed to the electorate:

> EMILY: . . . if you don't listen to reason, it may be too late. . . .
> KANE: Too late for what? For you and this public thief to take the love of the people of this state away from me? (CC, p. 384)

The stunning loss at the polls is perceived by Kane as a rejection by this "lover"—and as a repetition on the public scale of his abandonment by his mother. Just as Kane attempts to reconstruct the physical fragments of the past, so also does he desperately strive to regain the devotion of the public through his fanatic promotion of Susan Alexander. Susan's walking out on Kane represents but another repetition of his original, childhood trauma. Kane desperately clutches the glass ball that becomes his pacifier and that reminds him of "Rosebud," a word he utters plaintively, and which perhaps gives him some insight into his actions.

It is significant that Kane purchases countless statues of Venus, the love goddess. He thereby attempts to compensate in marble—in objects that he can possess one hundred percent—for the loss of maternal love and the security of his childhood. Kane reduces human beings to collectibles, just as the wizened Cruz annually summons one hundred guests to his mansion at Coyoacán—ostensibly to celebrate the New Year but in reality to pay homage to him—to perform at his command. Kane marries a woman whom he does not love—Emily Monroe Norton, the niece of the president, as a means of ascending to national political power. The whole future course of the relationship between Kane and Emily—their basic incompatibility, Kane's ruthless exploitation of her, and finally his abandonment of both her and his son—are summed up in Bernstein's flippant remark concerning Kane's behavior prior to his marriage:

> LELAND: World's biggest diamond. I didn't know Charlie was collecting diamonds.

BERNSTEIN: He ain't. He's collecting somebody that's collecting diamonds. Anyway, he ain't only collecting
statues. (CC, p. 361)

Kane's insensitivity, his regarding Emily as just one more prize to be
added to his collection, is paralleled by Cruz's claiming of Catalina
from her father as a prize of war. Like Emily with Kane, Catalina, the
sheltered daughter of a Porfirian aristocrat, grants Cruz the social re-
spectability necessary for his political advancement—even in a
postrevolutionary society.

There is a distinct neogothic quality to both *Citizen Kane* and
La muerte de Artemio Cruz. In the film, this is particularly evident
in the opening and closing scenes in which the huge, disintegrating
Xanadu, evoked at night, emerges from the mists as a phantasmagoric structure, mysterious and foreboding. As Naremore states: "In
Kane, space becomes demonic, oppressive; ceilings are unnaturally
low, as if they were about to squash the character—or, conversely, at
Xanadu rooms become so large that people shrink, comically yet ter-
rifyingly dwarfed by their possessions."[13] An air of demonism suf-
fuses both the palatial estate of Xanadu and the opulent world of the
monastery at Coyoacán. In *Citizen Kane*, the outsize material possessions seem ready to devour the inhabitants. This looming and
menacing quality of the material world finds a particularly powerful
image in the scene in which Susan Alexander reclines listlessly before the gargantuan fireplace, which looms above her like a huge
gaping maw that is threatening to devour her. As Kane stands in
front of the fireplace, the immense flames behind him attest to the
infernal nature of the world that he had fashioned as a paradise
realm. When Kane orders his guests to attend a picnic, the file of cars
slowly and silently driving across the Florida sands seems much
more like a death march than the celebration of a festive occasion.
And the picnic itself is evoked in a rapid series of grotesque, nightmarish images—strange birds, roasting flesh of the animal slaughtered to provide the picnic fare, rhythmic but tormented music.

In *La muerte de Artemio Cruz* the same hallucinatory atmosphere is conveyed, although by means of a different technique.
Welles creates his bizarre world by concentrating on a seemingly
real but actually expressionistic exterior setting. Fuentes, with the
conceptual advantage that the written word has over the visual
image, penetrates directly into the warped mind of Cruz, who mentally twists what is ostensibly a celebration of life into a ritual
of death. Undercutting the sumptuousness of the banquet are the
morbid images floating through Cruz's consciousness. Like Kane

at Xanadu, the wizened Cruz is obsessed with demonstrating his power, which he longs to impose directly and sadistically over those around him. As Cruz watches the drunken revelers, he envisions a swift, violent attack on them by the enormous rats that lie in wait in the beams of the monastery. Fanatically questing for self-preservation and self-renewal, Cruz is imbued with the demonic spirit of an Aztec god, demanding the blood sacrifice of his guests in order to nourish himself:

> and in his sensitive ear heard the secret shuffle of immense rats, black fanged and sharp muzzled . . . that at times scurried impudently across the corners of the room, and that waited, in the darkness, above the heads and beneath the feet of the dancers, by the hundreds and thousands waited, perhaps, for an opportunity to take them by surprise, infect them with fevers and aches, nausea and palsy . . . if he raised his arm again for the servants to drop the iron door-bars, the ways of escape . . . ; then his retinue would find themselves obliged to remain with him, unable to abandon ship, forced to join him in sprinkling the corpses with vinegar and lighting perfumed faggots, in hanging rosaries of thyme around their necks, in brushing away the green buzz of flies, while he commanded them, to dance, dance, live, live, drink. (pp. 253–254)

In this expertly constructed work, Cruz's terrifying vision is but the phantasmagoric expression of what the protagonist has practiced throughout his life. Cruz allows others, even his own son, to die in his place, forges a new life for himself on the sacrifices of others, and even at the hour of his death calls for repeated blood sacrifices of those like the unknown soldier, Regina, and Bernal who gave up their lives once for him. In the same way, Kane relentlessly sacrifices those around him—Leland, Susan Alexander, Emily, even his own son—all of those attracted by his spellbinding presence. The bitter words of Cruz's daughter Teresa, cast aside by her father because she could not fulfill his egomaniacal purpose: "Even what he loved, he destroyed" (p. 196) find their equivalent in the life of Kane.

As we have seen, fragmentation is both a basic theme and an important structural technique in both of these works. In *Citizen Kane*, dialogue is continually interrupted, and much of the movie seems to be like the *March of Time* newsreel, affording us mere glimpses into the life—and into the soul—of Kane. Throughout *La muerte de Artemio Cruz*, the fragments of first-, second-, and third-person narrative symbolize not only Cruz's multiplicity of selves but

also the incompatibility of those selves and the inability of Cruz—
on his deathbed as throughout his life—to integrate self-serving ego
and self-negating conscience, *yo* and *tú*, opportunism and idealism.
Similarly, the splintered, at times highly compartmentalized selves
of Kane—his brutality and his tenderness, his shyness and his ag-
gressiveness, his vaunted idealism and his rapacious opportunism,
his imaginative exuberance and his rigidity, his love of country and
his monstrous *amour propre* are all strikingly conveyed through the
technique of fragmentation of dialogue, scene, and point of view.

Cruz leads a split life, maintaining a mere façade of a marriage
with Catalina while living openly with his mistress Lilia at Coyoacán. He also is a split personality, outwardly maintaining a supreme
aloofness, not even allowing his guests to approach him, but in-
wardly yearning for reunion with his son. As the dancing couples
summoned by Cruz to his New Year's Eve celebration whirl about
before him, their conversations are not recorded objectively by the
omniscient author but are instead filtered through the consciousness of the protagonist. Instead of coherent dialogue, only free-
floating fragments of conversations are perceived, as the dancers approach, withdraw, and approach again. The partial, confused, kaleidoscopic patterning of the conversation is similar to the random,
illogical movements of a consciousness at the prespeech level.
Taken as a whole, the montage produced by concatenation of the
fragments constitutes an exteriorization of Cruz's own misshapen
identity, a mocking echo of his own life, and a microcosm of the narrative structure as a whole:

> "... lovers, about twenty years ago ..."
> "... how can he give suffrage to that gang of Indians ..."
> "... and his wife alone at home, never ..."
> "... questions of high politics; we received the ..."
> ....
> "... they're investing a hundred million ..."
> "... it's a heavenly Dali ..."
> "... and we'll get it back in a couple of years ..."
> "... the people at my gallery sent it over ..."
> "... in New York ..."
> "... she lived several years in France; deception ... they say
> ..." (p. 255)

The disintegration of Cruz's physical self and the shattering of his
spiritual self attested to here are stunningly evident from the very
beginning of the novel, expressed through the extreme fragmenta-

tion of language that characterizes Cruz's first-person monologue. Similarly, at the outset of *Citizen Kane*, the dropping by Kane of the glass ball—the object that, ironically, is the only one of his numerous possessions that still retains any meaning for him, and the smashing of the ball into fragments, one of which reflects and distorts the image of the nurse at his bedside—provides an adumbration of the incessant fragmentation that will characterize the entire film. It also foreshadows the distortion of Kane by others and by Kane himself.

Another example of the skillful use of fragmentation in the film is provided by the enormous jigsaw puzzles that Susan Alexander incessantly labors over in an attempt to fill the vacuum of her life at Xanadu. The actions of Susan in composing the puzzles are paralleled by the actions of the reporter Thompson as he doggedly attempts to fit together all the pieces of Kane's life—the interviews and the partial impressions that he has received concerning Kane. In one of the concluding scenes, the camera in an overhead shot pans over huge mounds of boxes, in a vision that is but the magnification of the huge crossword puzzles—fragments of Susan's own shattered existence, and pieces of the immense mystery that is Citizen Kane.

The continual emphasis on fragmentation also strikingly underscores the theme of the tragic incompleteness of both lives. It is significant that for all of its imposing splendor, Xanadu is never finished. Supposedly built for Susan Alexander but in reality another monument to Kane's ego, the incompleteness of the edifice signifies not only the truncated relationship between Kane and Susan but also the unfulfilled, the *manqué* nature of Kane himself. Another indication of Kane's stunted existence is that the major part of his treasures at Xanadu are never uncrated—they are essentially worthless to him. Similarly, Artemio Cruz is denied—throughout his lifetime and even on his deathbed—the fulfillment that he is seeking. Ironic testimony to the horrendous power of materialism that converts Cruz into a deathbed Midas is that although the anguished Cruz struggles desperately to recall the face of his dead son, he is unable to summon that image to consciousness, and yet the memories of his possessions—even at the very moment of his death—are amazingly precise and elaborate: ". . . pass close touching, smelling, tasting, smelling the sumptuous robes—the rich marquetry—the gold frames—chests of bone and tortoise-shell—locks and hasps—cutters with iron corners and key escutcheons—fragrant benches of ayacahuite wood—choir benches—baroque robes and miters" (p. 298). Unable to break down the wall of his fierce pride in order to respond to Catalina's attempts to achieve a reconciliation with him,

Cruz fails to attain even the resignation and contentment of his paternal surrogate, Don Gamaliel, who derives a perverted satisfaction from rehearsing his own funeral. The calculating and cold-blooded Gamaliel dies secure in the knowledge that in the opportunistic Cruz he has found a successor—a true son, one that the introspective and romantically idealistic Gonzalo never could have been—a successor in ruthlessness. But neither Kane nor Cruz have a successor—both indirectly destroy their sons, and Teresa has no reality for Cruz, who fails to attend her wedding. When the audacious, conniving Jaime Ceballos dares to approach the aged Cruz, in what is another example of the cyclical time patterning that characterizes the work—a repetition of the boldness of the young Cruz in confronting Don Gamaliel—the monarch of Coyoacán summarily rejects his own double in opportunism. Instead, like the withered Kane, Cruz remains trapped in an idealistic past, absorbed in an inner dialogue, a dialogue with his dead son—the only one whom Cruz judges worthy enough to be his successor. Ironically, Cruz now must become his son's successor by keeping alive his memory:

> "You accepted things as they are; you became realistic. . . ."
> "Yes, that's it. Like you, Don Artemio. . . ." He asked him if he
> had never wondered what lies on the other side of the sea; for
> to him it seemed that all land was much the same, only the
> sea was different. "Like me . . . !" He said that there are is-
> lands. . . . ". . . did you fight in the Revolution, risk your hide,
> to the point that you were about to be executed . . . ?" Sea that
> tasted like bitter beer, smelled of melon, quince, straw-
> berry. . . . "Eh . . . ?" "No, I. . . ." A ship sails in ten days. I
> have booked passage. . . . "Come to the banquet before it's
> over, eh? You hurry to gather up the crumbs. . . ." You would
> do the same, Papá. . . . ". . . on top for forty years because we
> were baptized with the glory of that. . . ." "Yes. . . ." ". . . but
> you, young man? Do you think that that can be inherited?
> How are you going to continue. . . ?" Now there is a front and I
> think it is the only front left. (p. 260)

Kane's grasping of the glass ball—after Susan leaves him and again at the hour of his death—is a striking manifestation of his deep desire to unify present and past in order to gain spiritual wholeness. Similarly, in *La muerte de Artemio Cruz*, the dying protagonist struggles determinedly to effect a *cambio de piel*, in order to reconstruct and renew himself. Completely alienated from those around him—Catalina, Teresa, the priest who has come to administer the last rites—rejecting all their attempts to console him because he recognizes the hypocrisy of these comforters, who are interested only in the whereabouts of his will, Cruz is forced to take refuge in self. The once mighty Cruz now comes to envy the lowly sponge for possessing a power that he is denied—the marvellous capacity to regenerate a complete self from a mere fragment.

It is significant that the only time when the unifying form, the first-person plural *nosotros*, is employed in Cruz's monologue is to depict his adventures at Cocuya with Lorenzo. Yet these brief moments of unity, of spiritual transcendence between father and son, are but a prelude to their inevitable and permanent separation. Kane's attempts to unify self and Other also are thwarted. It is ironic that the young Kane, playing exuberantly in the snow, should shout "the Union forever!" as part of the mock Civil War battle that he is fighting—at the exact moment when his mother is signing the document which will dissolve her family forever. Both Kane and Cruz die in spiritual isolation. The only unity ever attained among Cruz's three antagonistic selves is an extremely ironic one, as, at the end, all three voices merge as a prelude to Cruz's death.

In both works there is a constant interplay between free will and fate. Despite the tremendous wills of both of these protagonists, despite the immense power that they wield over thousands of persons, both Kane and Cruz are reduced to puppets. The fatalism of both works is emphasized by the fact that the lives of the flamboyant protagonists are explored as pasts, or, in the case of Artemio Cruz, as a past relived as only an illusory future. The dying Cruz cannot modify the past except in his febrile imagination; the possibilities for self-recreation and self-transcendence are presented when it is really too late for Cruz to choose again, even if he decided to:

> you will break the silence that night and will speak to Catalina asking her to forgive you; you will tell of those who have died for you to live and will ask her to accept you as you are
> . . .
> you will stay on with Lunero at the hacienda, you will never leave your place
> you will stay with your teacher Sebastián, as he was, as he was, and will not go to join the revolution in the north.
> (p. 238)

Citizen Kane is also a fatalistic work, one that creates a false future similar to the one operating in *La muerte de Artemio Cruz*. As McBride points out, referring to the manner in which the life of

Kane has been structured: "A system has been created in which all of Kane's actions are now in the past tense—and hence no longer of any effect. Welles' use of time counterpoints Kane's apparently powerful actions with the audience's foreknowledge that those actions will fail and that he will remain as he was shown at the beginning of the two hours: destroyed. The events of his life as we will see them exist in a limbo of moral futility."[14]

Film and novel evoke their respective protagonists from ironic perspectives—both as exalted potentates and as towering examples of self-destruction, they are finally brought down because of their intransigence and egomania. Kane is photographed in the company of the leaders of Europe; Kane is shown as the master of Xanadu, like the biblical Noah commanding that two of every kind of animal be brought to populate his island empire, his private universe. Yet each time that the self-deified Kane is presented, there occurs a change in point of view, that radically alters our impression of Kane by reducing him from puppetmaster to puppet. Many times the dynamic and exuberant Kane is presented as the apparent victor only to be mocked—by a remark of Leland, by an ironic juxtaposition, by a clumsy action, as when at a dedication ceremony he accidentally drops wet cement over his expensive coat or, most strikingly, by an abrupt change in perspective, as the camera angle changes in order suddenly to deflate Kane's image as conqueror. When Kane first appears at an election rally, he is already savoring his imminent victory as governor, with the path to the presidency seeming to open up before him. Yet Kane the man himself is dominated by a huge poster of himself, symbolizing the triumph of the mere hollow image over the man, the image that can be shattered just as quickly as it was inflated. As Kane pompously and self-righteously continues his speech, the camera pulls back to focus on the target of Kane's attacks—his opponent, Boss Jim Gettys, who, as Naremore points out, "stands high above the action, the stage viewed over his shoulder, so that he dominates the frame like a sinister power. It is Gettys who is truly in control of this campaign. . . ."[15] Thus Welles provides a visual adumbration of the downfall of Kane even while the central action depicts him at the height of his power and glory.

Another swift undercutting of the imperious Kane comes when he arrogantly states to Susan as he stands in front of the monstrous fireplace at Xanadu, "This is our home, Susan." Yet the camera depicts a Kane who is just the opposite of the grandiose baron of Xanadu role that Kane wants to play. He is shown as a miniature, dwarfed by the immense logs in the fireplace, and his words seem to refer not only to Xanadu but to the mammoth flames of the fireplace—the hellworld that his own will has constructed for both Susan and himself.

A similar undercutting—both thematic and structural—of the imperiousness of Cruz appears repeatedly in Fuentes' novel. The prime mechanism through which the vaunted I is deflated is the second-person consciousness, which becomes stronger as the I-narrative becomes increasingly atomistic and incoherent, to indicate the disappearance of Cruz the rapacious *conquistador*. The power of the second-person voice over Cruz is indicated stylistically, by the lengthy, convoluted sentence structure, the phrases that pyramid over one another and seem to acquire a life of their own, while the I-narrative, which through Cruz's life has been the dominant voice, now lapses into incessant and sterile repetition. Cruz's subconsciousness at first links him, through a weird dream, with the *conquistador* Cortés. Like the arrogant Spanish *marqués* in the sixteenth century, Cruz emerges as the twentieth-century master of the New World. Yet this dream of Cruz's is a paradoxical one; it raises the vision of his grandeur and of his victory over men and over time, only to undercut the allusion by showing the conqueror conquered. The self-assurance of Cruz, who like the original *conquistadores* founds a personal empire on the blood of his victims, is emphasized through the use of an imperative future: "for you will have created night by closing your eyes, and from the bottom of that inky ocean there will sail toward you a stone ship that the noon sun, hot and drowsy, will comfort in vain: ship of thick blackened walls raised to defend the church against the attacks of pagan Indians and to unite the military and religious conquests. . . . You will advance down the nave to the conquest of your own New World" (p. 31).

Testimony to the careful way in which *La muerte de Artemio Cruz* has been structured is that this dream of conquest is given a chilling actualization within the third-person narrative of December 31, 1955, in which the omniscient author depicts Cruz's self-styled role of emperor of Coyoacán. Like the gods, Cruz attempts to score a victory over time, to gain immortality—but his victory is shown to be a spurious one. Cruz succeeds in preserving only a misshapen, soulless husk of a self, and is mocked by his guests as "la momia de Coyoacán." This final defeat has been adumbrated by Cruz's dream, in which the Conqueror, striding through the nave, seemingly invincible, is mocked by the idols that the Indian sculptors have placed within the church—hidden presences that they endow with Christian masks. Like the Spanish *conquistadores*, the arrogant Cruz too will be conquered from within. The impassive stone idols symbolize all-conquering death: "angels and saints with faces of the sun and moon, with harvest-protecting hands, with the index fingers of guide dogs, with the cruel, empty, useless eyes of idols and the rigorous lineaments of the cycles. Faces of stone behind kindly rose masks, ingenuous and impassive—dead, dead, dead" (p. 32).

Like Welles, Fuentes also uses structural devices to provide an ironic perspective on his protagonist. The Mexican author adroitly utilizes the cinematic technique of foreground and background action as he juxtaposes the silent figure of Cruz's wife Catalina, who is struggling with her conscience and against her temptation to submit physically to Cruz, with a backdrop that depicts the conqueror Cruz. The narration of June 23, 1924, skillfully interweaves the passivity of Catalina, mired in indecision and anguish, with the activity of Cruz, portrayed in the process of relentlessly destroying the power of the *hacendados*—not to establish a revolutionary system, as he pretends, but instead to build his own empire. This scene provides another example of the excellent fusing of theme and structure. The omniscient author time and again interrupts Catalina's brooding monologue and, through the use of flashbacks and spatial montage, records Cruz's rapid rise to provincial hegemony. Catalina's thoughts are repeatedly cut off by the action narrative depicting Cruz, just as her life has been suddenly and brutally interrupted by the bold and forceful Cruz. Yet the juxtaposition of Catalina and Cruz is an ironic one, for although Cruz masterfully dominates the old aristocratic order and eliminates all his enemies, this solitary and seemingly fragile woman who nevertheless possesses an intense will successfully resists him, allowing only her body to be surrendered. The ending of the scene shows the conqueror once again conquered—forced to take an Indian girl as mistress.

The great and lasting appeal of *Citizen Kane* and *La muerte de Artemio Cruz* is that both film and novel are total creations, traditional and experimental, historical and mythic, epic in that they capture the spirit of whole countries, lyric in their sensitive portrayal of the inner worlds of the protagonists. Both works are highly structured, perhaps even over-structured, and yet both are open creations in their central ambiguity and in the unresolved problems that they pose. Both combine action and conquest with philosophical concerns, as each probes the metaphysical problems of time, memory, death, and immortality. Both represent a dramatic break with the previous history of their respective genres. As Cowie states, referring to the expert craftsmanship of *Citizen Kane*: ". . . *Citizen Kane* marked much more than the bright spark of a new decade, and it is tempting and justifiable to divide cinema history into the pre-1940 and post-1940 periods. The gangster films, comedies and

Westerns of the Thirties had all established an elaborate iconography of their own. But dialogue and situation took precedence over style and expression."[16]

La muerte de Artemio Cruz is an eclectic work of art, expertly combining the novel of character, plot, and action with the narrative of innerness, as it deftly explores the consciousness and even the subconscious mind—and the collective unconsciousness—of its protagonist. *La muerte de Artemio Cruz* pays homage to the novel of the Mexican Revolution—to Azuela's *Los de abajo* and *Andrés Pérez, maderista*, to Guzmán's *La sombra del caudillo*, while at the same time going beyond these classic works of Mexican literature to explore psychological and metaphysical dimensions, and to experiment with language and style, particularly in the second-person narrative.

These two masterful creations are epic in scope, tracing the destinies of both a character and a country. Both are striking examples of a stylistic *tour de force* and yet neither is dated; both are open creations that are as relevant to the 1980s as they were to the times when they were created. The variations in mood, tone, and style found in *Citizen Kane* are emphasized by Gottesman: "How, for instance, do the mysterious, impressionistic, dreamlike qualities of the opening sequence relate to the factual, objective, realistic characteristics of the newsreel? What are the functions of the magical invocation and the documentary capsule?"[17] Similarly, *La muerte de Artemio Cruz* encompasses a tremendous range of styles, tempos, and tones: eloquent and halting, declamatory and implorative, denunciatory and exalting. The crisp, factual, historical narrative containing description and dialogue that characterizes the third-person segments contrasts markedly with the associational, highly emotionalized welter of images in Cruz's first-person monologue, and also with the dense, overwrought, at times surrealistic vision presented by the second-person voice: "Chorus, sepulcher, voices, pyre: and you will imagine in the forgotten region of consciousness the rites, the ceremonies, the endings: burial, cremation, embalming: exposed upon the height of a tower, so that it be not the earth, but the air itself will rot you; sealed in the tomb with your dead slaves; wailed by hired mourners; buried with your most valuable possessions, your company, your black jewels: death watch, vigil" (p. 240).

Another significant parallel between *Citizen Kane* and *La muerte de Artemio Cruz* is their extreme intensity. In both film and novel, every scene, every character, every incident serves to reflect, to illuminate—or to problematize—the life of the protagonist. Fuentes has characterized himself as "a putter-inner, not a taker-outer."[18] The reader of this highly intricate, baroque narrative is at times overpowered by the dazzling display of images. The supercharged quality of Welles' style and the techniques used to achieve that intensity are analyzed by Naremore:

> The short focal-length of the lens enables him to express the psychology of his characters, to comment on the relationship between character and environment, and also to create a sense of barely contained, almost manic energy, as if the camera, like one of his heroes, were overreaching.
>
> This highly charged, nervous dynamism of imagery and action can be found everywhere in *Kane*, and is produced by other techniques besides photography. Fairly often Welles will stage important moments of his story against some counterpointing piece of business, as if he were trying to energize the plot by throwing as much material as possible onto the screen.[19]

Both novel and film are expansive in their sweep of time and history and intensive in their probing into the hidden lives of their respective protagonists. *Citizen Kane* has been characterized by Higham as "a work of confidence and excess, as bold as a fresco, and it reminds one again that the cinema has continued a nineteenth century fiction tradition of size and grandeur when the novel (in English at least) has largely shrunk to the trivial."[20] There is little doubt that *La muerte de Artemio Cruz* is also a work "of confidence and excess" and that Carlos Fuentes has done more than any other Latin American novelist and perhaps even any other novelist in the world writing today to restore the novel to the prodigious stature that it maintained in the nineteenth century, when its scope encompassed generations of families and the portrayal of entire societies.

Another aspect that both works have in common is the significant role that is given to the viewer/reader, who can no longer remain a mere passive recipient of verbal and visual images, but is given the freedom to put together the fragments of the protagonists' lives and to render his or her own value judgment. The reader/viewer is compelled to be active, to bring order to chaos, to synthesize the myriad perspectives and to come to grips with the problematic nature of the two protagonists. In attempting to discover unifying factors to the works, the reader/viewer duplicates the attempts of the dying Cruz to find a transcendental meaning to his life and those of the reporter Thompson to discover the true meaning of the paradox that is Charles Foster Kane. Does *Citizen Kane* condemn or ultimately vindicate its protagonist? Critics are divided in their opinions. Although some see in the film a strong indictment of American materialism and of the power of the media, others see it as lauding Kane. As Crowther states unequivocally: ". . . at no point in the picture is a black mark actually checked against Kane. Not a shred of evidence is presented to indicate absolutely that he is a social scoundrel. As a matter of fact, there is no reason to assume from what is shown on the screen that he is anything but an honest publisher with a consistently conscientious attitude toward society."[21] In his final evaluation of Kane, Higham is reluctant to assume the role of what Julio Cortázar would describe as the *lector cómplice* collaborating with the artist in completing the creative endeavor: "One is left only with the wish that Welles had drawn his own conclusions about this friend of the working man, the Jeffersonian, the fascist, the master of empires, instead of leaving us with an enigma as baffling as a great stone Easter Island face."[22]

We might ask as well, is the paradoxical hero of Fuentes' novel to be condemned or exonerated? Although both Fuentes and Welles are moralists, and both subject the lives of their protagonists to relentless scrutiny, neither is didactic. Cruz and Kane are evoked with a mixture of damnation and reverence. The lives of both protagonists confound easy moral judgment, particularly when the persons surrounding them—the lackey Bernstein, the dissipated and senile Leland, the shrill and shrewish Susan Alexander in *Citizen Kane*; and the sycophantic Padilla, the acidulous Teresa, the grasping Catalina, and the cold-blooded Don Gamaliel in *La muerte de Artemio Cruz*—are portrayed as far less sympathetic characters than either Kane or Cruz. Although in one episode Cruz appears as the coward and traitor, deserting his men, leaving them to die on the battlefield, in another scene he is a bold and courageous hero, riding straight into the enemy and scoring a victory over them. In one encounter a crude and blatant opportunist, in the next he is evoked as cultured and sensitive, questing for an ideal and a genuine love with Laura. Unlike the fawning, hypocritical Catalina and Teresa, who sanctimoniously attend to him and whose feeble attempts at reconciliation serve only as a shabby mask of their avarice, Cruz remains defiant, unapologetic, and brazenly impenitent. His greed is coupled with a bold lust for life that the dour, crabbed women in their petty miserliness can never understand. They will reap the material benefits of his wealth but are deprived of Cruz's capacity to enjoy it—the sensualism that even in his final hours he continues to exult in.

Like the release of *Citizen Kane*, the publication of *La muerte de Artemio Cruz* at first confounded many tradition-minded critics, who praised the third-person action segments of the narrative because they could readily understand them and who even wished that Fuentes had written the entire novel from this orthodox perspective, so characteristic of the novels of the Mexican Revolution. Ironically, the intricate second-person narrative, a paradoxical form that contributes so much toward making Cruz a three-dimensional person, initially received a markedly negative response from several critics who were confounded by its excesses. Yet with its breathtakingly expansive scope that incorporates not only the conscience of a character and a nation but a universal consciousness, from genesis to the apocalypse, a theme that Fuentes later developed masterfully in *Terra Nostra*, the second-person narrative is the most original—and the most profound—aspect of the novel.

No comparison between *La muerte de Artemio Cruz* and *Citizen Kane* would be complete without consideration of the respective geniuses behind each of these creations. The similarities between Welles and Fuentes are striking: both are intense, explosive talents; both tackle projects that other creative artists shy away from. Actor, writer, director, Welles has done movie versions of Shakespeare's *Macbeth* and *Henry IV*, Kafka's *The Trial*, and Tarkington's *The Magnificent Ambersons*. Novelist, essayist, dramatist, film reviewer and script writer, diplomat, and teacher, Fuentes too demonstrates a remarkable range of talents. Tightly condensed short stories of the fantastic and the macabre like *Aura* are followed by mammoth displays of history, philosophy, visual art, and theology such as are found in *Cambio de piel* and in Fuentes' eight-hundred page work *Terra Nostra*. Hermetic, metaphysical works like *Cumpleaños* are succeeded by dazzling spy thrillers like *La cabeza de la hidra*. In works such as *La región más transparente*, Fuentes boldly attempts to portray not only the totality of modern Mexico—all social classes, from *los de abajo* to the remnants of the Porfirian elite, but also to encapsulate the whole of Mexican history, from the Aztec epoch to the present, in a display of imaginative power that has no equal in Mexican letters. And in *Terra Nostra* Fuentes' imaginative constructions are even more dazzling—whole civilizations, the Rome of Tiberius, the Spain of the Hapsburgs, the New World from its cosmogony to its apocalypse. The *cambio de piel* motif, a central one in Fuentes' works, characterizes the artist himself. Like Welles, Fuentes has an extraordinary capacity for self-transformation and self-renewal.

In addition to being consummate artists, both Fuentes and Welles are masterful showmen as well. Both love to dazzle and to confound their audiences, as Welles did in his electrifying radio broadcast on the Martian invasion of America. Both are bold experimenters. Both artists display eclectic tastes; both are fond of dialectic, of constant thesis and antithesis that result in a compelling tension and a marked ambiguity in their works. The remark of Johnson, commenting on the use of opposites in Welles' work, can also apply to that of Fuentes: "The struggle between tradition and progress, old and new, order and disorder, is one of the most powerful forces behind Welles' work. It is reflected in his American background and his love of Europe, and in his filmmaking that embraces both Shakespeare and modern American thrillers."[23]

There is no more fitting way to conclude our presentation than to quote a director who, like Orson Welles, is a master of the cinema: François Truffaut. Like Fuentes, Truffaut was also greatly influenced by *Citizen Kane*, and the French director's eloquent summation of the film can be applied almost verbatim to *La muerte de Artemio Cruz*:

> We loved this film because it was complete: psychological, social, poetic, dramatic, comic, baroque, strict, and dramatic. It is a demonstration of the force of power and an attack on the force of power, it is a hymn to youth and a meditation on old age, an essay on the vanity of all material ambition and at the same time a poem on old age and the solitude of exceptional human beings, genius or monster—or monstrous genius.[24]

Notes

1. Alfred MacAdam and Alexander Coleman, "An Interview with Carlos Fuentes," *Book Forum*, 4, no. 4 (1979): 680–681.
2. James Naremore, *The Magic World of Orson Welles* (New York: Oxford University Press, 1978), p. 83.
3. "RKO Cutting Continuity of the Orson Welles Production, *Citizen Kane*," in *The Citizen Kane Book* (Boston: Little, Brown and Company, 1971), p. 312. Subsequent references are included in the text, preceded by CC.
4. Orson Welles, "*Citizen Kane* Is Not about Louella Parsons' Boss," in *Focus on Citizen Kane*, ed. Ronald Gottesman (Englewood Cliffs, N.J.: Prentice Hall, 1971), p. 68. This article was originally published in *Friday* 2, February 14, 1941, p. 9.
5. Roy A. Fowler, "*Citizen Kane*: Background and a Critique," in *Focus on Citizen Kane*, p. 88.
6. Interview with Welles conducted by Juan Cobos and Miguel Rubio, "Welles and Falstaff," *Sight and Sound*, 35 (Autumn 1966): 158–163.

For an extensive examination of the theme of lost paradise in Fuentes' novel, see Lanin A. Gyurko, "Self-Renewal and Death in Fuentes' *La muerte de Artemio Cruz*," *Revista de Letras* (São Paulo), 15 (1973): 59–80.

7. Although citations are to the Sam Hileman translation, *The Death of Artemio Cruz*, occasional additions by the author are enclosed in brackets.

8. Naremore, *Magic World*, p. 94.

9. Robert Humphrey, *Stream of Consciousness in the Modern Novel* (Berkeley: University of California Press, 1965), p. 67.

10. Joseph McBride, *Orson Welles* (London: Secker and Warburg, 1972), p. 50.

11. William Johnson, "Orson Welles: Of Time and Loss," in *Focus on Citizen Kane*, p. 26.

12. Naremore, *Magic World*, p. 43.

13. Ibid., p. 50.

14. McBride, *Orson Welles*, p. 37.

15. Naremore, *Magic World*, p. 86.

16. Peter Cowie, *A Ribbon of Dreams: The Cinema of Orson Welles* (New York: A. S. Barnes and Company, 1973), p. 20.

17. Ronald Gottesman, "*Citizen Kane*: Past, Present, and Future," Introduction to *Focus on Citizen Kane*, p. 6.

18. Interview with Fuentes conducted by Emir Rodríguez Monegal, in *Homenaje a Carlos Fuentes*, ed. Helmy F. Giacomán (New York: Las Américas, 1971), p. 43.

19. Naremore, *Magic World*, p. 50.

20. Charles Higham, *The Films of Orson Welles* (Berkeley: University of California Press, 1971), p. 46.

21. Bosley Crowther, review of *Citizen Kane*, *New York Times*, May 4, 1941, in *Focus on Citizen Kane*, p. 50.

22. Higham, *Films of Orson Welles*, p. 24.

23. Johnson, "Orson Welles," p. 32.

24. François Truffaut, "Citizen Kane," trans. Mark Bernheim and Ronald Gottesman, in *Focus on Citizen Kane*, p. 130. The original article was published in *L'Express* (November 26, 1959).

Jaime Alazraki

Theme and System in Carlos Fuentes' *Aura*

It has been said of *Aura* that because of its fantastic element it belongs to the Gothic genre. A closer examination of the narrative reveals, however, that such a classification is misleading. The Gothic novel, like the fantastic short story of the nineteenth century, seeks to shake up the reader and generate in him a certain fear or horror. Roger Caillois defines this type of narrative as "a play with fear": in a world domesticated by the sciences, the fantastic narrative opens a window on the unknown, and through it the reader's fears and chills slip in. H. P. Lovecraft, practitioner and theoretician of the genre, similarly defines the fantastic by its capacity to frighten the reader. "A story is fantastic," he says, "simply if the reader experiences a deep feeling of fear and terror, the presence of unusual worlds and powers." Louis Vax has also observed that "fantastic art should introduce imaginary terrors into the bosom of the real world."[1]

There is no doubt that what Freud called the uncanny is present in *Aura*. It is less clear, on the other hand, whether its function is to terrify the reader. The supernatural exists in *Aura* as it does in poetry; more than a duel with fear, it is an effort aimed at poetic knowledge. Octavio Paz has said of *Aura*:

> Through love Fuentes perceives death; through death, he perceives that zone we once called sacred or poetic, but that now lacks a name. The modern world has not invented words to designate the other side of reality. It is not strange that Fuentes is obsessed with the wrinkled and toothless face of a tyrannical, insane, infatuated old lady. She represents the old vampire, the witch, the white serpent of Chinese stories: the old lady of murky passions, the outcast.

Paz's highly charged language makes redundant almost everything else that has been written on *Aura*: "The eroticism is inseparable from the horror, and Fuentes outdoes even himself in the horror, both erotic and grotesque. Fierce joy. If it is not sacred, it is something no less violent: desecration."[2] Poetry, then, in the sense of a search for that other side of reality that literature seeks beyond appearance; poetry in the sense of a force that defies and devastates our symmetrical constructs of numbers and concepts to discover, underneath those ruins, a forgotten fire.

The possible sources of *Aura* have been repeatedly pointed out, perhaps excessively: Henry James' *The Aspern Papers*, Stevenson's *Dr. Jekyll and Mr. Hyde*, Pushkin's *The Queen of Clubs*, Faulkner's "A Rose for Emily," Alfonso Reyes' "The Dinner." I myself could add to this incomplete list Rider Haggard's *She*, the story of a woman immune to the ravages of time and on whom youth is a mask which, as with Felipe's, finally falls down. But the list would only be complete with a scrutiny of all or most of Fuentes' readings. It has been said that when asked about the literary sources of two Mexican authors, Alfonso Reyes answered: "2000 years of literature," in itself a shortened reformulation of a remark by Borges: "It is well known that Whistler was asked how much time he had needed to paint one of his 'Nocturnes' and that he answered 'all my life.' With equal rigor he might have said that he had needed all the centuries that preceded the moment in which he painted it."[3] More daringly, the Russian formalists believed, in Victor Shklovski's words, that "images do not come from anywhere, they are God's." Shklovski goes on to say:

> The more a literary period is known, the more one is persuaded that the images which we considered as the creation of this or that poet were borrowed by him from another poet, almost without modification. The task of poetic schools is none other than the accumulation and revelation of new methods to dispose and elaborate the verbal material, and it consists in the disposition of the images rather than in their creation. The images are given; in poetry, images are more remembered than fashioned.[4]

Perhaps the only source that matters in *Aura* is the one which Fuentes himself has revealed in the epigraph that heads the narrative: Jules Michelet. Ana María Albán de Viqueira has studied what *Aura* owes to Michelet's *La Sorcière*. We shall not repeat her arguments but we shall detail some of Michelet's texts related to *Aura*. "Woman," says Michelet, "is born a fairy . . . , through love she changes into a sorceress, thanks to her cunning and maliciousness she becomes a witch, she rules destiny and numbs pain."[5] But woman is not only a witch, by nature, she also possesses the gift of parthenogenesis. "Alone, she conceived and gave birth. To whom? To a being identical to herself who has all appearances of reality. It has been seen, it has been heard. Everyone could describe it" (p. 37). Here the embryo of *Aura* is already stated. Ana María Albán has shown that even the name Aura comes from Michelet and it means "a spirit that penetrates and lives in the woman possessed by a satanic force" (pp. 48, 102). According to the spiritualists, "an 'aura' is a subtle form that surrounds the human body, a phenomenon related to materialization or, what amounts to the same, the formation of substances that emanate from the medium and assume the form of persons or objects. These phenomena of materialization are generally produced by neuropaths in a dimly lit room, in the presence of people who are almost always under the power of hypnosis."[6] The name Felipe also comes from *La Sorcière*. It is invoked by the witches during the celebration of the black mass, and so are the names Saga and Consuelo, "a delightful woman who believed she saw God and the devil reconciled" (p. 28). Also from *La Sorcière* comes the color green that Aura and Consuelo wear in their youth, for it is the color of Satan, prince of the world (p. 82). The flour doll with which Aura plays has its source in *La Sorcière*: "Woman," says Michelet, "keeps in her heart the memory and the compassion of the ancient gods now changed into spirits. In spite of persecutions, that fidelity is expressed in small rag or flour dolls, a representation of the gods of ancient religions: Jupiter, Minerva, Venus" (p. 65). Also the surrealist image of the cats "chained together and who wallow around within a surrounding fire" has its origin in a tradition noted by Michelet: "In the bonfires on St. John's Day chained-together cats were burned. . . . That very day a billy-goat was sacrificed to the gods Priapus, Bacchus and Sabazius," which immediately calls to mind the billy-goat Aura slaughters in the kitchen (p. 124).

The plants that grow in the patio of the large house on Donceles Street are the same plants cultivated by witches and whose description and use appear in *La Sorcière*. The ritual of the wedding dress, the extra table setting, the song composed by the deceased husband, his last suit, and the bitter wine, all elements mentioned by Michelet, appear in *Aura*. Finally, among the philters and enchantments cited by Michelet, the most efficient is the erotic wafer; during the celebration of the black mass, the witch was considered altar and offering, a practice performed to the letter in *Aura*:

Aura, squatting on the bed, places an object against her closed thighs, caressing it, summoning you with her hand. She caresses that thin wafer, breaks it against her thighs, oblivious of the crumbs that roll down her hips: she offers you half of the wafer and you take it, place it in your mouth at the same time she does, and swallow it with difficulty. Then you fall on Aura's naked body, you fall on her naked arms, which are stretched out from one side of the bed to the other like the arms of the crucifix hanging on the wall, the black Christ with that scarlet silk wrapped around his thighs, his spread knees, his wounded side, his crown of thorns set on a tangled black wig with silvered spangles. Aura opens up like an altar. (pp. 107–109)

The ingredients of Fuentes' narrative, then, come mostly from Michelet's *La Sorcière*. This fact, far from surprising, confirms Shklovski's assertion about images as children without parents or children of an Adamite father. Raymond Queneau wrote, tongue-in-cheek, that every literary work is an *Iliad* or an *Odyssey*; he was alluding to that idea which stands as one of the foundations of Borges' work: "literature as the diverse intonation of a few metaphors."[7] Borges is perhaps, among contemporary writers, the most honest and radical in accepting the notion of literature as a second language to which contemporary semiotics has familiarized us in a definitive way. Borges, John Barth has observed, accepts the apparent exhaustion of literature and "writes an original and notable work whose implicit theme is the difficulty, perhaps the lack of necessity, of writing original works of literature."[8] If, as Shklovski affirms, the writer is "an organizer of materials who assembles one piece next to the others,"[9] one must look for *Aura*'s originality not so much in the sources from which the bulk of its story comes, in this element or in that motif, as in the disposition of its materials. The materials matter much less than their organization. Literature, is, in the end, the constant rereading of a few texts, and "Pierre Menard, author of the Quijote" is nothing but a poignant caricature of this idea. Lévi Strauss distinguishes between the immediate contents of the first language and the content of form as a second language, and Octavio Paz has pointed out that poetry's only message lies in its form. In an even more definitive way, Roland Barthes has said that "literature is nothing more than a language, that is, a system of signs: its being is not in its message, but in its system."[10]

Our modernist poets understood only too well this notion of literature since they rewrote themes and motifs that were in European

poetry from Romanticism onward but which had not been expressed
in the Spanish language: they produced a music unheard before in
Spanish and their greatest accomplishment was to forge a new language on which Spanish contemporary poetry depends. Ana María
Albán observes that Michelet's *La Sorcière* is a key book for the
study of *Aura*. It is so from the point of view of its materials, as are
to a greater or lesser degree the other works with whose theme *Aura*
bears some affinity. But if one literature differs from another "not so
much because of the text as for the manner in which it is read,"[11]
Borges *dixit*, and if the task of the writer is not so much to invent
new images as to rewrite the old ones, those which have always ex-
isted, one must look for *Aura*'s originality more in its expression
than in its content, less in its signifieds than in its signifiers, although the latter may derive from and be indebted to the former.
Paradoxically, in almost everything I have read about *Aura* I have
found very little that addresses itself to the study of its expressive
system. The virtuosity of its prose is recognized, but the ins and outs
are left untouched; and yet it is here where its efficacy as a verbal
system rests.

Essentially *Aura* is a powerful love story: old age and death are
exorcized so that youth and love may triumph. The story of Aura is
the story of Consuelo, and the story of Felipe Montero, the reverse of
the story of General Llorente. Such magic is produced by means of
witchcraft and sorcery, warding off satanism and resorting to herbs
of parthenogenetic power. But this story, thus reduced to its skele-
ton, impresses us more for its truculence than for that poetic chord
that *Aura* strikes as a text with the same magic Consuelo exercises
at the level of plot.

There is a superimposition of the figures of Consuelo and Aura
and of General Llorente and Felipe Montero, as if one emanated from
the other: a game of lost voices. Those who have studied the narrative prefer to speak of doubles or *Doppelgänger*, a concept so abused
by criticism that, as Albert J. Guerard said, it has become a commonplace that no longer means anything.[12] The key here seems to be
the notion of superimposition: superimposition of two characters
who unfold continually and are present and past at the same time,
old age and youth. Alina Reyes, in Julio Cortázar's short story, "Lejana," is the inversion of this order: the young Alina unfolds into the
old beggarwoman of Budapest. It is not by chance that Cortázar has
said that he would have liked nothing as much as to have been the
author of *Aura* and that he feels, according to his own declaration,
an uncontrollable envy toward Fuentes as the narrative's author.[13]
Consuelo and Aura superimpose on one another. Aura is the incor-

poreal atmosphere, the "aura" of Consuelo that at times separates from the old witch to become the character with whom Felipe falls in love: "With the torn folds of the skirt in her hands, turns toward you and laughs silently, with the old lady's teeth *superimposed* on her own, while her legs shatter into bits and fly toward the abyss . . ." (pp. 95–96). Toward the abyss, toward that territory to which Paz alluded, from which Consuelo summons her on the levels of the signifieds and from which Fuentes summons her on that of the signifiers. The effectiveness of the narrative rests on that double-entry resurrection: the operation Consuelo performs through witchcraft and magic, Fuentes executes through language. The text also participates in that superimposition: the old witches' chronicle told by Michelet generates its own aura, an atmosphere in which the narrative finds its poetic habitat, the medium in which the miracle can take place, but now as a literary act.

A second superimposition at the level of the tale occurs when Aura, after making love with Felipe, becomes Consuelo's own echo: "Señora Consuelo smiles at you nodding her head, smiling at you along with Aura, who moves her head in rhythm with the old lady's: they both smile at you, thanking you. . . . The two of them get up at the same moment, Consuelo from the chair, Aura from the floor. Turning their backs on you, they walk slowly toward the door that leads to the widow's bedroom . . ." (pp. 111–113). With whom has Felipe made love? The answer awaits at the bottom of the narrative. Until then, Consuelo and Aura superimpose, converge, and diverge with one another; they are two women and yet the same woman. The text as a system that encodes the story participates in a similar symbiosis. The atmosphere that unanimously has been praised as its most achieved feature rests also, as does Consuelo's witchcraft, on its most immediate level. The narrative begins as a realistic story: Felipe is seeking employment, he reads an advertisement in the newspaper, and feels sure that he has found the job he has been looking for. But when he walks along Donceles Street he realizes that no one lives in the old downtown area and that the address given in the newspaper is in the midst of "old colonial mansions, all of them converted into repair shops, jewelry shops, shoe stores, drugstores" (p. 9). This is the first superimposition, the first in a series of strange overlaps that create the atmosphere of the narrative. The second superimposition comes immediately afterwards when Felipe finds that next to the number of the house he was looking for, Donceles 815, there is a second number, "*formerly 69*": a commercial district that was formerly residential and where the house he seeks is located, numbers that were or are other numbers. Before the paragraph ends a figure appears who, when she feels she is being seen, withdraws from the window to "the greenish curtains that darken the long windows." The window, like the slide in Nicholas Roeg's film *Don't Look Now*, already contains the essentials of the story: the greenish drapes, which anticipate the green skirt of Aura as her satanic origin, and that body "which draws back" when looked at (p. 9), which anticipates the ethereal figure of Aura who disappears into the shadows from which she came.

The atmosphere of the narrative is not an appendage added as a facile ruse. Like the genesis of Aura, the atmosphere grows organically from the narrative itself. Almost everything in the narration shares this double quality: the narrative superimposes itself on the atmosphere which emanates from it, and the atmosphere anticipates inadvertently, in a slow and patient display of magical illusionism, what afterwards the story will convey through the plot.

Even before Felipe enters the house, there is one more example of disquieting superimposition: the door knocker that Felipe raps— "that copper head of a dog"—is that and something else: "a canine fetus in a museum of natural science" (p. 11). It is hard not to think of the homunculus of Paracelsus, of the Golem of the Kabalists, of the sorcery that changes the old Consuelo into the young Aura. Before Felipe closes the entrance hall door there is a final contrast: "the long line of stalled cars that growl, honk, and belch out the unhealthy fumes of their impatience . . . and the door that opens at the first light push of your fingers" (p. 11). The transition already indicates the entrance into a world whose laws are very different, whose reality is like an impalpable mist which at any moment is going to vanish before that harsh reality "of the street."

Of all the devices that generate the atmosphere that surrounds the narrative, the counterpoint between light and dark is perhaps the most intense and insistent: "You close the door behind you and peer into the *darkness* of a roofed alleyway. . . . There isn't any *light* to guide you." Already, from this first sentence on the third page, an interplay of shadow and light is at work: they act as the two coordinates that weave and hold the narrative. It is not a matter of two extremes—darkness and light—but of a gamut of hues that regulates clarity and shadow according to the necessities of the narration: "A thin carpet, badly laid. It makes you trip and almost fall. Then you notice the *grayish filtered light* that reveals some of the humps" (p. 13). It is impossible to review all the instances of this interplay, which is a model of atmospheric chiaroscuro, but we should mention a few. We read of "scattered lights . . . braided in your eyelashes, as if you were seeing them through a silken net," of "dozens of flickering lights," of "that galaxy of religious lights," of "the light from the candles and the reflections from the silver and crystal," of "the light [that] blinds," of "soft glow," and of "a diffuse, opaline light."

The house is always in darkness, but in the bare hall there is a lighted center portion. The condition of the house, walled in by new buildings which have taken away its light to force the owners to sell, is repeated within the house itself: around the few patches of light high walls of darkness rise. Only in Felipe's room does there filter through a "flood of light": it makes sense since Felipe assumes the point of view of the reader, and his perplexities and questions are those of the reader. The darkness and shadows define the territory of Lucifer, and Felipe moves through it confused and bewildered. Clarity and darkness form two circles, two territories, clearly delimited in the dining room: "You separate the two different elements that make up the room: the compact circle of light around the candelabra, illuminating the table and one carved wall, and the larger circle of darkness around it" (p. 43). One circle contains the other, one circle imprisons the other and ends up by absorbing it, leaving scarcely the hint of a reflection coming from the dark: the return of Aura as filtered light, coming from the shadows, a luminous illusion, a dream that slices the dark crust of the night.

Parallel binomials perform a similar function in the creation of the atmosphere: the rabbit, white, a sensual flower, light-ridden, Saga-Sibia; and the mice next to the chest: ignored, black, denied, undesirable creatures of shadow and loathing; the *liquid* eyes of Señora Consuelo contained "at the back of its *dry* cave"; "those sounds that can't be heard" (pp. 23–25). In contrast to the repugnant eyes of Consuelo, of which "the black dots of the pupils" outlined on the yellowish cornea recall the blackness of the mice, Aura's eyes suggest the memorable image of Magritte: "those eyes of sea green . . . that . . . surge, break to foam, grow calm again, then surge again like a wave" (p. 27). And there is the black Christ on the white-washed wall next to the image of Luzbel in the demonic iconography: the pain on the one opposite the pleasure of the other. Other examples: the imploring and sorrowful mewing of the cats destroying the silence of the morning: "another door without a latch" (p. 31), "the mirror covered with fog" (p. 32), "the servant never even glimpsed" (p. 69), "cold fingers" (p. 17), "an intermittent sheen" (p. 13), "a troubled smile" (p. 105), "a happy grimace" (p. 105), "the taste of honey and the taste of gall" (p. 105); and toward the end: "a voice muted and transformed" (p. 141), "fleshless lips" (p. 145), "toothless gums" (p. 145), "a time . . . no clock could ever measure" (p. 139).

Of all these links, which in their opposition form oxymoronic pairs, the one that startles us most is the confusion and the absorption of wakefulness by a dream-state: the first erotic encounter between Aura and Felipe occurs in that interstice. Equally singular is the contrast implicit in the shadow-plants of the garden: in that enclosed place the henbane, nightshade, great mullein, euonymus and belladonna grow (p. 44). They are the magical herbs which feed Consuelo's illusion and with whose vegetal shadow Aura's light is procreated.

The common denominator of these expressive means is a state of absence, a lack which defines a no-man's-land that is but the geography or atmosphere in which the narrative exists. The counterpoint between the noisy and commercial world of the street and the dark silence that fills the residence of Donceles Street; the constant counterpoint between light and shadow that creates a penumbral space; and related counterpoints such as dream and wakefulness, the white rabbit and the black mice, the black crucifix and the white wall, Christ's pain and Lucifer's pleasure, the dark repulsive eyes of Consuelo and the light, blue-green ones of Aura, point to a similar relationship: Aura will come from the shadows, like an emanation from darkness, from a no-man's-land which, like the house on Donceles Street, is where it should not be, in the void between dream and wakefulness. Just as Felipe says to himself, "you're seeking your other half" (p. 117), the whole narrative is the search for a lost half, for something which is not where it should be, for the flesh of fleshless lips, for the teeth of toothless gums, for the temperature of the temperature-less fingers, for the sound of the silent voice, for a time that no clock can record. And this quest of the narrative as code is parallel to that other quest of the narrative as message: the search for Consuelo's lost youth and General Llorente's dimmed love. Aura (Consuelo's youth) can only live in that environment of slaughtered billy-goats and dense silences, gardens of shadow-plants and moss odors, humidity and rotten roots, shadows and penumbras, dreams and chained-together cats enveloped by fire, in the same way that the story of Aura, the narrative as literary creation, can only live in that expressive medium subtly forged by Carlos Fuentes.

One more unifying element in *Aura*'s expressive system is the second-person narrator. Fuentes also uses it in *La muerte de Artemio Cruz* and it has antecedents in Mary McCarthy, Rex Stout, Tom Lea, William Styron, and Michel Butor, among others. To what internal needs of the narrative does this choice respond? Certainly it is neither fortuitous nor arbitrary. The narrator is also the protagonist: Felipe Montero unfolds into these two functions, but not in the traditional manner of the first-person narrator who is also a character. The second person allows Felipe to be the subject and the object of the narration at the same time, the narrator who tells his own story and the character whose will has been mortgaged by the narrator. The second person generates a distance, separates the narrator from the character by establishing a two-fold condition that is of a piece with the theme: the narrator produces a script that the character performs, the narrator is and is not the character. He is the character and in turn, through that distance which the second person makes possible, he assumes the point of view of the reader, thus creating the illusion that the real narrator of the narrative is the reader. Is this dualism not the same one underlying the relationships of Consuelo-Aura and Felipe-General Llorente? Once again we have a clear case of superimposition, entities that confound each other forcing the narrator to assume a dual identity, to be himself and the other. The second person, moreover, to a greater degree than the first or the third, produces the impression of a narrative that takes place before our eyes, in a present that neither assumes any future nor needs to depend on the past: "You leave a tip, reach for your briefcase. You wonder if another young historian, in the same situation you are, has seen the same advertisement, has got ahead of you and taken the job already. You walk down to the corner, trying to forget this idea. As you wait for the bus, you run over the dates . . ." (p. 5). And is not this narration in the second person, which relies entirely on the present, the most fitting point of view for a story that attempts to deny the past through the present? Isn't this point of view the most suitable for a story as ethereal, fragile, and fleeting as our own present, which as soon as it happens is already ceasing?

Finally, the superimposition of two different languages—the Spanish of the narrative and the French of General Llorente's memoirs—performs a similar function: a language other than that of the narrative reveals the key to the story. ("The herbs do not strengthen the body, but rather the soul" [p. 133].) Those who have seen in the use of French a mere display of vanity do not realize that this playing with two languages is part of the total game: Consuelo and Aura on the level of characters, light and shadow on the level of the atmosphere that sustains the story, second-/first-person as a narrative dualism, Spanish-French as two languages which fit the one into the other, restating the binomial present-past as the enigma and its key. Summarizing: the division of the characters, their dual nature as beings of light and shadow, of reality and unreality, is joined, or almost inlaid, in a literary medium—the text—which participates in the same binarism, in the same game of reality and unreality. Theme and system shake hands, and from this act of necessary solidarity oozes the atmosphere of the narrative. In this textual space, the story achieves its narrative being, its poetic reality, that fascination that stirs the reader and interrogates him from a zone which has always been the realm, perhaps the only one, of literature. Paz said that we do not have a name for that geography; he meant poetry.

Notes

1. Roger Caillois, *Imágenes, imágenes* . . . (Buenos Aires: Sudamericana, 1970), pp. 12, 21; H. P. Lovecraft, *Supernatural Horror in Literature* (New York: Abramson, 1945), p. 16; Louis Vax, *Arte y literatura fantásticas* (Buenos Aires: Eudeba, 1965), p. 6.
2. Octavio Paz, "La máscara y la transparencia" in his *Corriente alterna* (Mexico: Siglo Veintiuno, 1967), p. 49.
3. Jorge Luis Borges, *Discusión* (Buenos Aires: Emecé, 1964), p. 11.
4. Victor Shklovski, "El arte como artificio" in *Teoría de la literatura de los formalistas rusos*, ed. Tzvetan Todorov (Buenos Aires: Signos, 1970), p. 56.
5. Jules Michelet, *La Sorcière* (Paris: Calmann Lévy, 1878). We follow the pagination indicated by Ana María Albán de Viqueira in her article "Estudio de las fuentes de *Aura* de Carlos Fuentes" in *Comunidad* (Mexico), August 1967, pp. 396–402.
6. Ana María Albán de Viqueira, "Estudio de las fuentes," p. 398.
7. Jorge Luis Borges, *Otras inquisiciones* (Buenos Aires: Emecé, 1964), p. 17.
8. John Barth, "Literatura del agotamiento" in *Borges: el escritor y la crítica*, ed. J. Alazraki (Madrid: Taurus, 1976), p. 175.
9. Shklovski, "El arte como artificio," pp. 55–70.
10. Roland Barthes, *Ensayos críticos* (Barcelona: Seix Barral, 1967), p. 306.
11. Borges, *Otras inquisiciones*, p. 218.
12. As quoted by Robert Rogers, *The Double in Literature: A Psychoanalytic Study* (Detroit: Wayne State University Press, 1969), p. 2.
13. Evelyn Picon Garfield, *Julio Cortázar* (New York: Ungar, 1975), p. 8.

Frank Dauster

The Wounded Vision: *Aura, Zona sagrada,* and *Cumpleaños*

Carlos Fuentes' shorter fictions raise a series of provocative and puzzling questions which fascinate critics and readers. *Aura* particularly has evoked very different readings, although *Zona sagrada* and especially *Cumpleaños* have also inspired variant and often illuminating interpretations. However, few have seen the threads which unite the three books, although many have commented independently on the mythic underpinnings, the fragmentation of normal time patterns, and the complicated allusions to pre-Hispanic thought which are common to the three. Margaret Sayers Peden has pointed out the mythic prototypes, the use of a sacred or hallowed region and the demonic possession which are so important in all three.[1] Richard Callan has examined both *Aura* and *Zona sagrada* from a Jungian perspective, and comments that both reflect a conscious use of depth psychology.[2] Susan Schaffer has examined "The development of the double in selected works of Carlos Fuentes"[3] focusing particularly on the three texts in question. There are, however, other similarities, perhaps most notably the implications of the unreliable narrator. These resemblances are so strong that the novels appear to be three stages in a process of psychotic breakdown and healing, a theme foreshadowed in such short stories as "Tlactocatzine, del Jardín de Flandes," from *Los días enmascarados*.

Aura: The Disordered Vision

Aura is certainly one of the most fascinating of Fuentes' works. Its use of witchcraft, its harking back to archaic rituals, its defiance of normal chronological time, have all exercised a profound attraction on its readers. Clearly, it is structured about two sets of doubles, Consuelo de Llorente as Aura and Felipe Montero as the long-dead General Llorente. Through her satanic rituals, Consuelo creates a double, an alternative personality, identical to herself when younger, which she controls and through which she has physical sex with Montero. But, in a fashion less clear, Montero is also a recreation of the general: "You stare and stare at the photographs, then hold them up to the skylight. You cover General Llorente's beard with your finger, and imagine him with black hair, and you only discover yourself: blurred, lost, forgotten, but you, you, you" (p. 137). Somehow Montero is identical to Llorente, as Aura is to Consuelo. Nor is this equivalence quite as abrupt a discovery as it might seem; the morning after celebrating the erotic mass with Aura, Montero comments, "You put your hands on your forehead, trying to calm your disordered senses: that dull melancholy is hinting to you in a low voice, the voice of memory and premonition, that you're seeking your other half, that the sterile conception last night engendered your own double" (p. 117). This may be almost literally true; to what extent the Felipe Montero who entered the house at 815 Donceles is the same Felipe who recognizes himself in the photograph we cannot tell. Even earlier, of course, there has been a clue: Aura-Consuelo murmurs to Felipe, "you're my husband" (p. 77), a statement whose implications Felipe is unable at that point to assess.

Now there is no way to attribute this amazing identity to some sort of ritual practice of Consuelo, as is the case with Aura. Although she conducts an erotic ritual which seems very close to a black mass, it is never indicated that Felipe has been altered physically. Possibly he is a reincarnation of the general; the fragmentation or slippage of time is one of Fuentes' continuing favorite themes, and something close to reincarnation or at least continuing consciousness across time is a major strand in *Cumpleaños.* But there is no real indication of this in *Aura,* and in any case, it would make the Felipe-Montero identification quite different from the doubling of Aura and Consuelo. How then do we understand the eerie identity of the two? Obviously, it cannot be sheer coincidence; Consuelo, at her advanced age, hardly proposed to wait until someone exactly like Llorente finally appeared. There must be another explanation.

Richard Callan has suggested that *Aura* may be a subjective experience, either a dream or something close to it:

> The story may be understood in either of two ways: First, the events up to the second night happened to Felipe but everything else is a phantasmagoria, beginning with his first dream, the first in many years, and that a nightmare. The Aura he knows thereafter is out of character with the timid girl he

first met: he "awakens" from the nightmare with a cry to find
Aura lying, naked and succubus-like, on top of him (p. 35).
This erotic dream is presented as fact, throwing the subsequent action into the domain of revery. The second view, preferable and more likely, is that the entire second story is a
hypnagogic drama like the famous one that Jung analyzes in
Symbols of Transformation. It further resembles the Miller
fantasies in having an abortive outcome. In this case there
would be not three persons in the list of characters, nor even
two, but only Felipe Montero and his archetypes. . . .[4]

This is an intriguing hypothesis, but there is a related interpretation which goes a step further. One clue lies in Fuentes' idio-
syncratic use of the narrative *tú*. This stylistic characteristic has
been approached in many ways, but it is possible to regard it as a
variant of the first person singular, that is, of the protagonist as narrator. The unspecified narrator may well be Felipe Montero; we are
reading Montero's memory in action. But this interpretation places
the action of the book in a different perspective. Given the odd situations and esoteric rituals which he describes, it is legitimate to wonder whether the entire narrative is not suspect, whether we are not
dealing with a classic case of the unreliable narrator as madman.
   Such would not be a unique case in recent Spanish American
fiction; Sábato's *El túnel* is a prime example. It is intriguing that
critics accept Castel's final madness but ignore the possibility that
he may have been mad from the book's beginning. Considering
Sábato's treatment of psychosis in *Sobre héroes y tumbas*, this is not
a fanciful notion. Other contemporaries employ many of the same
techniques and raise the same questions. Cortázar would probably
reject standard notions of schizophrenia, and he is obviously dealing
with other conceptions of reality; many of his characters are at least
partially locked into another kind of reality. But this is precisely one
of the forms of schizophrenia, and a traditionally oriented reader
might well see many of Cortázar's protagonists as clinically mad. It
is not overly daring to approach Fuentes in somewhat the same way,
particularly since *Aura* is not only *about* some odd doubling, but
such doubling is the essence of the book.
   There are some other curious references which support this
reading. Montero's entrance into the odd house at 815 Donceles is
the entrance to the labyrinth; he walks blindly, with no idea of
where his steps will take him. The atmosphere of the house—perpetual darkness, labyrinthine halls, the humid odor of rotting vege-

tation, the scurrying of rats and stench of scorched cat fur—is such that we may certainly see in it the infernal vision, a world gone mad, or perhaps the world perceived by a madman. Wherever else this house may exist, it surely dwells in Felipe's mind. There are also some anticipations of the behavior of Mito in *Zona sagrada* which underline this interpretation: Felipe finds a refuge in the house; he makes very little effort to leave, once he has entered, and permits the packing and transfer of his few belongings almost without protest. His willingness to accept the arrangement with Consuelo is presumably financial, but his easy acceptance indicates a disposition or even an eagerness to abandon the difficulties of life outside as much as the desire for significant financial gain. In sum, the house, and especially Aura's room, is a place of refuge, a "zona sagrada" where Felipe finds shelter from the menacing city outside. There is certainly an anticipation of *Cumpleaños* in the empty streets with their disordered names and numbers, and the shadow of one who hides when Montero looks at the window. This is not intended as an exclusive reading of a book which is, after all, one of the most deceptively complex in recent Mexican letters, but it seems clear that on one level of meaning, at least, *Aura* may be read as the record of one man's delusion.[5]

Zona sagrada: The Descent into Madness

Zona sagrada permits of no such cavils; it is clear that by book's end, Mito is unable to function. The novel is, in one sense, a series of scenes from a descent into madness, a graphic voyage into hell. There are a number of resemblances to *Aura,* some of which have already been mentioned. Particularly important are the mythic structure, here carried to an extreme degree of complexity, embodying both pre-Hispanic and Greek mythological scaffolding, and the characteristic flight from normal time: "The protean structure of the novel also reflects the attempts of the characters to re-create and thus perpetuate themselves through constant change. They seek to defy the ruinous course of chronological time that will lead them inevitably toward debilitation and death."[6] One of the chief resemblances is the supreme unreliability of the narrator, trapped in a destructive oedipal situation. His beloved apartment, his sacred place, is something out of a *fin de siècle* dream; the books are all "decadent," the most admired work of art is by Aubrey Beardsley. The apartment also contains a picture of Sarah Bernhardt, not surprisingly an actress, like Claudia Nervo. To what extent does she replace a portrait of Claudia, which might be too perilous for Mito's fragile psyche? He is obsessed by incestuous compulsions, barely able to function in the world. He is potentially if not actively homosexual, repelled by heterosexual love and the female body, as we see in his violent reaction to Bela.[7] He is a sadist (witness his cruelty to his dogs), participates in a grotesque and probably fantasized orgy involving reversal of sexual roles, and teeters about in Claudia's lingerie. Finally, he is reduced to total dissociation as he adopts the role of the dog, completing the sadomasochistic compulsion which animates him. To accept the version of reality, whatever that may be, offered to us by Mito is to willfully ignore the fact that he is incapable of anything even remotely close to an objective narrative. His tale is hopelessly suspect.

Like *Aura*, *Zona sagrada* is built about a series of doublings or fragmentations of characters, but it is a much more complex work and employs them more extensively.[8] There are additional similarities: both involve an ambiguous relationship between a young man and an older woman, clearly sexual in *Aura* and openly oedipal in *Zona sagrada*. In this light, the Consuelo-Aura splitting may be seen as Montero's hallucinated effort to disguise the reality of a profound incestuous attraction. Both books involve witchcraft; Mito's orgiastic dream or hallucination or fantasy with the starlets is not unlike Montero's blasphemous relationship with Aura, and Gloria Durán has studied extensively the role of the witch in both novels.[9]

It is in the extensive doublings involving Mito and Claudia that *Zona sagrada* finds its structure. Claudia is several women in the novel; Gloria Durán even remarks that "Claudia is more than one person and, like the Consuelo of *Aura*, can project herself in other forms; she is in fact woman in general, or the archetype of woman as mother, lover or wife. What remains to be seen is that Claudia not only has doubles of herself, but that she is a double, part feminine and part masculine."[10] Whether Claudia is in fact hermaphroditic, as Durán suggests, or whether this is simply an image of her fostered by a disordered Mito is questionable. Certainly, as Mito presents her to us, she is polyvalent; not only does she have multiple mythic equivalents (Penelope, Circe, Coatlicue, the archetypal witch, etc.), but, William Siemens suggests, she is also the moon goddess Selene, thereby associating her with Nuncia of *Cumpleaños*.[11] She is also several other characters in the novel. One is her efficient and mannish alter ego, Ruth:

> The secretary would be, once more, the go-between. That procuress with her eternal two-piece suit and her powdered face

and her short hair, that excrescence of the freedom which my mother, somehow, conquered for all of them. Ruth, faithful as only that parallel procreation can be, not a mirror but the incubus, the intimate, the fat dog or the well-fed rabbit.[12]

The tone is chillingly reminiscent; the last sentence has a startling echo of Consuelo, even to the rabbit. Ruth is Claudia's other self, her masculine side, so much so that Mito suspects a lesbian relationship. But we discover that the mirrors are only reflections of other mirrors; behind the glamorous and eternally feminine movie star lie the mind and heart of a moneylender or an international financier, while Ruth, for all the deliberate masculinity of her manner and attire, at times reveals a much more open and human person. More than opposites, they are complementary.

Claudia is also doubled in Mito's one heterosexual love, Bela. Bela first appears made up to resemble Claudia and wearing her clothing, whereupon Mito becomes violent and strikes her savagely. Her later efforts to establish a relationship with Mito are frustrated by his apparent inability at anything more than a hesitant physical union, and by Claudia's rage. Bela is Claudia, and his possession of Bela—if it indeed takes place, since the episode's resolution is most ambiguous—is incest. Claudia reacts strongly because she perceives Bela as a rival and because Claudia may be dangerously aware of the doubling. All the young women with whom she surrounds herself are Claudia's doubles in another sense, they are her vicarious youth. But Claudia must surely realize what sort of monstrous situation she has created; perhaps she is frightened by how dangerously close a Mito-Bela relationship comes to overt incest.

The most obvious doubling in the novel is that of Mito and Giancarlo. The latter refers to them as brothers: "Friends, Guglielmo? Brothers? Even though it be temporary, *caro.* Brothers born of the same mother" (p. 107). And Mito repeats the theme: "Apollo and Dionysus, born together . . ." (p. 144). Jill Levine has expressed the relationship clearly:

Here the protagonist . . . is drinking a Campari with his Italian friend and, perhaps, lover, Giancarlo Adelphi, to whom the narrator refers in the familiar "tú," in the best tradition of the Nouveau Roman. This "tú," immediately suggests a mirror, a double. Giancarlo's presence is not really felt except as a reflection of the protagonist-narrator. Later we understand that Giancarlo is something more than a double: he is also a symbolic brother of Mito. The relationship between them is not only homosexual but also incestuous; its real significance is revealed toward the end of the book, in the chapter "Card Tricks," when Mito enters his mother's hotel room in Rome and finds her making love with Giancarlo. Then, the latter calls him: "Brother."[13]

There are serious oddities about these two "brothers," not the least being the epigraph from Borges' "Las ruinas circulares": "Quería soñar un hombre" ("He wanted to dream a man"). The Borges tale deals with a man who dreams another, only to find at his death that he too is the creation of another's dreams. What better clue to the nature of Mito's relationship with Giancarlo? The latter excels at all those things in which Mito is singularly adept; like Mito, Giancarlo lacks a father and has a disinterested mother. Like Mito he is thoroughly narcissistic, sexually disoriented—witness for example the episode of the dolls (p. 102)—almost certainly homosexual. In the wild ride to Positano and the episode in the subway tunnel, he is potentially suicidal, an attitude apparently shared by Mito, if we may believe his last words in the novel:

> And he, now, in her arms, will not want to abandon life, will want to remain buried in her and will be afraid of death just as both of us, before being born, were afraid of life.
> Not I.
> That is my victory. A dog knows how to die unsurprised.
> (pp. 190–191)

In addition to these striking similarities, Mito talks to Giancarlo constantly, even when Giancarlo is not present. Is he, in the first person singular of *Zona sagrada*, talking to himself, much as Montero does in *Aura*? There are even moments when Giancarlo seems to be acting in Mito's name:

> *Cretino*, and if I succeed in humiliating her?, and if I act in your name?, and if I break her and transform her and offer you her in all her weakness, behind her aggressive words and false strength?, and if I extract her whole story, bit by bit, and afterward tell you about her loves, her deceptions, her ambition, the repugnance she's felt, how coldly she's calculated?, if I surrender your real mother to you, naked, maskless, insulted, finally revealed by an imagined man who offers her the last surprise: the surprise that, despite all appearances, I don't reflect her?, and if your mother finally admits that one flees

loneliness only to find humiliation?, do you want to see her like that, do you want me to give her back like that? (p. 183)

This is, by any standard, an extraordinary paragraph, even if we discount the ambiguous "imaginado." It is so close to what Mito desperately wants, perhaps without ever articulating it to himself or even daring to think it out in those terms, that we must consider the possibility that the speaker is not another person, a flesh-and-blood Giancarlo, but a repressed side of Mito which takes form and speech in this hallucinated other self which he has conceived. Callan and Siemens have come to the same conclusion. Callan sees Giancarlo as a phantom created by Mito's disturbed psyche in a desperate effort to struggle against the destroying Circe—interestingly, he also sees Bela as in large measure imaginary. "But who is Giancarlo that he should take such loving care of Guillermo? Is he real? I think that he has little if any reality outside of Mito's psyche (the same holds for Bela)." And again:

> Part III, which occurs after Claudia's departure from Mexico, probably takes place entirely in Mito's mind, as does a great portion of the book. For example, Giancarlo may have been only a fellow student he saw and admired at a distance, and their friendship all a fantasy. We know from Jung that "when a person remains bound to the mother, the life he ought to have lived runs away in the form of conscious and unconscious fantasies."[14]

Siemens goes further, stating flatly that "The novel has a fictional reader as well, a double created by the narrator and called Giancarlo Adelphi."[15]

The crucial resemblance is, of course, the sexual attraction to Claudia, who is, as Mito remarks, also Giancarlo's mother. In Mito's case the incestuous passion is never realized, while Giancarlo, apparently and rather precipitously starring in a film with Claudia, becomes her lover. But the whole episode of the film and of the bedding of Claudia and Giancarlo is dubious; it is impossible to determine where fact ends and fantasy begins; Siemens calls it "imagined."[16] The letter from Bela and the episode of Claudia and Giancarlo embracing in the hotel room are not objectively verifiable, and there are elements of behavior which fairly cry out that this cannot really be taking place.[17] It is hardly likely that Giancarlo, aware of Mito's distressed state and of his feelings for Claudia, would turn from her embrace and call Mito, "Hermano" (p. 178). Nor does it seem likely that in Mito's condition, Giancarlo would engage in the mad adventure of the trains. Such behavior seems much more consistent with the hallucinations of a deeply disturbed psychotic who is still attempting through his fantasies to avoid facing the real nature of his problem, even while overtly suicidal.

More than once Mito has what appear to be visions or hallucinations. The episode of the orgy, with its parody of homosexual rape, and the following scene with Claudia howling madly certainly seem to be hallucinations. In the same fashion, the episode of the filming appears hallucinated; it reads like a mad von Stroheim ordering about a series of assistants whose names are all clearly from Brecht: Jenny, Bilbao, Mahoganny. . . . Since this episode is juxtaposed with Mito's now homicidal remarks about revenge and cannibalism (pp. 176–177), it seems clear that we cannot trust anything he says:

> Don't you understand me? Don't you accept me? Then I have other weapons. Cain's. Oedipus's. I will invoke the elements. With a hand I will draw the storm over the garden of the monsters, with the other I will raise the dust of its bed; wrapped in mud and water I will corner you in the bottom of the open mouth of that baroque Demon where you look for refuge, not knowing that I have assumed the powers of the fallen angel, of God's double. (p. 166)

In view of Fuentes' fondness for inside jokes—the parodic filming, among others—it can hardly fail to strike us that Mito even calls himself the double of God. He has been operating for so long with alternative personalities that he now begins to think of himself as still another.

Given Mito's initial instability, it is unlikely that his narrative, particularly of the later and more bizarre adventures, is trustworthy, a conclusion reinforced by his remarks about having been released from a clinic, the episode of transvestism, and the final collapse. Giancarlo is nonexistent, a twin conjured up by Mito. Unable to accept the real nature of his condition and unable to alter it, he creates an alter ego, a person who shares those things he would be, who is more heroic and more brilliant than he, and who may safely bed the desirable Claudia without disastrous psychic damage. Except, of course, that it does not work, and Mito is led into the final collapse, the desperate effort to become the object of his desire.

Even the last pathetic chapter, where Mito accepts his existence metamorphosed into a dog, totally removed from sanity, is based on a complicated set of doublings. In his degradation, Mito sees himself as a dog, one of the ineffectual begging creatures who have been the victims of his sadism. What better opportunity for one who needs to be humiliated, reviled, mistreated? This is, after all, his relationships with Claudia, and his existence as a dog is simply a logical extension. In his madness, he has translated into literal terms the metaphoric nature of his previous reality. His masochistic obsession has become factual reality. And even here the diseased vision lives: if Gudelia, who wears Claudia's clothing, is a cruder version of Claudia, then who is the coarse Jesús who lives in Mito's apartment, wears Mito's clothes and noisily fornicates with the complaisant Gudelia? In this mirror world of doubles lies the truth of Mito's pathetic vision, of the disturbed world created by his distorted psyche.

Cumpleaños: The Vision Redeemed

Of the three works under consideration, *Cumpleaños* is the densest and most difficult, and its publication was greeted with a certain degree of consternation. McMurray has suggested that most of the action is a dream;[18] others have proposed that the protagonist is dying and that the novel is a deathbed epiphany. The problem is complicated by the riddle of Siger of Brabant, a polemical thirteenth-century Averroist philosopher, and by the novel's resolute defiance of normal chronology. There are, however, important similarities between the three novels; the doublings anticipate the blurring of identity which is an important theme of *Cumpleaños*, the great whole or one Being, which is a favorite speculation of both Borges and Latin Averroism, one of whose leaders was Siger of Brabant. Fuentes has remarked that "*Cumpleaños*, which I wrote after *Cambio de piel*, is a companion novel to *Aura*, no? They form a diptych in a way."[19] *Cumpleaños* is many things; it presents many of Fuentes' literary obsessions, but it is also possible to see it as the final stage in the trilogy *Aura–Zona sagrada–Cumpleaños*, and to read everything between the awakening for the birthday and the recognition of London as a psychotic episode.

The opening scenes recall Sábato's exploration of the underside of madness in *Sobre héroes y tumbas*; the hallucinated London is reminiscent of Fernando Vidal's psychotic vision of Buenos Aires in the "Informe sobre ciegos." Curtains cover blind walls, straight corridors have corners; the nightmarish city, so reminiscent of Borges' City of the Immortals and equally outside normal time and normal space, is also London, or rather all Londons, coexisting in one here and one now. It is a city of terrifying narrowing halls, collapsing walls, unexpected abysses and oddly mutable physical features, recalling nothing so much as the psychotic vision of the protagonist of *The Cabinet of Dr. Caligari*.[20] It is not our intent to reduce *Cumpleaños* to a psychological novel; the book is a complex meditation on the nature of time and the continuity of mind through time, and probably other things as well. It has important religious overtones, as witnessed by the ritual wounds, the stigmata and the use of the trinity of man, woman, and child in both the vision and the reality of George's middle-class home. But it would be stubborn not to recognize in *Cumpleaños* the psychological contexts of the two earlier works.

George's initial experiences in the alien world into which he awakens are of total dissociation: his senses are unreliable, he cannot tell whether he is dressed or naked, and the woman Nuncia insists that there is no such person as he.[21] Yet, considering the terrifying nature of the experience, he seems startlingly at ease, and the child seems quite accustomed to him:

> It is natural for him to greet me. This must be his house. In any case, he was here before I. He must be the first occupant. It is natural.
> It is not natural for him to add, immediately, in his best company voice: How nice that you have come back.
> Then I once again take possession of my privilege.[22]

There are several striking remarks here, the first the casual comment that it is natural for the child to act as he does, since the situation is anything but natural. More startling is the obvious fact, expressed first by the child and then by George, that he has been here before. Whatever this city may be, George has been here before, and here he is at home.

The body of the novel appears to be a psychotic episode, a vision of George's life and childhood, perhaps triggered by his son's birthday, but also somehow related to the death of his father, of which there are variant versions, and to George's apparent responsibility for that death. Nuncia, the child, and the horseman all function as doubles of George, his wife, and son, although the exact intent is hardly clear. At times, Niño seems to be George as a child; much of what he says and does finds a response in George's memory.[23] We see George's nostalgia for his own lost childhood as he watches Niño's accelerated maturing. Niño cannot be dismissed as George's memory of himself as a child; on one level, the child seems to represent Siger, and there is also the whole religious context. But it does seem clear that he represents the process of George's childhood, compressed, accelerated, and subject to George's own distorted view of it.

One of the most perplexing aspects of the book is the doubling of George and the stranger. At times George appears to be a child and the stranger is his father:

> Today I saw you fornicate with my father—I said to Nuncia in a low voice. She did not recognize me. And the child took advantage of that instant of my apparent opposition to the woman, he took me by the hand, he led me to the remote point where the willow grows. There, without giving me an opportunity to react, he slashed my forearm with a tiny stiletto, he raised the sleeve of his velvet jacket while I stood stupefied at the sight of my own blood, he thrust the small dagger into his own arm, he placed it against mine and mixed our blood.
>
> We have sealed the pact again, he murmured, strangely docile and moved. We have never been separated. We can never be separated. Somehow, we will always live together. Until one of us succeeds in reaching what he has most wanted in life.
> (p. 54)

These extraordinary paragraphs, with their oedipal echoes in the last lines, the Freudian suggestions in the initial statement, and the identification of George and the child, strongly suggest that we are dealing with something very close to *Zona sagrada,* although far more obscure.

Nuncia also has a variety of roles: in addition to her ambiguous part in the Siger context, she appears at times to be both George's wife and his mother, and like Claudia, she has been identified with a whole series of goddesses, some malevolent, some benevolent. Nor are all the doublings strictly along sexual lines; in an episode reminiscent of *Zona sagrada,* George is also Nuncia. The doublings of Nuncia are so complex and so shifting that it is tempting to regard them as the disordered images of a mind incapable of ordering its perceptions coherently.

Cumpleaños relies so heavily on these doublings that certain key episodes are almost exercises in fragmentation of characters, to the extent that all personality becomes inextricably interwoven. McMurray comments that "the theologian, George, the child, Christ, and the Devil are all the same person." Adriana García de Aldridge, in her intriguing tracing of Celtic elements, remarks that George is an architect and that Siger "mentions to him that in one of his incarnations he was a builder of dolmens."[24] Clearly, both George and Niño are at times Siger of Brabant, re-created or reincarnated in search of proof of his theories. But George is also the Niño who, as he grows, becomes George, and there is the mysterious horseman, George's absolute physical double. Gloria Durán interprets the rider as a symbol "of the other self, the personal unconscious." She relates the symbol of the horse to both death and the erotic drive and accepts the interpretation of the novel as dream.[25] This illuminates the Claudia-Mito relationship, since *Zona sagrada* includes cryptic references to a young woman who rides each morning on the beach at Positano, and Claudia is on several occasions described as riding horses in some of her most important roles. It seems clear that the horseman-double of *Cumpleaños* is a continuation or at least another version of the relationship symbolized in the earlier novel by this same figure of a rider. George, however, unlike Mito, is beginning to organize his psyche, and his horse-riding double is a man: himself. The rider seems to represent George's life seen from outside, an autoscopic vision. He observes his absolute double, i.e., himself, engaging in sexual activity with Nuncia; this dissociation goes to the extreme that the two apparent portions of George's identity function as simultaneous lovers. But George's wound is healing, and he recognizes the situation. He is aware that the rider is himself and that he must face the rider and be rid of him: "Only my constant presence at Nuncia's side could exorcise the double, the ghost, whatever it was . . . anything except myself . . ." (p. 68).

The ending of *Cumpleaños* is hardly less puzzling than other aspects of it. George is restored to London and to today, but with a seemingly heightened perception and an enriched experience, albeit also with the menace of Nuncia's threat that the whole frightening adventure could happen again. There is a critical passage which indicates that George has had a vision, a perception of the true nature of the world, which has given him, if not freedom, at least the key to it:

> I have seen five lotus floating in the garden pool. For no reason, they reminded me of the promises made. Here; in this garden, in these rooms. I looked at the lotus and thanks to them, I realized that I could remember my life in this place. As on another occasion, I asked myself: Will I, then, be able to remember my other life when I leave this one? Twice only my companions, the child and the man, half-opened the curtains of that past which must have been mine. I knew the love of my mother and the death of my father. I learned that neither

he nor she were free; I knew the elementary, clear truth: to be engendered, to be born, to die, are acts foreign to our freedom; ferociously, they mock what we, precariously, try to build and to win in the name of free will. (pp. 94–95)

This experience seems to refer to George's awareness of multiple lives, but it also replicates the kind of perception lying at the core of the Jungian concept of integration, the purified result of psychotic experience. From a somewhat different point of view, it is the Aristotelian perception as presented by Francis Fergusson, the vision which comes from suffering and which leads us to the further business of living. Those who make it safely through the experience are more whole than before; the crippling wound heals and the psyche is strengthened, albeit terribly altered. George seems to have passed the ordeal and is ready to resume the process of life, more alert to its multiple dimensions if more scarred by its dangers.

Aura, Zona sagrada and *Cumpleaños* look very much like three stages in this process: Montero's entrance into the delusion, Mito's psychotic destruction, and George's return to life, scarred but healed. For George, experience is no longer separated into the worlds of inside and outside, as it was for Mito and Montero. He has learned, in terrifying and difficult fashion, to reconcile the opposites, to abandon the tempting but fatal sacred place and, through fear and suffering, to find liberation and wholeness.

Notes

1. Margaret Sayers Peden, "The World of the Second Reality in Three Novels by Carlos Fuentes," *Otros mundos, otros fuegos. Memoria del XVI Congreso del Instituto Internacional de Literatura Iberoamericana* (East Lansing: Latin American Studies Center, Michigan State Univ., 1975), pp. 83–87.
2. Richard Callan, "The Function of Myth and Analytical Psychology in *Zona sagrada,*" *Kentucky Romance Quarterly,* 21, no. 2 (1974): 261–274, and "The Jungian Basis of Carlos Fuentes' *Aura,*" *Kentucky Romance Quarterly,* 18, no. 1 (1971): 65–75.
3. Susan Schaffer, "The Development of the Double in Selected Works of Carlos Fuentes," *Mester,* 6, no. 2 (May 1977): 81–86.
4. Callan, "The Jungian Basis," pp. 73–74.
5. For other readings, see my "La transposición de la realidad en las obras cortas de Carlos Fuentes," *Kentucky Romance Quarterly,* 19, no. 3 (1972): esp. 314–315.
6. Lanin Gyurko, "The Myths of Ulysses in Fuentes's *Zona sagrada,*" *Modern Language Review,* 69, no. 2 (April 1974): 316.

7. Carlos Fuentes, *Zona sagrada*, 3d ed. (Mexico: Siglo XXI, 1967), p. 70. All further references will be to this edition.

8. Susan Schaffer has discussed the number of trinities in *Zona sagrada*, another anticipation of *Cumpleaños*, in "The Development of the Double," p. 84.

9. Gloria Durán, *La magia y las brujas en la obra de Carlos Fuentes* (Mexico: UNAM Press, 1976).

10. Ibid., p. 95.

11. William Siemens, "The Devouring Female in Four Latin American Novels," *Essays in Literature*, 1, no. 1 (Spring 1974): 119.

12. Carlos Fuentes, *Holy Place*, trans. Suzanne Jill Levine, in *Triple Cross* (New York: E. P. Dutton and Co., 1972), p. 24.

13. Suzanne Jill Levine, "Zona sagrada: Una lectura mítica," *Revista Iberoamericana*, 40, no. 89 (October–December 1974): 618.

14. Callan, "The Function of Myth," pp. 271, 274.

15. Siemens, "The Devouring Female," p. 118.

16. Ibid., p. 119.

17. This discussion occasionally uses the phrase "verifiable truth" and its variants. Obviously, we are dealing with a fiction and such phrases are only approximations to indicate the relationships between what Mito perceives and what we suspect may have happened.

18. George R. McMurray, "*Cumpleaños* y 'La nueva novela,'" in *Homenaje a Carlos Fuentes* (New York: Las Américas, 1971), p. 387.

19. Herman P. Doezema, "An Interview with Carlos Fuentes," *Modern Fiction Studies*, 18, no. 4 (Winter 1972/73): 498.

20. Manuel Durán was the first to notice this resemblance in *Tríptico mexicano* (Mexico: Sep Setentas, 1973), p. 121.

21. This whole episode is clearly analogous to birth and, in the total context of the novel, suggests that it might bear analysis in the light of Carl Sagan's speculations about the role of the birth experience in producing the religious search and the phenomena of visions reported by those who have been resuscitated after apparent death. See Carl Sagan, *Broca's Brain* (New York: Random House, 1979), pp. 301–314, "The Amniotic Universe."

22. Carlos Fuentes, *Cumpleaños* (Mexico: Joaquín Mortiz, 1969), pp. 15–16. All references are to this edition.

23. Luis Leal has commented on the autobiographical suggestions of the text in saying, "el viejo también es Siger de Bramante, pero también es George, que puede ser Carlos Fuentes" ("La nueva narrativa mexicana," *Nueva Narrativa Hispanoamericana*, 2, no. 1 [January 1972]: 91).

24. McMurray, "*Cumpleaños*," p. 396; Adriana García de Aldridge, "La dialéctica contemporánea: 'Tiempo propio–tiempo total' en *Cumpleaños*," *Revista Iberoamericana*, 45, nos. 108–109 (August–December 1979): 529.

25. Gloria Durán, *La magia y las brujas*, pp. 178–179, 192.

Malva E. Filer

A Change of Skin and the
Shaping of a Mexican Time

Octavio Paz writes in *The Labyrinth of Solitude* that Mexicans are, for the first time in their history, "contemporaries of all mankind." This claim to full membership in a world of expanding and diversified culture is also at the core of Carlos Fuentes' fiction and essays. The collected articles of *Tiempo mexicano* [1] are a result of his concern with this subject, while the novel *A Change of Skin* attempts to recapture his Mexican experience as part of the universal historical drama. "We are contemporaries through the word," he says, echoing Paz's idea. "In order to name ourselves, we have to name the world; and the world, to name itself, has to name us." [2] The effort to encompass an infinite reality makes of Fuentes' novel a labyrinth of time, such as the infinite novel left by Ts'ui Pên in "The Garden of Forking Paths." [3] Its goal is unattainable, as acknowledged by a narrator who bears the family name and shares the madness of Balzac's character Louis Lambert. [4] We are told, indeed, in Fuentes' novel, that "madness may be the mask too much knowledge wears" (p. 337). Freddy Lambert will leave us on "the morrow of an impossible feast," but his "personal happening" is, for him and for his readers, a forceful and transforming experience. The text, while discrediting itself as an adequate means of representing reality, claims none the less to be truthful to it. For further assurance, a quotation from Michel Foucault, introducing the main body of the novel, tells us that all indicators pointing to the lack of truth of the written texts are yet another sign that the signs in a book do resemble the truth. [5] *A Change of Skin* is Fuentes' most ambitiously designed work before *Terra Nostra*. The following pages analyze some aspects of this novel as they relate to the author's view of Mexico and that country's possible role in a culturally pluralistic world.

Fuentes' choice of time and setting points to the deeper meaning of his book. The day is Palm Sunday, April 11, 1965, on the eve of Holy Week; the place is Cholula, where Mexican history has deep roots and where voices of the past still break into the present. This is a unique stage on which to represent the drama of a Mexican history that has been made, says Fuentes, by the coexistence of diverse, even conflicting cultures: the mythic and cosmic conceptions of the Indians; the Spanish version of Christianity; the individualistic values of the European bourgeoisie; and the faith in science, reason, and progress borrowed from the industrially developed countries. "To choose only one of these historical lines," he believes, "is impossible or undesirable; instead, it is possible and desirable to attempt a fusion of their respective values and, having achieved that synthesis, to go further" (*Tiempo*, p. 39). The novel's description of Cholula's church stresses the overlapping of traditions: Christ, as conceived by the natives, has his wounds covered with blood and feathers; the baptismal fonts are the ancient pagan urns where the hearts of the sacrificed were cast; the Arabic arches stand on the tezontle-stone floor; the sixteenth-century chapel combines an austere simplicity with the rich Renaissance-style ornamentation that was imposed by the Romantic spirit of the last century.

Religious syncretism also is evident at Cholula. In *Tiempo mexicano*, for instance, Fuentes refers to the Indians' concept of cyclical time and to their belief in a founding God, a belief which caused them to understand Christ not as the Savior but as the God of the Origins. According to Fernando Benítez, whose expertise in Mexican Indian culture Fuentes greatly admires, the ceremonies of the "coras" during Holy Week attribute the Creation to Christ. In the Indians' understanding of the Passion, Christ's sacrifice does not redeem humanity, but his blood assures that the sun will not die and Quetzalcoatl's maize will continue to grow on this earth. The ancient Mexican gods, says Fuentes, were conceived as protectors against change, for the Indians thought that the future could bring only destruction. In fact, memory of their origins and fear of the future dominated the society of the Aztecs. Religion, politics, and art were each a form of exorcism, a way to postpone the catastrophe. The Aztecs accepted the inevitability of change, but not without first building elaborate safeguards. Every fifty-two years, a cycle was closed, and the past had to be "cancelled, denied, destroyed or covered like the seven successive pyramids at the ceremonial center of Cholula" (*Tiempo*, p. 27). Human blood was required to win another reprieve, so that new life could grow.

A Change of Skin is clearly centered around this theme of a cyclical time (represented by the seven pyramids), the idea that "the end of a cycle required, as homage to the arrival of the new, that the old should disappear" (p. 294). Fuentes believes that Mexico has kept the original conception of sacrifice as necessary to maintain the order of the cosmos. This, he holds, is Moctezuma's real revenge, and the "final victory of the Indian world in Mexico."[6] The novel summons the whole world to participate in the sacrificial exorcism of Cholula, for guilt is universal and the apocalypse can be averted only by cancelling the past. Western civilization is tried and convicted, as man seeks to free himself from "the old schizophrenias of the Greco-Christian-Judaeo-Protestant-Marxist-industrial dualism" (p. 236). The ceremony involves, as in the ancient ritual, the offering of human blood, here represented by the execution of one of the characters. An introduction to the last part of the book carries the announcement that the narrator, now identified as Xipe Totec, Our Lord of the Flayed Hide, is changing his skin. Finally, at the close of the novel, he indicates that he is an inmate of Cholula's asylum for the insane, a place symbolically named Our Lord Lazarus, "he of the resurrections" (p. 461).

In order to build up to its climax at the Gran Cu of Cholula, the text strives to produce a kaleidoscopic view of our own times. Frequent incursions into past centuries show that progress is mere illusion, that past and future exist here and now. Violence is presented as being the same, no matter who the perpetrators are or who their victims, in evocations that switch from the cruelties of both Spaniards and Indians to the atrocities of the Inquisition, the concentration camps, Hiroshima, and Vietnam. The open-ended, inexhaustible list also includes the Molotov-Ribbentrop pact, the Moscow trials under Stalin, and Trotsky's murder. Everybody is implicated, even the beatniks who judge and condemn the preceding generation. "There is no historical progress, . . . only a repetition of a series of ceremonial acts."[7] This is part of Fuentes' intended message in the novel. "Man makes no progress," says Javier in his never-completed book. Every child "must repeat everything for himself and for the world, . . . as if nothing had ever happened before his birth" (p. 448). Jakob, a Holocaust survivor, declares: "We'll try and fail and try again and fail again, and go to the end of the ancient contradictions in order to live and repeal them, ridding ourselves of our old skin and exchanging it for the fresh new skin of the new contradictions, those that will await us then" (p. 441).

Fuentes believes that Mexico, aware of its own overlapping of cultures, should avoid an illusion of progress that has proven self-destructive to those societies where it has succeeded most. In both *Tiempo mexicano* and *A Change of Skin*, he compares the United States' "mechanical ruins" of progress with the "natural ruins" of Mexican underdevelopment: "If Mexico is nature in ruin," says Javier in the novel, "the United States is machines in ruin. In Mexico everything is a ruin because everything is promised and no promise is kept. In the United States all promises have been kept. Yet it is a ruin just the same" (p. 81). The author clearly feels that his country still has time to avoid the mistakes of its more prosperous neighbor. Since their independence, Latin American nations have followed the "triumphant model" of progress, empiricism and pragmatism. By so doing, says Fuentes, they have adopted the ideologies of their exploiters, the "antiutopian time of progress, of being" as against the "moral time" of that which should be, and can only be desired or imagined (*Tiempo*, p. 31). The philosophy of the Enlightenment, with its denial of the past as barbaric, irrational, and superstitious, was eagerly accepted by those societies that wanted to eradicate their Indian and colonial past and join the optimistic march of progress. However, that ideology was based on the assumption that Europe was the center of the earth, and its culture, the only acceptable model. In our time, states Fuentes, the way has been opened for a new view of the world conceived as "a plurality of cultures that presupposes a plurality of values" (p. 32). He detects also a new determination in countries that are seeking to combine "the power of technology with the energy of their own traditions."[8] In this context, Latin America is described by Fuentes as a "polyculture where the past lives hidden alongside the façade of progress," where an opportunity still exists to choose "from several times and a plurality of values in order to construct a better human society."[9]

The narrator of *A Change of Skin* assembles memories that run through centuries of human experience and failure. He needs to take possession of the past before he can cancel it. His evocation of the characters' voices is an attempt to reenact and render meaningful his own Mexican experience made of Greek and Judeo-Christian tradition, of Indian myths and Spanish Catholicism, of European culture and the American manufactured world. Before the start of a new cycle, he tries to mold that experience into a totality. This is the novel's "impossible feast." In fact, the writer's immediate problem is, according to Fuentes: "How to employ a fragmented, sequential discrete medium—language—yet achieve the impression of totality of wholeness, and above all, of presence."[10] Javier, mirroring the narrator, pursues his own elusive totality in *Pandora's Box*, only to discover that "words could not conquer the fragmentation of reality" (p. 195).

Although to recapture total reality is admittedly impossible, the novel does succeed in reviving the time of "being" and "progress," even though it falls short of imagining the new, utopian, Mexican time. The cyclical concept of life would seem not to allow for anything but the repetition of the past. In fact, Fuentes' narrative is consistent in presenting a pessimistic view of the world, according to which the new is always condemned to acquire the negative features of the old. From his first novel, *Where the Air Is Clear*, to *A Change of Skin*, he critically examines his country's past and present, decrying its inability to break away from old and self-destructive patterns. In *Terra Nostra* and *The Hydra Head*, his more recent novels, he imagines Mexico's future, but only as a fatalistic recurrence of the past.[11] Yet, it would be incorrect to identify the author's own position with this pessimistic outlook. In essays and lectures Fuentes has expressed his belief in Mexico's ability to build "a generous and revolutionary utopia," based on the cultural realities resulting from its coexisting histories. To that effect, a "screening effort" must be made, to "effectively separate the oppressive, dead weight from the living and liberating realities" (*Tiempo*, p. 40). The aim should be a "creative recreation," as represented by two great poems of Mexican literature: *Death without End* by José Gorostiza and *Sun Stone* by Octavio Paz, where Western linear discourse struggles with the spirit of Indian cyclical time in order to reestablish reality on a new foundation.

Freddy Lambert admires and envies the poet's ability to produce a synthesis of language and time. Indeed, one can hardly read Fuentes' novel without remembering poetic images from *Sun Stone*, such as the following:

> a face of flames, face that is eaten away,
> the adolescent and persecuted face
> the years of fantasy and circular days
> that open upon the same street, the same wall,
> the moment flares up and they are all one face,
> the procession of faces of this calling,
> all of these names are unified in one name,
> all of these faces are now a single face
> all centuries are now a single instant
> and throughout the centuries of centuries
> the path to the future shut by these two eyes[12]

A Change of Skin may be read as an exploration of the possibilities of prose fiction to create its own synthesis of language and time. More specifically, the text can be interpreted as an effort to rescue the reality of Mexican experience by creating its fiction. "We are resolved to invent our own reality," says Octavio Paz. "Spanish American literature . . . is both a return and a search for tradition. In searching for it, it invents it. But invention and discovery are not terms that best describe its purest creations. A desire for incarnation, a literature of foundations."[13] That desire, we believe, is Fuentes' main motivation in writing his novel. On the other hand, the "revolutionary utopia" must await its fiction; his characters are still going through the pains of their self-criticism.

The narrative is built on the recreated experiences of the protagonists: Javier, a Mexican intellectual who failed as a writer and became a United Nations bureaucrat; Elizabeth, his Jewish wife, who may be a Mexican but remembers herself growing up in the New York of the Depression; Franz, a Czech Nazi refugee, who designed the buildings of Terezin's concentration camp, and did not try to save his Jewish girl friend; Isabel, an uninhibited but somewhat faceless young Mexican woman. The ambiguity concerning Elizabeth's origin makes it possible for her to represent a feminine image of an American or Americanized view of reality, mingled with the complexities of her Jewish background. She is a product of mass education, increased intellectual and sexual awareness, and cosmopolitan life. Her frustration and neurosis are the price that she pays for these privileges. Isabel, the young and definitely Mexican woman, is presented as the least conflictive of the characters and, at the same time, as an unfinished product. She already lives in the sexually liberated world built by the older generation and takes it for granted. Not sharing and not understanding Javier's interpretation of Mexican life, she finds his writing laughable and his concern pointless. Her following remarks best describe her attitude: "I give up trying to understand you. It's like all that complicated nothing you wrote about the Indians, in your little notebook. So what? Who cares about the Indians? I certainly don't. Do you think I give a damn about that stupid Pepsicóatl?" (p. 279). She is a blasé, uprooted pursuer of her own pleasure. Her behavior typifies the imported and superficial sophistication that Fuentes considers a hindrance to the creation of Mexico's own future. Is she condemned to repeat Elizabeth's life, as Javier fears? In order to prevent this, he kills her, in one of the possible outcomes of the novel. Symbolically, Javier strangles Isabel with the shawl that Elizabeth had given to her.

The four characters and the narrator are joined by a group of six hippies who are the judges and destroyers of the past; among them is Franz's executioner. Other places and circumstances come alive: Prague on the eve of the war; New York in the thirties; Buenos Aires in the forties; a summer on the Greek beach of Falaraki; Mexico during the years of the Cristeros' war and throughout the following decades up to the time of the novel. Javier's memories of his childhood and adolescence are particularly vivid, as he evokes the oppressive environment of the old, gloomy house in Calzada del Niño Perdido. He portrays a moment of Mexican history and a social class while remembering the tragedy of his father's bankruptcy and the restrictions of a home life ruled by his mother's unrealistic middle class values. Economic defeat and tragedy also make up the memories of Elizabeth, as the daughter of poor Jewish immigrants in New York City. In all cases, the text meticulously seeks to re-create the past and describe the present. Actual streets and buildings, movies, popular music, books, the cultural and political milieus are recalled by the narrator, who seems as determined as Fuentes to name the world or, as the Beatles' song promises, to give us back our time. It is irrelevant that he wasn't there, and is only reporting what he heard. It is of no consequence either that Elizabeth has lived, through her imagination, more than one life. We have been everywhere in this world of printed words and television newscasting, of movies and records, advertising and fashion. The upheavals, the anguish, and the inventions of our century are depicted by the novel, and rightly so, as our common property, our collective adventure. Faced with the narrator's skepticism about the veracity of her Falaraki story, Elizabeth offers a reconstruction of the time that is, in fact, a collection of news items:

> The best-seller that year was . . . was . . . *Anthony Adverse*. . . . Hitler gobbled up Austria, Mussolini pulled out of The League of Nations. We listened to Kate Smith and Kay Kyser and laughed at Jack Benny. Father Coughlin was spouting off. Huey Long was killed, I think. Cárdenas expropriated the oil companies. Garbo loved Taylor. . . . Léon Blum's cabinet fell. . . . John Steinbeck published *The Grapes of Wrath* and John Ford made the movie with Henry Fonda. (pp. 77–78)

The list continues, followed by similar paragraphs throughout the novel, apparently suggesting that this is the stuff of which reality is made. In fact, says Fuentes, "history is fiction" and reality, "apocryphal,"[14] a view we are familiar with from Borges' *Ficciones*. As if to prove the point, Freddy Lambert includes in his memories some of the main characters of Fuentes' previous novels.[15]

A *Change of Skin* has been compared to Cortázar's *Hopscotch*, an earlier attempt by a Latin American writer to convey his experience of contemporary life. Indeed, Javier shares with Oliveira a demolishing intellect and a total paralysis of will. While *Hopscotch* recaptures its author's Argentinian experience, *A Change of Skin* is, not surprisingly, a Mexican version of our time. Fuentes' intimate knowledge of his country's history and concern with its present realities emerge from within the book's universal framework. We find in these crowded pages numerous descriptions and critical comments dealing with Mexico City, the Mexican people and the unresolved conflicts of their way of life. The text, as much as the characters, repeatedly returns to modern Mexico from far away places and distant times. On one of these occasions, we are told: "Javier decided that the time had come to return to Mexico City, that he needed Mexico again, that if he did not face and overcome its terrible negations he would always believe that he had taken the easy road and his writing could have no value" (pp. 130–131). Javier would go out and "roam all over the city," looking for contrasts, images, words, profiles, masks. He was trying to find his words in that world that belonged to him. However, despite a declared interest in Mexico's Indian past, he feels that his country's uneducated and mostly Indian citizens are like creatures of another species. To them, "we are Martians," Javier says. "We don't speak as they do or think as they do. . . . If we do see them, it's like the zoo. . . . We are their enemies and they know it" (p. 111). He tries to break the barrier by provoking a fight in which they beat him up. The humiliating experience, sought with masochistic determination, momentarily dissolves the social and intellectual distance that separates him from that group. He was now "on their side of the cage" (p. 113). Javier's attempt at sharing the experience of the oppressed is rather unconvincing, but sufficiently indicative of the guilt that is typical of socially concerned intellectuals. Most of the time, though, he is satisfied with his role of interpreter and critic of Mexican society. His remarks generally echo the author's views. They are also close to the ideas of Octavio Paz, whose friendship and works have been credited by the novelist with being an "original and permanent inspiration" for his own books (*Tiempo*, p. 59).

Fuentes thinks of Mexico as a country wearing a series of masks in the course of its history: At its origin, "a skin of stone, mosaic and gold," then "the baroque and frozen order of liberalism and modernity," and the mask of "peace and progress" under Porfirio Díaz. They were the masks of slavery and hunger that were broken by the revolution. He says that the exceptional, unmasking moments of Mexican history force the country to see itself in its own "depth of latent myths, palaces in ruins, tragic miseries, grotesque coups, painful betrayals," and "useless deaths" (*Tiempo*, pp. 65–66). Popular language in Mexico is, according to Fuentes, a mask of repressed violence, and so is the language of elegance, modesty, and excessive courtesy. In the novel, Javier's description of his city dwells on the contrast between the elegance of residential neighborhoods and the atmosphere of hostility surrounding them. He feels the threatening presence of "those dark-skinned millions with their intolerable passivity, their sudden violence, their unhappy smiles, their jeering sadness, their brutality and rancor." One wonders what our social critic can offer to that mass of people, marked by "centuries of humiliation and frustrated revenge" (p. 199).

"We cannot return to Quetzalcóatl," states Fuentes, "nor will Quetzalcóatl return to us" (*Tiempo*, p. 33). Mexico should not settle, however, for "Our Lady the Pepsicóatl," which is the time being forced upon it by the "modern world": "a technocracy without cultural values, without political liberties, without moral aspirations and without esthetic imagination" (*Tiempo*, p. 41). Javier knows, also, that the clock cannot and should not be turned back. "Or do you really think," he pointedly asks, "it would have been better if the Spaniards had been defeated and we had gone on living under the Aztec fascism?" (p. 431). His frustration and guilt feelings are evident, however, when he faces his own experience. Javier illustrates the limitations and agony of an intellectual whose social ideas have not made a dent in the fabric of reality. He is paralyzed by an excess of knowledge and destructive skepticism. This type of personality and behavior recurs in Fuentes' novels. He portrayed it for the first time in *Where the Air Is Clear* through his characterization of Rodrigo Pola, also an ineffectual writer. *A Change of Skin*, while exposing the selfishness and parasitism of Javier, suggests on the other hand the opposite model of Vasco Montero, a successful poet who is actively committed to the social and political struggles of his time. In the last pages of the novel, Javier admits his failure and condemns himself: "The world didn't change. It denied me and refused to notice me . . ." (p. 407). He declares his passive, irrelevant life to be as guilty as Franz's Nazi past, and more cowardly: "What was action in him in me was only possibility, latency. In me it lacked all greatness, all courage. I have been a kind of larva Franz" (p. 408). "A soul of jelly, like Javier's, is far more guilty than mine," says Franz (p. 445). This is also the opinion of the narrator who, unhappy with the turn of events leading to Franz's execution, would like to change his story.

The novel's verdict is clear: Javier should not survive, the possibilities of his experience have been exhausted. It is safe to assume also the author's agreement with a negative evaluation of this character. Lonely intellectual exercises, such as those engaged in by Javier, are not what culture is all about, according to Fuentes. He understands culture to be a collective and disciplined effort to address all the needs of human life, from economic satisfaction to the fullest development of each human being (see *Tiempo*, p. 35). Javier represents the type of "innocuous" intellectual that the author criticizes and rejects. Obviously, he is not the kind of human material with which to achieve a creative synthesis of the past and invent, as Fuentes envisions, Mexico's own model of development. Freddy Lambert knows it, as he knows it all, in his own mad wisdom.

Fuentes' novel, both through its narrator and through Javier himself, aims at a reality that is different from the one which Javier represents. As pointed out by Julio Ortega, *A Change of Skin* "pursues another world, another time: the new space where reality is invented."[16] This was also Javier's ambition, stated at the beginning of his aborted book: "A novel discloses what the world has within itself but has not yet discovered and may never discover" (p. 262). However, Fuentes' narrator and characters are trapped by a text that, like the life it recaptures, devours its own creatures as well as their hopes. The future, symbolized by a bundle of rags (or a child), is swallowed and digested by the present, a yellow dog whose "hunger is far from being sated" (p. 462). Time is, in this novel, the eternal consumer that must, like the god Kronos, devour its children in order to exist. Freddy's narration remains, challenging death with the power of its own creation. Writing a story is, like the ceremony at Cholula, a way to postpone the final destruction. "The 'lies' we spinners of tales tell," says Lambert, "betray the 'true' . . . in order to hold away . . . that day of judgment when the beginning and the end shall be one" (p. 422). In Fuentes' novel, we may conclude, not only are Mexicans the contemporaries of all mankind, but all mankind has been made to participate in the exorcism, and the shaping, of a Mexican time.

Notes

1.   Carlos Fuentes, *Tiempo mexicano* (Mexico: Joaquín Mortiz, 1971).
2.   Carlos Fuentes, prologue to *Los signos en rotación y otros ensayos*, by Octavio Paz (Madrid: Alianza Editorial, 1971), p. 13.
3.   Jorge Luis Borges, *Labyrinths* (New York: New Directions, 1964).
4.   Fuentes associates Balzac's character with the narrator of his novel in conversations with José-Miguel Ullán, published as "Carlos Fuentes: Salto mortal hacia mañana," in *Homenaje a Carlos Fuentes*, ed. Helmy F. Giacomán (New York: Las Américas, 1971), p. 340.
5.   Michel Foucault, *The Order of Things* (New York: Vintage Books, 1973), p. 47.

6. Fuentes quoted by Emir Rodríguez Monegal, "Carlos Fuentes," in *Homenaje*, p. 31. This view of Mexico as a country constantly demanding the sacrifice of its people appeared in Fuentes' first novel, *Where the Air Is Clear*, and has recurred in his later novels, with special emphasis in *A Change of Skin*. Lanin A. Gyurko discusses the subject in "El yo y su imagen en *Cambio de piel* de Carlos Fuentes," *Revista Iberoamericana*, 76–77 (July–December, 1971): 689–709.

7. Fuentes quoted by Monegal, "Carlos Fuentes," p. 41.

8. Quoted by Richard Eder in "For the Writer Carlos Fuentes Iran Crisis Brings Déja Vu," *New York Times*, January 9, 1980.

9. Carlos Fuentes, "The Writer in an Alien Culture," *Point of Contact*, Spring 1979, p. 14.

10. Ibid., p. 7.

11. Lanin Gyurko deals with Fuentes' pessimistic outlook, as conveyed by his fictional works, in "El yo y su imagen," p. 690, and, more recently, in "Individual and National Identity in Fuentes' *La cabeza de la hidra*," *Latin American Fiction Today: A Symposium*, ed. Rose S. Minc (Gaithersburg, Md.: Hispamérica, 1979).

12. Octavio Paz, *Configurations*, trans. Muriel Rukeyser (New York: New Directions, 1971), p. 11.

13. Octavio Paz, *The Siren and the Seashell* (Austin and London: Univ. of Texas Press, 1976), p. 179.

14. Fuentes quoted by Monegal, "Carlos Fuentes," p. 40.

15. Among his earlier characters mentioned in *A Change of Skin* are Norma Larragoiti, Jaime Ceballos, Régules, Padilla, and Artemio Cruz.

16. Julio Ortega, *La contemplación y la fiesta* (Lima: Ed. Universitaria, 1968), pp. 80–81.

Roberto González Echevarría

Terra Nostra: Theory and Practice

In an essay that had a wide distribution in the sixties, Alejo Carpentier maintained that the novel is above all a form of knowledge, not an object of aesthetic pleasure:

> The Spanish picaresque, born unwittingly from the comical nucleus of *Lazarillo de Tormes* and continued until the premonitory autobiography of Torres de Villarroel, fulfilled its true novelistic function, which is to violate constantly the naive principle of being a story destined to cause "aesthetic pleasure to its readers," to become instead an instrument of analysis, a way of knowing epochs and men; a way of knowing that goes beyond, in many cases, the author's intentions.[1]

As on many other occasions, Carpentier is echoing here an idea of Unamuno's: the knowledge of man and of his time can be achieved through the artistic observation of the local culture.[2] Carpentier's essay, "Problemática de la actual novela latinoamericana," proposes a vast theory about the relationship between texts and contexts in the Latin American narrative, that is, a synthesis of ideas with a long history in Spanish-language intellectual circles.[3] These ideas, linking the peculiarity of local culture and history to literary production, are the main preoccupation of essayists such as Unamuno and Ortega in Spain, and of Alfonso Reyes, Mariátegui, Henríquez Ureña, Lezama, Paz, and many others in Spanish America.[4] The central concern of these writers was to distinguish what is specifically Spanish or Spanish American in their own literatures, and to show how this peculiarity issues from a broader code, a culture that renders that difference intelligible. These ideas culminate in *Terra Nostra*, where they are subjected to a very severe test, and where they show, by "going beyond the author's intentions," the very complex fashion in which novelistic theory and practice are articulated using such presuppositions. If the very term "culture" is based on a metaphor of tilling the earth, *Terra Nostra*, from its very title, announces its intention to provide the ground for a mutual understanding—a telluric communion, a *common ground*. *Terra Nostra* could perhaps be seen as the last gasp of the *novela de la tierra*.

The relationship between *Terra Nostra* and these ideas is so strong that the novel comes with a sort of manual in which the theory about the "knowledge of men and epochs," and the instruments for its achievement, are revealed to the reader. I am referring, of course, to Fuentes' essay *Cervantes o la crítica de la lectura*, where one reads: "In a certain way, the present essay is a branch of the novel that has occupied me for the past six years, *Terra Nostra*." Also, under the heading "Bibliografía conjunta": "In the measure in which the present essay and my novel *Terra Nostra* are born out of parallel impulses and obey common preoccupations, I indicate in what follows the twin bibliography of both works."[5] It is not unusual, of course, for a novel to appear with one or several expository pieces that "explain" its origin and execution. Among Latin American books, such is the relationship between Carpentier's *El reino de este mundo* and *La música en Cuba*, and more recently between Severo Sarduy's *Cobra* and his *Barroco*. In the case of Fuentes, there is a similar relationship between his essay *La nueva novela hispanoamericana* (1969) and several of his earlier novels. In a way, what I propose to do here, which is to fit the theory expounded in *Cervantes o la crítica de la lectura* to the practice of *Terra Nostra*, is analogous to my study of *El reino de este mundo* and its relation to *La música en Cuba* and various other essays of Carpentier's. I intend therefore to pry apart that relationship to see how the impulse to intelligibility and knowledge present in that essay is thwarted in the fiction; how, against the explicit and implicit intentions of both the essay and the novel, the latter renders the link between cultural specificity and literature questionable. In the case of *Terra Nostra* this approach will also allow me to make some observations about the recent history of the Latin American novel.

And what do we find in that "twin bibliography" at the end of *Cervantes o la crítica de la lectura*? In addition to the names of some recent theoreticians and critics like Derrida, Foucault and Cixous, and many others extremely familiar to the Hispanist like Américo Castro, Valbuena Prat, and Stephen Gilman, there are, of course, Cervantes, Fernando de Rojas, Juan Ruiz, and Quevedo, not to mention the Spanish editions of the *Suma contra gentiles* and the *Summa theologicae*. Needless to say, not all of these books play the same role in both of Fuentes' books, and there are others, not included in the bibliography, that have a very prominent place in *Terra Nostra*—namely, several important novels by Latin American writers: *El siglo de las luces, Rayuela, Tres tristes tigres, El obsceno pájaro de la noche, Libro de Manuel, De donde son los cantantes*. It is evident, therefore, that *Terra Nostra* is an inquiry into the origins of the culture of Spain and Latin America, through an analysis of the literary myths created by them. Such a study of culture through mythology has its most remote source in Plato, of course, though it was Vico who legitimized it in modern times. The most recent source of Fuentes, however, is the Spanish "Generation of '98" and the *Modernistas*. It is difficult to avoid the sensation, when reading *Terra Nostra* or *Cervantes o la crítica de la lectura*, that Fuentes is moved in these books by anxieties very similar to those found in *Vida de don Quijote y Sancho*, "El sepulcro de don Quijote," *Don Quijote, don Juan y la Celestina, Clásicos y modernos*, or *La corte de los milagros*. (*Meditaciones del Quijote* also comes to mind, and Ortega's *Obras completas* appears in the "Bibliografía gemela.") The figure who links these Spanish writers and Fuentes is Américo Castro, for whom there are three entries in the bibliography: *El pensamiento de Cervantes, España en su historia*, and *La realidad histórica de España*. Castro also serves to ground on a historical "reality" the Orientalist metaphoric penchant of the *Modernistas*, who often cast Latin America and Spain in terms of Asia. There is a clash in Fuentes' novel between the historical knowledge of the origins of culture pursued by the *Noventaiochistas* and the artificial image of Hispanic culture given by the *Modernistas*. This clash is, of course, within an ultimately homogeneous literary ideology that envelops modern literary production in Latin America since the middle of the nineteenth century and that is beginning to give way now.[6]

It does not matter here that the books by Américo Castro exemplify three very different moments in the ideological evolution of the Spanish professor. Fuentes' link with Spanish intellectual history is determined first by the overall importance that the relationship between Spain and Mexico has had in this century. The exile to Mexico of great Spanish intellectuals—many of whom had been disciples of Ortega and through him had delved into the thematics of the "Generation of '98"—is one of the most important chapters in the history of ideas in Mexico. To this one must add the intense and tortured perception by Mexican intellectuals and artists of Spain's role in the origins of Mexican history. The "return" to Spain evident in both of Fuentes' books is clearly also a return to origins in search of identity, of a beginning that informs the present. The best known interpretation of the paradoxical love-hate relationship with the mother country is Octavio Paz's *El laberinto de la soledad*, a book written under the influence and even the tutelage of the exiled Spanish intellectuals mentioned, and one that has had a lasting impact on Fuentes' work. In a sense *Terra Nostra* is still a reaction to Paz's 1950 book. If in *El laberinto* Paz spoke of a schism at the core of the Mexican's soul, torn by his scorn of a whorish mother (Malinche) and his admiring hate for a violent father (Cortés), Fuentes attempts a reconciliation in *Terra Nostra*—a reconciliation that would include not only an acceptance of the liberal Spain whose tradition Paz already claimed, but also of the dark, violent, and retrograde Spain that most Latin Americans and Spaniards abhor.

The "twin bibliography" reveals, then, what every reader of *Terra Nostra* suspects: that Fuentes' voluminous novel represents a considerable effort to achieve an absolute knowledge of Hispanic culture, a knowledge binding its two branches on both sides of the Atlantic. The novel, after all, centers on the moment that would be the beginning, in history, of its modern peculiarity: the sixteenth century, when America was conquered and Spain underwent telling historical upheavals. As one reads in *Cervantes o la crítica de la lectura*: "The three dates that make up the temporal references in the novel can also serve to establish the historical background of Cervantes and *Don Quijote*: 1492, 1521, and 1598."[7] The dates correspond to historical events that are reenacted several times in the novel: discovery of America, defeat of the *comuneros*, death of Philip II. If the literary figures—Celestina, Don Quijote, Don Juan—serve as an access to knowledge of the culture in which they are engendered, the historical events and figures give the blueprint of the history from which that culture unfolds. *Cervantes o la crítica de la lectura* builds the foundation for the construction of *Terra Nostra*, gives the bases of its intelligibility in the widest possible sense. Culture and history are a structure of knowledge, a key for the comprehension of everything that precedes the text and gives it meaning.

The ideological underpinning of Fuentes' construct on Hispanic culture and history is Américo Castro's theories of Spanish history. Fuentes' appropriation of Castro's views is somewhat more insouciant that Juan Goytisolo's.[8] And it is not clear from *Cervantes o la crítica de la lectura* or from *Terra Nostra* if Fuentes is aware that *El pensamiento de Cervantes*, which emphasizes Cervantes' debt to Italian Humanism and was written in the early twenties, and *España en su historia*, published in 1948 after Castro had proposed his theories on caste-struggle, are hardly compatible: nor are we sure if he knows that a vast gulf exists between *España en su historia*, which stresses the Arabic component of Spanish culture, and its "re-writing" (published in 1954 and retouched many times under the ti-tle *La realidad histórica de España*), which gives far more impor-tance to the Jewish element. Be that as it may, Fuentes promotes the idea, derived from Castro, that Hispanic culture is fragmented owing to the struggles between Jews, Moors, and Christians that resulted in the victory of the latter and the violent suppression of the former. Such fragmentation, which would have broken a previous harmonic fusion of Arabic eros, Jewish wisdom, and Catholic militant ecume-nism, is responsible for the contradictions, clashes and contrasts that have characterized Spain and her American colonies since the sixteenth century. Although Américo Castro and his disciples have exhausted the possibilities of relating this fragmentation to the birth of modern Hispanic literature, usually appealing to an Existentialist ideology, Fuentes manages to supply a version in a new key.

The fragmentation is now rendered as the separation between words and things that Foucault perceives as the transition from a medieval *epistemé* to a "classical" one in his *Les Mots et les choses*. Given that Foucault begins his book by analyzing two Spanish works—*Don Quijote* and *Las meninas*—it is not difficult to see how Fuentes would be tempted to conclude that the fragmentation of codes in the modern world originates in Spain. But one can hardly agree with him, particularly because the ideological foundations of Castro and Foucault are so divergent, and because Foucault, though dealing with Hispanic works, does not touch upon any other Penin-sular examples to support his analyses. We know, however, that Fuentes is really seeking a "literary" link to connect these theories; that link is none other than Lukács in the guise of Octavio Paz. At the beginning of section II of *Cervantes o la crítica de la lectura*, Fuentes alludes to Paz's *El arco y la lira* to explain how the epic is the literature of a unified community, whose homogeneity is re-flected in the lack of ambiguity of the epic text and of the epic hero, while the novel is the literature of a fragmented society, whose plu-rality and ambiguity are reflected in the novelistic text and hero. Anyone familiar with Lukács' *Theory of the Novel* will recognize without much difficulty the source of these ideas. In *El arco y la lira* Paz uses this view of the novel as a contrast to poetry, in which uni-fication is sought through plunging into the abyss of language and its promise of a return to a oneness of meaning. In *Cervantes o la crítica de la lectura* Fuentes makes a similar use of Lukács, though now he has also brought in Américo Castro and Michel Foucault. A synthesis (or reduction) of the implicit argument of Fuentes' essay would run as follows; the caste struggle (Castro) resulted in a fracture, a separation between words and things (Foucault), that produced the modern novel (Cervantes), which is the product of fragmented societies (Lukács). But the plot does not end in such a catastrophe.

If the novel reflects the fragmentation of Hispanic culture and history, Fuentes proposes a reconciliation analogous to the one he pursues between Latin America and Spain. The return to a basic set of figures and events is a demolition prior to a reconstruction that reader and writer will accomplish through a ritualistic exchange. Projecting onto Joyce a capability that he would wish for himself and that is similar to Cervantes', Fuentes writes in his essay:

> Joyce tells the reader: I offer you a *potlatch*, an excremental ownership of words, I melt down your bars of verbal gold, throw them in the sea and challenge you to make me a gift that is superior to my/your/our words according to a new legality in the making, I challenge you to abandon your lazy, passive, linear reading to participate in the rewriting of all of your culture's codes, going all the way back to the lost code, to the reserve where savage words circulate, the words of the origin, the words of the beginning.[9]

Terra Nostra is, then, an effort to reach back to those original words found in a prediscursive logos which retains the keys to a homogeneous Hispanic culture, a reserve that is a common ground whence those keys have emanated throughout time and history. In spite of the "criticism of reading" that the essay appears to promote, *Terra Nostra* attempts to abolish all possible criticism through a return to the origins of language, a golden age where there is no mine or yours, a moment before dispersion that is an apotheosis of the legible. Such a plenitude of meaning would be the kind of knowledge that Carpentier and the "Generation of '98" wished to attain, and also a reunification of *las dos Españas*, with Latin America included for good measure.

Reading is not an abstract issue in *Terra Nostra*, but a concrete problem that begins with the very size of the book and also includes a variety of modernist narrative techniques plus an avalanche of cultural allusions. There is no question of aesthetic pleasure, in the sense Carpentier spoke of, but of discipline; few works bite so much into the reader's real life. Of course, these problems of reading lead to more theoretical issues and hark back to the question of knowledge and culture, of intelligibility posed at the outset. In a brilliant article, Lucille Kerr maintains that *Terra Nostra* is a book in which the quest for absolute knowledge is frustrated, in which the author, whose hypostasis is El Señor in the novel, succumbs before finding the key to the labyrinth that he himself has wrought, and with the solution of which he has been teasing the reader to lead him along the 783 pages of the text:

> The thematic and structural paradoxes are still as dominant at the end as they were at other points in the novel. In and of themselves, these mysteries have a power over the reader; Fuentes' strategy is to increase their potential force by pretending to underscore their decipherability. The author manipulates us to make us believe in an ultimate truth that he, as author, pretends to possess. But in the end he refuses to reveal or invent it. In this way, Fuentes himself pretends not to desire or to be able to play that privileged role of the truthful voice, since the problems about which he writes in *Terra Nostra* are ultimately unanswerable in the extraliterary world as well.[10]

There is a great deal to be learned from Kerr's scrupulous analysis, and in the end I must agree with her that in the text power gives way to the impossibility of knowledge, and that even when such power attempts to exert control from a strategic weakness, many of the enigmas remain unsolved. I believe, however, that Kerr gives up too soon on the riddles of *Terra Nostra*, that the relentlessly numerous cultural and historical allusions are more decipherable than she allows. A text is not the dialectical potential of paradox—a reservoir of mutually cancelling contradictions—but the rhetorical performance of contradiction. The moment of illegibility does arrive, in a manner not too dissimilar from Kerr's description, but first there is a very sustained display of knowledge and "readability." It is in that interval that the issue of culture and literature is played out, against the ideological background sketched in *Cervantes o la crítica de la lectura*. The metaphor of "mystery text" that Kerr applies to *Terra Nostra* is very appealing, but there is much more in the novel than the solution of a discrete enigma: *Terra Nostra* pursues a broad self-recognition and collective self-discovery that the many recognizable cultural and historical allusions make very clear.

No matter how much the apparent dispersion, *Terra Nostra* repeats, unifies, and reduces Spanish and Latin American history to a set of literary and historical figures, almost all of them from the 1492–1598 period. It is evident that the characteristics of El Señor come from various Spanish kings, but El Señor, even if in the future he is projected as Francisco Franco, is Philip II. The Chronicler is

Cervantes, even if inescapably he may appear to be Carlos Fuentes in the future. The young woman with tattooed lips is Celestina. The multiplying shipwrecked young man is the protagonist of Góngora's *Soledades*. Guzmán is Antonio Pérez, though perhaps also Guzmán de Alfarache. These figures, it is true, are multiplied, not by differentiation, but by repetition. The most spectacular case is the whole New World, which turns out to be the double of the Old: "Quetzalcoatl, Venus, Hesperia, Spain, identical stars, dawn and dusk, mysterious union, indecipherable enigma, but cipher for two bodies, two lands, cipher for a terrible encounter" (p. 485). On the level of these repetitions, the problem in *Terra Nostra* is not so much that of obscurity, but of a blinding clarity. From a thematic or ideological perspective the text displays here concepts about Hispanic culture whose sources we have already seen. Philip II incarnates authoritarianism and orthodoxy, which are but sublimations of a burning concupiscence. Don Quijote, Don Juan, Celestina, and the shipwrecked youth project various facets of the split matrix-figure of Philip: unshakable faith that obliterates reality and covers it with a fiction, the uncontrollable desire that tricks and violates, the all-powerful sensuality that corrupts everything, the lack of identity that is supplemented with ornate language. At this level time and space lose their differentiating power: to the West, the Escorial, a temple of death, becomes an Aztec pyramid, a temple of death; to the past Philip becomes Tiberius Caesar and to the future Franco (and the Escorial the Valle de los Caídos) or Maximilian. But are these figures truly the same? Has Fuentes hit upon founding myths, a reservoir, a "lost code," the "savage words," the "words of the beginning"? Has he not rather returned to what has always already been said? Is he not collating instead texts that scatter in his own the clutter of history? The clarity of the hieratic figures of the origin turns out to be instead the pollution of time and history, not original words, but the used words of the *Modernistas*, the artificial words of the worldly. *Terra* stands not for the virgin soil of the Garden, but the earth of the trash heap of time; Fuentes' mystification in *Cervantes o la crítica de la lectura* about the possibility of going back to original words, to a prelapsarian common ground, is opposed by the novel's insistence on the proliferation of the particularizing details of history. History is like the bric-a-brac of *Modernista* poetry, a decor without support, veiling the absence of support. The text, like history, is a question of the unfolding of para*dox* into contra*diction*, and of the undissolvable residue of what is said, of the *dicta*. Against the mystification of myth the text offers the proliferation of history; against the clarity of repetition, the density of difference.

Terra Nostra suggests (inevitably) a way of domesticating, on the level of enunciation or performance, the issue of repetition and difference. Lucille Kerr has also noticed with great insight the importance of murder in all structures of power set up in the text. The assassination of the double is the violation that inaugurates temporality, history. As one annihilates the similar, repetition is broken, difference established, and temporal succession begun. The presence of death is really the needed ingredient to set in motion the *potlatch*, the give and take of time in the world. But of course, there is a paradigmatic story of Christ's sacrifice and *Terra Nostra* not only includes it, but makes it a part of the most historically remote time-segment in the novel, where it becomes another origin, set at the time of Tiberius Caesar, the first authority figure, the first dictator in *Terra Nostra*. Christ is like the Father, but submits himself to the unrepeatable individuality of time. The irony that does not allow this act to become dogma in the novel is Tiberius' own murder, which is only the first of what will be many repetitions of the story of Christ. At the very moment when *Terra Nostra* is going to claim a clear beginning, the unrepeatable also glides into repetition, but a repetition that differentiates through deformation. Tiberius dies to reveal the thirst for knowledge and power implicit in Christ's sacrifice; knowledge is always a mask for power. It is not difficult to see here a clear correlation between the figure of Christ, the dictator, and the author himself. It is above all in this correlation that one detects that, contrary to the generous exchange between writer and reader that Fuentes posits in *Cervantes o la crítica de la lectura*, contrary to his claim that a shared knowledge of culture will come from shared rewriting, his will is to exert authority and power over the reader.

It is, therefore, not in a feast that the Señor/Author circulates the codes containing knowledge, a shared knowledge that would become culture (Hispanic, Hispanic American), but in a polemic struggle with the reader. Given that the master signs are unreachable, that knowledge prior to the use of language is not available, the Señor/Author uses the knowledge of history to control the reader. Culture becomes thus the repository not of pristine knowledge, but the conglomeration of the trivia of history. The Encyclopedia/Señor, The Master of Bibliographies, the Master Scriptor encrypts in writing, preserving rather than sharing. The very choice of dictators is revealing of this attitude. Philip II not only controlled the vast Spanish Empire, but did so through writing. He was the King Bureaucrat, Secretary to Himself. Tiberius Caesar also ruled through writing, governing by correspondence his Roman Empire. I have shown elsewhere how in the modern dictator-novel in Latin America the figure of the dictator—he who dictates, whose voice is an authority before writing—is demystified and replaced with that of the secretary, a subordinate who usurps power from the ruler by being able to supplant truth and knowledge with simulacra. In *Terra Nostra* such power has not been relinquished; the subaltern god, the son, has not slain the father, but pretends to be both father and son to contain knowledge of both history and the mastercodes from which it issues. The Dictator/Scriptor incarnates a duality that leaves out the reader. There is in this egotistical suppression of the other a *performed* insight into Hispanic culture that in some ways confirms Unamuno's, Baroja's and Valle Inclán's worst premonitions about the Spanish and by extension the Spanish American man.[11] We see, then, in this real contact between reader and book an insight into men and epochs that validates indirectly Carpentier's assertion about the role of the novel as a form of knowledge.

The Latin title of *Terra Nostra* contains, in a curious way, an emblem of the sort of contradiction that I have examined here: a hoarding, a preservation of knowledge encrypted in a writing that is not to be shared, but that is used to exert power over the reader. It is obvious that by writing the title in Latin Fuentes is "naming" the origin-oriented thematics of his novel, that origin in which presumably writer and reader will share common words, unpolluted by time. But Latin is not a shared language; it is an abstract, unspoken code, the chiseled letters of monuments, not the language of exchange. Our common code—Spanish—has dissolved the cryptic atemporality of Latin by splitting its pristine vowels, by diphthongizing the accented, long $\bar{e}$ and $\bar{o}$ into *ie* and *ue*. *Terra Nostra* would be *Tierra Nuestra*, extending the vowels, giving them time and differentiating them phonetically and graphically. Like the Dictator/Scriptor, who monstrously wishes to contain both the voice of authority and the inscribing, disseminating power of writing, *Terra Nostra*'s title pretends to be a shared language in which there is no time, no difference, no exchange. The encyclopedic knowledge—both because of its vastness and its hasty, pell-mell origin—of the figure of the author therein obtained is that of a resentful, egolatrous, and solemn possessor of truth. Once these mechanisms in the novel are unveiled, we become aware that *Terra Nostra* wishes to pass its ideological bulk as truth; that though its mystifications are more insightful than its ideology, the latter is part and parcel of the very structure of the novel, of the very attitude that the text assumes before the reader.

There is another possible reading of *Terra Nostra* that undermines the one I have just performed, and through which the novel is linked less obliquely to the *Modernista* version of Hispanic culture, rather than to the "Generation of '98." Here the source of Fuentes' experiment is to be found in a Borges story, "El jardín de los senderos que se bifurcan," even if that source is disguised as Guilio Camillo's Theatre of Memory.[12] The key both to Camillo's work and the novel mentioned in Borges' story is the same: simultaneity, complementarity. Fuentes' novel attempts the same by giving various mutually exclusive solutions to several episodes. In "El jardín de los senderos que se bifurcan" Yu Tsun relates the discovery that the British sinologist Stephen Albert has made in reference to the novel written by his ancestor Ts'ui Pên: "In all fiction, when a man is faced with alternatives he chooses one at the expense of the others. In the almost unfathomable Ts'ui Pên, he chooses—simultaneously—all of them. He thus *creates* various futures, various times which start others that will in their turn branch out and bifurcate in other times. This is the cause of the contradiction in the novel."[13] A series of violent deaths is related to the labyrinthine novel of Ts'ui Pên: he is killed by an unknown assassin, Stephen Albert is killed by Yu Tsun to thereby transmit a message, and Yu Tsun writes on the verge of execution for his crime. The seriousness of the matter, one might say, led Borges to merely sketch the plan for the novel and its impossible nature rather than actually write such a book. Be that as it may, it is important to note that Borges has chosen as his novelist the representative of a millenary culture, one whose collective self-recognition we would expect to be easier. Yet every act of communication of knowledge is thwarted and leads to death. Yu Tsun "writes" at Albert's death and thereby condemns himself to death. The close correlation between knowledge, writing, death, and the novel in Borges' story forecloses the kind of rewriting of the codes of culture that Fuentes proposes in *Cervantes o la crítica de la lectura* and attempts to carry out in *Terra Nostra*. Writing is the accumulated residue of all those codes gathered on the verge of death, which is both the total absence of knowledge and absolute knowledge. The presence of Orientals, but more so of the Orientalist Stephen Albert, links the story to *Modernismo* and its image of history and culture as Museum.[14] In the Museum the Tinkerer, like the writer, rearranges objects that bespeak of death, not the origin. Borges' story is the most powerful link in Latin American literary history between *Modernismo* and postmodern fiction, not because of its eccentric theory of the novel, but because it offers this image of the writer.

Terra Nostra's end, which chronologically is also the beginning, contains such a caveat, rendering the intervening seven hundred pages as a disclaimed foundation. At the end, which occurs in 1999 in Paris, there is a game of cards being played by a group of characters drawn from recent Latin American fiction: Oliveira (*Rayuela*), Cuba Venegas (*Tres tristes tigres*), Humberto Peñalosa (*El obsceno pájaro de la noche*), and others, including Pierre Ménard. The cards being used are topics of Latin American history and literature: dictatorships, police goonsquads, prisons, etc.

> "Full house!" shouted Buendía. "Masferrer's Tigres, Duvalier's Tonton Macoutes, and the Brazilian DOPs, plus an Odría and a Pinochet."
> "That's shit, you're wiped out, you and your momma and your papa." Oliveira crowed triumphantly, spreading his four Prisons on the card table: the cisterns of the Fort of San Juan de Ulúa, Dawson's Island, the cold plain of Trelew, and the Sexto in Lima . . .
> "O.K., top that. . . ." (p. 762)

This game is being played on the verge of Apocalypse, and parodies the gathering of various tellers in Boccaccio's *Decameron*, who have however fled to the city to save themselves from the plague. The nature of the "cards" and of the "players" themselves, plus the fact that the game is being played while the world is on the brink of extinction, is a comment on literature, its relation to history and to a knowledge of the artificiality of writing that is not too far from that of Borges' story. In mobilizing so many literary figures, from Celestina to Yu Tsun, from Doña Inés to Cuba Venegas, *Terra Nostra* demonstrates that the language that unites us, that the *tierra nuestra*, are not the words submerged in a logos before language, but the already uttered words that are circulated in works like *Don Quijote*, *Vida de Don Quijote y Sancho*, and "Pierre Ménard, autor del Quijote."

Terra Nostra ends where the most radical new Latin American fiction begins, calling attention to a curious phenomenon in the history of the Latin American novel: that the established novelists who rose to fame during the Boom have become the epigones of a younger group whose most important figures are Severo Sarduy and Manuel Puig. Fuentes in *Terra Nostra*, Mario Vargas Llosa in *Pantaleón y las visitadoras* and *La tía Julia y el escribidor*, Juan Goytisolo in *Count Julian* have all abandoned the novel of cultural knowledge in favor of fictions in the vein of Sarduy and Puig in which indeterminancy in all realms and the "universalizing" force of popular culture demystify literature's claim to a deep insight into

Hispanic culture through a fusion with myth, language before writing, or any sort of primitivistic ideal. *La traición de Rita Hayworth* and particularly *De donde son los cantantes* had already undermined projects like *Terra Nostra*, or even recycling and renewing gestures like *Count Julian* or *Pantaleón*, to such a degree that there is a certain pathos in the end/beginning of Fuentes' book.

Notes

This article is work-in-progress toward a book dealing with the relationship between the concept of culture and the idea of literature in modern Latin America. The research for this project was made possible by a grant from the Social Science Research Council and the ideas were tested in a National Endowment for the Humanities Seminar that I directed. I wish hereby to make public my gratitude to both SSRC and NEH for their generosity and to my colleagues of the seminar for their reactions and encouragement.

1. Alejo Carpentier, "Problemática de la actual novela latinoamericana," in his *Tientos y diferencias* (Montevideo: Arca, 1967), p. 7. My translation.

2. In his famous prologue to *El reino de este mundo*, Carpentier speaks with admiration of Unamuno. He alludes to the Spanish thinker in many other instances, as recently as 1980, in an article published only a few months before his death ("La difícil pureza idiomática," *Revolución y Cultura*, no. 89 [January 1980]: 16–18). Latin American writers have felt closer to Unamuno than to other Spanish thinkers because, being Basque, he felt marginal to Spain in a way similar to that of his colleagues from across the Atlantic. I have given some details on this in my essay, "Borges, Carpentier y Ortega: dos textos olivados," *Revista Iberoamericana*, 42 (1977): 697–704.

3. I have traced these ideas and their relation to Latin America in the first two chapters of *Alejo Carpentier: The Pilgrim at Home* (Ithaca and London: Cornell University Press, 1977), pp. 15–96.

4. A further elaboration of this topic will appear in my article, "El concepto de cultura y la idea de literatura en Hispanoamerica," to be published in the *Actas* of the *Coloquio sobre Literatura Latinoamericana* that took place at the Universidad Simón Bolívar (Caracas) on February 28–29, 1980.

5. Carlos Fuentes, *Cervantes o la crítica de la lectura* (Mexico: Joaquín Mortiz, 1976), pp. 36, 111.

6. Carpentier's *El recurso del método* is the best "study" that we have of how *Modernismo*, though utilizing a philological thrust that is concerned with the origins of language, turns those "natural" origins into artifice, making nature and its display a museum. I have analyzed these ideas in my "Modernidad, modernismo y nueva narrativa: *El recurso del método*," *Revista Interamericana de Bibliografía/Inter-American Review of Bibliography*, 30 (1980): 157–163.

7. Fuentes, *Cervantes o la crítica*, p. 36.

8. Miguel Ugarte has studied competently Goytisolo's debt to Castro in his "Juan Goytisolo: Unruly Disciple of Américo Castro," *Journal of Spanish Studies: Twentieth Century*, 7 (1979): 353–364. Fuentes himself has written about this issue in his review of Goytisolo's *Count Julian* (*The New York Times Book Review*, May 5, 1974, pp. 5–7).

9. Fuentes, *Cervantes o la crítica*, p. 109.

10. Lucille Kerr, "The Paradox of Power and Mystery: Carlos Fuentes' *Terra Nostra*," *PMLA*, 95 (1980): 98–99.

11. In a long review of Octavio Paz's *The Other Mexico: Critique of the Pyramid*, Fuentes writes:

> Octavio Paz was struck by the continuity of a power structure, masked by different ideologies, serving equally well the needs of Indian theocracy, Spanish colonialism, and modern *desarrollismo*, development for development's sake. . . . When Paz pulls apart the final curtain of his drama, we are facing the unmentionable, the skeletons in the closet of our subconscious national life. His stage becomes a bare space where naked figures sing, weep, crawl next to a blood-stained wall, or dance in a festival that will soon be crushed by a violent physical intrusion. The light on that deepest of stages is the light of time: past, present and future. The figures chant a line from a poem by Octavio Paz: "Time hungers for incarnation. . . ." How to link power and society democratically in Mexico? The first step, says Paz, is critical freedom. Only in an open critical atmosphere can the true problems of Mexico be defined and discussed, and the conflicting history of Mexico, hungering for incarnation, come out into the open. *The Other Mexico* is a critique of what the Mexican revolution achieved and failed to achieve, as well as a modest but far-ranging proposal for a new revolution: for a peaceful reform of our conscience and purpose. ("Mexico and Its Demons," *New York Review of Books*, September 20, 1973, p. 16)

> In *Cervantes o la crítica de la lectura* Fuentes seeks a parallel solution as we saw, but in the execution of *Terra Nostra* the demon reappears to reinstate violence.

12. Fuentes' debt to Frances Yates' *The Art of Memory* is great, particularly in the chapter entitled "Teatro de la memoria," which is a synthesis of Yates' book. But the fundamental issues raised by Yates' research are already present in at least two of Borges' stories: "El jardín de los senderos que se bifurcan" and "Funes el memorioso."

13. Jorge Luis Borges, *Obras completas* (Buenos Aires: Emecé, 1974), p. 478; published in English as *Ficciones*, ed. and intro. by Anthony Kerrigan (New York: Grove Press, 1962), p. 98.

14. I am indebted here, of course, to Edward W. Said's *Orientalism* (New York: Vintage, 1978). See also "Modernidad, modernismo y nueva narrativa" (n. 6, above).

Mary E. Davis

On Becoming Velázquez:
Carlos Fuentes' *The Hydra Head*

Velázquez seeks the root of every myth in what we might call its logarithm of reality.—Ortega

The publication of Carlos Fuentes' *The Hydra Head* in 1978 did not arouse the critical furor occasioned by his earlier *Terra Nostra*. Perhaps the deceptive simplicity of detective fiction dampened the customary excitement for a new text from Fuentes. Beneath its slick surface, however, *The Hydra Head* is as baroquely patterned as are his earlier novels, and the conceit of the inept detective provides Fuentes with an opportunity to display his talent for wry humor. In a pastiche of texts from Dashiel Hammett, Shakespeare, Lewis Carroll, and Edgar Allan Poe, in combination with thirty years of detective movies, Fuentes alternates the tone of his text radically. Throughout the escapades à la Woody Allen of his several detectives, Fuentes continues his meditation upon the ambiguous nature of good and evil, of man within society, of identity and its labyrinth— the thematic constants of all his texts.

In *Terra Nostra* Fuentes wove allusions to an enigmatic painting through one strand of the plot. Now in *The Hydra Head* he threads certain paintings into the entire novel, and both the style of the artists and the subject matter of their paintings serve as analogues to character development within the novel. The protagonist Félix Maldonado begins his journey in the colorful world of indeterminate universal figures of the canvasses of Ricardo Martínez. He first encounters a Martínez painting in the magical setting of his meeting with Sara Klein: "The light of the open fire formed a halo about her; an enormous painting by Ricardo Martínez served as a backdrop. After twelve years, Sara Klein was suspended within a luminous drop in the center of his world" (p. 45). Not until after Sara's death does Félix have the courage to confront the significance of that painting: "he recalled the figures he'd seen the night of his last meeting with Sara Klein, the figures resembling the paintings of Ricardo Martínez. He'd been unable to describe them, because he hadn't dared to approach those creatures of misery, compassion, and horror" (p. 272).

One of Félix's doubles is a shadowy character named Trevor or Mann. Fuentes employs paintings at two significant points in Félix's encounters with this diabolical figure. Trevor's sister Angélica is sacrificed to the success of his espionage schemes, and Fuentes uses a canvas of the dead Ophelia by John Everett Millais to forecast her death. Trevor narrates: "I, on the other hand, dreamed uneasily of my dead sister, Angélica, floating in a river like a sylvan siren adorned with fantastic garlands" (p. 153). Later Fuentes arranges a dramatic scene of rooms within rooms and revelations within revelations as Trevor and Félix confront each other, finally understanding that they are doubles. Once again a painting serves as the mirror of consciousness, in this case, of Trevor's sense of bad faith: "I was distracted by the San Sebastian above the fireplace, a good example of sixteenth-century colonial painting. Félix's face may have resembled Velázquez, but his body was that of the martyr—with words as arrows. Deliberately, I returned to my chair and again buried my face in my hands" (p. 235).

As Félix achieves enough distance from his former life to judge it, he contemptuously refers to the current young lover of the nurse Licha as "el majo desnudo" ("your little Goya *Majo Nude*"). He himself had earlier been Licha's lover, albeit ephemerally, and he has learned through the sequence of adventures comprising *The Hydra Head* the vanity of almost all his amorous conquests. Only in the case of Sara Klein has Félix found and lost a woman worthy to serve as his *anima*.

More constant than that of any other artist is the appearance of Velázquez in *The Hydra Head*. By making "Las meninas" ("The Ladies in Waiting") the warp and woof of the text, Fuentes calls to mind the courtly world of the seventeenth century, the epoch in which Spain was still the center of a vast empire, but of an empire whose King preferred to shift his power to the Conde-Duque de Olivares, the insidious Sevillian who was instrumental in Velázquez's becoming the friend and court painter of Philip IV. Not only does Velázquez give us entrée into daily life in the palace, with his portrait of the princess, her ladies in waiting, dwarfs and dogs, but he also includes the royal parents in a mirror, and figures representing the Church and the bureaucracy hover in the dark background. For our purpose, more important than any of the royal figures or the palace itself is the self-portrait of Velázquez in the left foreground, a portrait from the close of his career, painted only four years before his death. Velázquez presents himself looking directly at us, musing, perhaps, on the curious group of figures who inhabit his canvas like *revenants*.

Velázquez's self-portrait functions on several levels within Fuentes' text. It mirrors Félix's process of individuation, and the personality of Velázquez himself gradually becomes the model for Félix's new sense of himself. Since Félix is an obtuse character given to self-analysis only because of the bizarre events of the plot, Fuentes must rely on the acuity of his reader to interpret Velázquez's developing significance in the life of his character. Velázquez's life at court provides the paradigm for Fuentes' exploration of the vacuum at the heart of power. Beyond his importance for Félix's character, Velázquez and his obstinate originality become exemplars for the creative imagination, and Fuentes will ultimately reveal himself, as Velázquez did in "The Ladies in Waiting," as "a portraitist portraying the portrayal."[1]

That Velázquez can serve as a double for Félix and for Fuentes should not surprise the reader familiar with Fuentes' entire canon. Multiple doubling is part of the process analyzed by Susan Schaffer:

> The "double" in Fuentes' more recent, enigmatic works is virtually overpowering as he attempts to analyze the ramifications of the dual personality of Latin American man. At times, Fuentes adheres to tradition relying upon pre-scientific and folkloric manifestations of man's spiritual shadow. Yet, Fuentes goes beyond this initial phase to create something unique which advances the idea of the *doppelgänger* in its development process. This step is the Mexican's successful utilization of multiple personages, wherein man becomes divided into three, four, or even an infinite number of duplicate selves.[2]

After his blending of European myths and historical figures with the pre-Columbian legend of Quetzalcoatl in *Terra Nostra*, Fuentes does not hesitate to insinuate Theseus, Trevor, Hamlet, the March Hare from *Alice in Wonderland*, Humphrey Bogart, Woody Allen, and Velázquez as multiples of Félix.

Far more significant than these often humorous multiples are the archetypal figures who present themselves to Félix during the course of his adventures. The old woman dressed in black rags at the Zócalo prefigures the old woman who exchanges a basket of baby chicks for one of packages of cocaine in the taxi—both intimate the Terrible Mother, but a matriarch bearing death rather than life. Death is appropriately omnipresent in this novel of pseudo-detection, and the Director General, the sinister figure who first warns Félix of the new life he has entered blindly, is himself a walking skull. He lives surrounded by artificial darkness, and his Citroën is as darkly cavernous as the carriage of death. At the close of the novel, Félix's last vision of the Director General blends him into his archetype: "The face of the Director General was disappearing behind the veils of sleep, until only two eyes of black glass glittered deep in a white skull" (p. 284). Captain Harding of the "Emmita" represents the initiatory old man for Félix, and his death becomes that of a surrogate victim. Félix's understanding of the integrity of Harding's life aids him in the recuperation of his own father.

The several women who surround Félix are all exemplary of various aspects of womankind, and as such they are blended together to form the archetypal enchantress, forever mystifying, forever beyond rational understanding. Félix's wife Ruth explains the constellation of lovers early in the novel: "You always put Sara on a pedestal. You went to bed with Mary. But for you either a pure, even intellectual, love or pure sex without love doesn't work. You need a woman like me to solve your practical problems, to handle the details of your career and your social life" (p. 37). Félix only dimly perceives the importance of the three women in his adventures, and at the end of the novel he desperately tries to reach "his faithful Penelope, and now he was returning defeated from the wars against an invisible Troy" (p. 280). At that point he discovers that his Penelope is the murderess of Sara Klein. Félix's failure to confront the archetype of Circe has led to the death of the only woman he could have loved.

Fuentes' art in conjuring up the momentary appearance of archetypal figures is comparable to one of the most striking aspects of Velázquez's style, as Ortega explains: "Here we have the unique pathos in Velázquez's art. In the picture, suddenly a man or a pitcher 'appears'—the question as to what it may be is unimportant. The important thing aesthetically is that this act of appearance is forever repeating itself, that the object is forever 'appearing,' coming into existence" (pp. 99–100). Fuentes, then, has utilized Velázquez's method, incorporating the universal figures from the style of Ricardo Martínez in order to surround Félix both with multiples of his own self and with more universal archetypes from the unconscious. In so doing he celebrates and laments both reality's appearance and its deeper significance.

Although Fuentes has always combined myth and reality in his novels, his combination of methods in *The Hydra Head* has freed him from the ironbound circularity of his earlier prose. Lucrecio Pérez Blanco maintains that "*The Hydra Head* is a circular novel."[3] His opinion would superficially appear well founded, and he cites the repetition of the scene in the taxi which contains the principals in the espionage plot as well as the repetition of Félix's encounter with the President to support his theory. However, as one examines these scenes carefully, there is a difference in the replay of each one, a difference which centers on the consciousness of Félix. The second time he is surrounded in the taxi, Félix knows the roles of the other characters. The second time he meets the President, his name is no longer Félix Maldonado. He has become, in appearance and reality, Diego Velázquez.

Ortega explains that Velázquez was not popular during his lifetime. "He made the most unpopular of discoveries: that reality differs from myth in that it is never completed" (p. 100). Fuentes may be said to explore the ramifications of this discovery. After novels progressively more circular, following on the heels of texts such as *Zona sagrada*, *Aura*, *Cumpleaños*, and *Terra Nostra*, in which mythic circularity almost absorbs the facticity of the characters, *The Hydra Head* represents a liberation of style. The reason that Félix must confront the President a second time may become clearer if we consider a parallel text.

In the prologue of *Los reinos originarios* (1971), Fuentes discusses the circular nature of pre-Columbian Mexican art:

> The meaning of ancient Mexican art consists, precisely, of elaborating a most ample time and space in which the implacable circle of the sustenance of the cosmos fits as well as the circularity of the perpetual return to origins and the whirling of all those mysteries which rationalization cannot accommodate.[4]

Creation of a mythic time and space demand the appearance of a god, and Fuentes interprets the function of Quetzalcoatl: "Quetzalcoatl fights with his appearance: he is the incarnation itself of the dilemma of all art. He is the only Mexican god who dares to appear with a body, with an identity. He breaks the fatality of the mask."[5] Félix's first encounter with the President resulted in the loss of consciousness, followed by his capture by the Director General and subsequent plastic surgery. Félix's progress through these ordeals gives him the chance to abandon his former mask for a real face, that of

Velázquez, and, armed with his new self, he must again confront the image of power.

The transformation of an overly punctual bureaucrat into an analogue of Velázquez demands the entire novel to effect. From an other-directed man with an institutional mask, Félix becomes once again the personification of imagination which characterized his youth. He ultimately is the Velázquez captured by Ortega: "In him we have one of those men most secretly resolved to exist only from within, to obey only their own resolutions, which were of the most tenacious and unalterable kind" (p. 85). The decision to become another (or to become himself) is made for him, much as was Velázquez's when Philip IV made him the court painter; as Ortega describes the event, "pure chance decided that Velázquez should live all his life inside a glass enclosure" (p. 96).

As the novel opens, Fuentes surrounds Félix with a series of mirrors: the doors of Sanborns, *cristales*, Bernstein's thick glasses, the Zócalo of Mexico City with its blinding sun—all forming a labyrinth of reflections leading to his confrontation with "the life-size reproduction of the Velázquez self-portrait hanging in the hall. It was one of their private jokes. When they'd seen the original in the Prado, they'd laughed in that nervous way one laughs to break the solemnity of museums, but had not dared say that Félix was the painter's double. 'No,' Ruth said, 'Velázquez is *your* double . . .'" (pp. 34–35). Félix must face Velázquez each time he enters his home, but on the day when his bureaucratic identity is dismantled, the self-portrait suddenly reveals to Félix his emptiness:

> The face in the mirror recalled the resemblance to Velázquez, the black almond eyes, the high olive-skinned brow, the short curved nose, Arab but also Jewish, a Spanish son of all the peoples who'd passed across the peninsula . . . a Mediterranean face, high prominent cheekbones, full sensual mouth with deep fissures at the corners, thick black wavy hair, wide-set but heavy eyebrows, and again the black eyes that would have been round, round to the point of obliterating the whites, were it not for the vaguely Oriental elongation, black moustache. But Félix's face did not have the smile of Velázquez, the satisfaction of those lips that had just tasted plums and oranges. (p. 35)

After he meets Sara Klein, Félix realizes that his angle of vision has changed. The figures of Ricardo Martínez not only hang on the wall behind Sara, but they have also seeped outside into the real world: "From the midnight mists emerged motionless figures huddled in the mud, like the figures in the painting by Ricardo Martínez. Félix wondered whether those shapes were actually Indians, human beings squatting in the middle of the night, wrapped in their dusk-colored sarapes, rent by the fangs of the blue fog" (pp. 51–52). The fear that attacks Félix as he sees these universal figures increases as he meets the President. He discovers that "the President suffered the same malady as Félix Maldonado. He had no face. He was nothing but a name, a title" (p. 57). Having realized the emptiness of his mask and of that of even the most powerful in his country's hierarchy, Félix is prepared for part II, which begins as he awakens from plastic surgery.

Fuentes presents Félix's return to consciousness as that of a baby just awakening to reality. When he at last sees himself in the mirror, he confronts "the reflection of a mummy swathed in bandages, with no apertures but the holes for eyes, nose, and mouth" (p. 62). The Director General informs him of the elaborate plan in which Félix's surrogate was killed and buried. Félix has no more of his former existence than a memory. "The man behind the name no longer exists" (p. 69). After his bandages are removed, Félix is astounded. "The face reflected in the mirror belonged to a different name, not Félix Maldonado" (p. 74). Félix escapes from his captors and registers in a hotel under the name Diego Velázquez: "He hesitated before signing the name of the artist he no longer resembled . . ." (p. 99).

Felix can solve the mystery of the murder of Sara Klein only by acting like Velázquez. "He had no evidence that she had died there except his own imagination and will. That was enough" (pp. 99–100). He unexpectedly sees again in the mirror the face he had thought lost forever. "He realized that the old resemblance to the Velázquez self-portrait that had been his and Ruth's private joke was returning with the beginnings of his moustache" (p. 100). The search for the killer leads Félix to his old friend Professor Bernstein, who ridicules Félix's conviction that he now is different. "'The only surgery performed on you was that of suggestion.' Bernstein smiled, but immediately erased the smile. 'It's enough to know that a man is being sought. After that, everyone sees him differently. Even the man himself'" (p. 135).

Shortly after the beginning of part III the reader discovers that Félix and his friend Trevor have collaborated through the action of the first two parts, as Trevor explains:

"For a few weeks, you'll be living a kind of voluntary hypnosis," I'd told him as I explained what he might encounter. "If not, our operation may fail."

"I don't like the word hypnosis," Félix had said, smiling his Moorish smile, so like that of Velázquez. "I'd rather call it fascination. I'll allow myself to be fascinated by everything that happens to me. Maybe that's the fulcrum between the exercise of will you're asking of me, and fate." (p. 144)

Because of his independence and imagination, Félix steadily moves closer to Sara's killer, and his face reveals his true character: "Somehow his moustache was obliterating the memory of the operation and returning to him the face that, if not exactly his own, more and more resembled the face of his private joke with Ruth, the Velázquez self-portrait" (p. 173). By the end of part III, Félix is closer to the killer but as far as ever from understanding the crime. "He was reaching the end of an adventure in which he couldn't be sure whether he'd been following some plan—either his own or another's—or whether he'd been the blind instrument of change, completely divorced from will" (p. 208).

The novel's last section is narrated by Trevor, who imagines Félix's adventures after he abandons Trevor's house. Trevor provides a recapitulation of the years of his friendship with Félix, and he describes his reencounter with him after thirteen years of absence. Trevor had changed, but Félix "was unchanged, Moorish, virile, the image of Velázquez's self-portrait, and tall for a Mexican" (p. 223). For Ortega, Velázquez's prime concern in painting was "to convert the everyday into permanent surprise" (p. 99). Félix's life has become a permanent surprise, a life for which his similarity with Velázquez has prepared him, as Trevor insists, "No one but you can worry out this mission. When something surprises you, you always react with imagination" (p. 223). Because Trevor is a dedicated fan of Shakespeare, the last part has a melodramatic quality not found earlier, a quality most notable as Félix reenters his own house. Only as he hears again the taped message from Sara Klein does he realize that his wife is her murderess:

Félix closed his eyes. He wished he could close them forever. He left the room, his eyes closed, he knew by heart the arrangement of his own home. He reached the front door and, as he opened it, opened his eyes. He had kept them closed for fear of seeing himself in the self-portrait Ruth and Félix Maldonado had laughingly bought one day in Madrid. (pp. 281–282)

Only after the adventures of the novel is Félix, momentarily as sightless as Oedipus, prepared to face himself, i.e., Velázquez, with the knowledge that the responsibility for Sara's death rests with his own house and, ultimately, within himself.

Never again is Félix called by his old name. He has become Diego Velázquez, and his new identity so painfully constructed is intact for his second meeting with the President. Fuentes has reiterated Velázquez's method of composition in "The Ladies in Waiting" in the construction of scenes within his novel. All the characters are caught in enigmatic relationships to power. Several scenes in particular—Félix's encounter with Sara Klein, his grand scene with Trevor in the double's house, and his final confrontation with Ruth disguised as the nun who killed Sara Klein—all would have been perfectly illustrated by Velázquez. Only he could have caught the ambiguity of the characters' relationships. In *The Hydra Head* as in "The Ladies in Waiting," the figures represented both have and do not have a firm contact with each other. The power of the artist maintains each in his private orbit, yet all in a universe of emblematic positions. Fuentes approximates the meditative nature of many of Velázquez's finest portraits, and just as the water jug has a personality equal to that of the old water seller, so that clear stone of the magic ring reveals far more than Trevor's assumed personalities.

As he arranges these vital scenes like Velázquez's tableaux, Fuentes focuses the heart of each scene within Félix's perception. Just as "Velázquez paints movements in one single, arrested moment" (Ortega, p. 105), so Fuentes makes Félix confront the self-portrait or its double in the mirror throughout *The Hydra Head*. And, finally, Fuentes reveals a new portrait of himself, thereby paying a last tribute to his seventeenth-century model.

Notes

1. José Ortega y Gasset, "Introduction to Velázquez," in *Velázquez, Goya, and the Dehumanization of Art*, trans. Alexis Brown (New York: W. W. Norton, 1972), p. 106. Subsequent citations will be identified by "Ortega" within the text.
2. Susan Schaffer, "The Development of the Double in Selected Works of Carlos Fuentes," *Mester*, 6, no. 2 (May 1977): 81.
3. Lucrecio Pérez Blanco, "*La cabeza de la hidra* de Carlos Fuentes: No-

vela-ensayo de estructura circular," *Cuadernos Americanos*, 221 (May–December 1978): 219.

4. Carlos Fuentes, *Los reinos originarios* (Barcelona: Barral Editores, 1971), p. 10.
5. Ibid., p. 14.

Margaret Sayers Peden

Forking Paths, Infinite Novels, Ultimate Narrators

I leave to the various futures (not to all) my garden of forking paths. —Borges

In any attempt to make a methodical or systematic statement about contemporary Spanish American writing, it is helpful to turn to the models offered in Jorge Luis Borges' fiction, "The Garden of Forking Paths."[1] As the noted sinologist Stephen Albert studied the enigma of Ts'ui Pên's heritage to his descendants—his "chaotic manuscripts," the book in which the hero dies in the third chapter, but is again alive in the fourth—he, the "barbaric Englishman," reached a conclusion overlooked by generations of students. He recalled that Ts'ui Pên had stated, at different times, that he was going to retire to construct a labyrinth, and that he was going to retire to write a book. Albert's intuition was that the two labyrinths were the same, that Ts'ui Pên had constructed "a labyrinth of symbols." Before discovering the fragment of letter cited above as an epigraph, Albert had conjectured as to what might constitute an infinite book. He arrived at two possibilities. One would take the form of a circular novel "whose last page was identical with the first, a book which had the possibility of continuing indefinitely" (p. 106); the second would be an unfinished book, a book written by each succeeding generation of his family, "a Platonic, hereditary work, transmitted from father to son . . ." (p. 106). In contemporary Spanish American literature, the form of the first model has most often appeared in poetry and brief fiction; we think, for example, of Octavio Paz's circular "Piedra del sol," Torres Bodet's "Dédalo," or Borges' own, "The Cyclical Night," as well as the fiction "The Circular Ruins." The second model is not unlike the structure of Gabriel García Márquez's *One Hundred Years of Solitude.* Though that book is written by a single scribe, the gypsy Melquíades, the repetitive chronicling of *soledades* creates the illusion of a continuing narrative with authorial responsibility handed down from Buendía to Buendía.

But with the discovery in the archives of Oxford University of the fragment bearing the exquisite calligraphy of Ts'ui Pên, Albert is given the clue to the correct interpretation of the mystery. The phrase "various futures (not to all)," suggested "bifurcation in time, not in space" (p. 107). "'The Garden of Forking Paths' is an enormous riddle, or parable, whose theme is time . . ." (p. 109). "This network of times which approached one another, forked, broke off, or were unaware of one another for centuries, embraces all possibilities of time" (pp. 109–110). And thus, Borges'—or Ts'ui Pên's—labyrinth leads us directly to the work of Carlos Fuentes, and, specifically, to his most recent novel, *Una familia lejana*,[2] the primary focus of this study.

Novels which adopt the landscape of the garden of the forking paths are not exclusive with Fuentes. As every student of the literature is aware, Julio Cortázar's *Rayuela* is a prime example of the multiple possibilities of fiction, and of life. It is precisely the alternatives—did Horacio throw himself from the window (chapter 56, the last chapter in the traditional order) or is he in a later chapter (following the directions for an alternate reading), head bandaged (a fall from a window?), being cared for by Gekrepten?—that created such a furor when this landmark novel was published. The metamorphosing characters in the fictional worlds of Severo Sarduy, Salvador Elizondo, and José Donoso similarly follow the forking paths, alternative routes creating multiple layers of reality, none of which alone is true, but which in combination form a tapestry of ever-changing design. But it is my contention that the most faithful weaver of the silk of changeable colors, the tapestry of flowing designs, is Carlos Fuentes. As we shall see, the forking paths appear in his earliest novels; recently, alternative realities have become the obsession of his fiction.

In *Una familia lejana* contradictions of fact, easily overlooked at first reading, begin on the first pages. When the reporting narrative "yo" sights his friend in the Automobile Club de France, he takes note of his pallor, but thinks to himself that when he had seen him following his return from a trip to Mexico, his normal pallor had been dissipated by the strong Mexican sun: "I had occasion to see him following his trip to Mexico . . ." (p. 9). But when a few lines later he greets his friend, he seems to contradict this information: "'I haven't seen you since you returned from your trip,' I said" (p. 9). This is not a glaring inconsistency; additionally, it may be consciously ambiguous. Has the narrator *not* seen his friend since his return, or not since the time he saw him *upon* his return? There is a shading here that allows for an alternative within the rules of normalcy.

A later contradiction also allows for a possible explanation. When a young guest, Víctor Heredia, arrives from Mexico, his host, the Comte de Branly, inquires when Víctor's father will arrive. The boy informs his host that his father will arrive that same afternoon (". . . and he said he would arrive that afternoon" [p. 24]). Within moments, however, he tells Branly that he has given orders to Branly's chauffeur to pick up his father at four the following afternoon ("I've already told Etienne to pick him up at four tomorrow afternoon" [p. 24]). Are these contradictions occasioned by boyish mischief—this is quite within the character of the young Víctor Heredia—or possibly, if improbably, from the trauma of contemporary travel, jet lag? Or when the Comte's servants arrive from shopping and explain that they are late in the performance of their normal chores because of a power blackout that occurred earlier that morning, can the reader assume that time, in the normal chronological sense, has been suspended?

A third instance is more notable since it involves a perceivable object, and not information reported in conversation. An omniscient narrative voice is describing the portrait of the Comte de Branly's father, a photograph taken shortly before the young reserve officer was to die at the age of thirty. The reader enters the Comte's thoughts: the Comte considers his father's profile to be his best feature (". . . his best feature his profile . . ." [pp. 26–27]). But in the same paragraph we read that the photograph has a peculiar quality, a diffuse light that seems to originate in the officer's silver-colored eyes. And just before the Comte goes to sleep, he passes his hand across the face of the photograph: "He covered his father's eyes and closed his own." It is now obvious that rationality is being subverted.

When the Comte drives his young guest past the suburbs of Paris to Enghien-les-Bains in search of a man who bears the same name as the youth, their quest is frustrated. They do not find the man at home, and decide to return to Paris. The Comte has two contradictory impulses: "Branly tried to interest Víctor in other outings" (p. 36), and, within a few lines, "on the return to Paris, my friend did not insist that they go out again" (p. 37). The reader must be wary of accepting as absolute fact any information he receives, either from the narrative voice or from the characters' conversations. To understand how these contradictions function within the framework of the entire novel, we need to consider for a moment its structure.

Basically, the novel is told within a period of several hours by the Comte de Branly to an unnamed (until the last pages) friend who is accompanying him at luncheon at a table overlooking the Place de la Concorde in the Automobile Club de France. The friend, in turn, records the story in first-person narrative. The action begins with their meeting in the club. During the long and lingering luncheon, and during the conversation in the club solarium, and subsequent swim, the narrative line, or, more accurately, lines, are recounted in flashback. These two principal characters remain in the club building until an accident in the pool necessitates removing the Comte to his home on the Avenue de Saxe. This moment occurs some seventeen pages before the end of the novel.

The setting of the first four chapters alternates between the Comte's mansion and the home of the second, or French, Víctor Heredia, at the Clos des Renards in Enghien. The fifth through nineteenth chapters, covering the period beginning with a second trip to Enghien in search of the French Víctor Heredia, and lasting several days while the Comte recovers from an automobile accident suffered there, though often involving scenes other than the French manor house, are narrated by the Comte as if from that location, though he is, of course, telling the story at the luncheon table in the club. In the nineteenth chapter two shifts in setting occur: the Comte leaves the Clos des Renards in the narrated story, and the two who are engaged in marathon conversation, the teller and the listener/recorder, move from the club dining room to the area of the solarium and the pool. From chapter nineteen until near the end of chapter twenty-one, the men remain in that area. In the last pages of the same chapter the two men go together to the mansion on the Avenue de Saxe. In chapter twenty-two, for the first time in the novel, the two men part, as the Comte's still-unidentified friend first visits the Clos des Renards and then returns to the Avenue de Saxe to call on the Comte. After this last meeting the friend, in the last chapter, leaves the Avenue de Saxe, wanders through the streets of Paris, and returns to the club pool to encounter his destiny. Essentially, from the time of the Comte's accident in the pool, and in spite of their two conversations, the Comte and his friend, who have been together throughout the novel, are separated. When they do move apart, the narrative follows the friend to the novel's end—which is necessarily incomplete, like any *story*, like any *his/tory*: "No one can remember every detail of a story" (p. 214).

From the first view of the Clos des Renards, the residence of the French Víctor Heredia, events are perceptibly unreal. Though fall has not yet arrived, dead leaves cover the avenue leading to the manor house, as well as the path in the adjacent woods; the Comte sees a strange vision in a second story window of the house ("a silhouette whose sail, like that of an ancient schooner, blended into indistinct waves of flowing hair—sail, fluttering curtains, white gown, all glimpsed fleetingly . . ." [p. 35]). From the site of the Clos des Renards the narrative moves in space across two continents, and in time through two centuries, following the lives of various Heredias.

From that moment of the arrival at the Clos des Renards the reader is never returned to objective reality—not after the Comte's recovery and departure, and especially not following the Comte's accident in the pool, his return to his town house, and the friend's separation from the Comte to meet his own destiny. The only pages in which the reader is led to expect a traditional reality are the opening pages, those first four chapters narrated in the club dining room, but covering a conventional exposition of the meeting between the Comte de Branly and two Heredias: Hugo Heredia, noted Mexican archeologist, and his son Víctor. Later in the novel when we read that the Comte approached his friend and invited *him* to dine, contradicting the now-accepted fact that the friend approached the *Comte*, we are no longer amazed by the incongruity. But those first refutations of fact in surroundings in which we are directed to expect normality, indicate that no reality may be assumed "normal" in this fiction. If once we could confine the nonnormal to a specific setting, a Gothic house, an enchanted wood, that privilege has been rescinded.

If not the contradictions, the coincidences should warn the reader that he is traveling into country where the rule of the ordinary is not honored. Consider, for example, a French madrigal that links together the widely diverse characters and moments in this novel. It is the tune played as the hours strike on an ornate antique ormolu clock belonging to the Comte de Branly in Paris; it is a tune whistled by the young Mexican Víctor Heredia in Cuernavaca, and echoed by an unknown voice from a *barranca*; it is the tune whistled by the mysterious son of the French Víctor Heredia in Enghien; it is the song sung by a waiter passing across an iron footbridge above the club pool. The madrigal also serves as the vehicle by which Branly is transported back to a key moment in his childhood, a moment in the Parc Monceau when he failed to take a step that would have welcomed into a circle of children a child staring through the beveled windows of a house on the Avenue Velázquez. In a different time he would have followed a different fork in the path. In that alternate reality, the story the Comte de Branly tells his friend would be a different story.

In my experience, the first overt statement of alternative fictions in Fuentes' novels appears in *La muerte de Artemio Cruz*,[3] in the pages where Artemio Cruz considers how his life might have been had he, at the key moments developed in each of the chapters, made a different decision: ". . . you will read and you will choose again: you will choose another life . . ." (p. 246). Here we have a listing of possibilities. The alternatives are not developed novelistically, but are projected in the reader's imagination as Artemio Cruz enumerates the moments that determined his life.

In *Zona sagrada*[4] the alternatives are not clarified, that is, they are not conclusive, but are structurally integrated in the figure of Giancarlo/Guglielmo, who may be the protagonist Guillermito's alter ego, his friend, his twin, or who may be the incarnated vehicle for his mother's destruction. Guillermo himself questions: "¿Camaradas, Guglielmo? ¿Hermanos . . . ? ¿Apolo y Dionisos?" (p. 107). Telegonus and Telemachus? In *Cambio de piel* Fuentes makes an enormous leap in his progressive fracturing of reality. The novel is a labyrinth of doubling: Elizabeth and Isabel may be two women, but are likely one; similarly, Javier and Franz. A chapter is dedicated to the archetypal doubles, William Wilson and Mr. Hyde. The garden of the forking paths has at this point in his career become the obligatory setting for Fuentes' novels.

In *Terra Nostra* the doubling of characters expands to the doubling of worlds. The Old World is projected onto the New, and reflected in a distorted mirror image in the Next World. Power, politics, religion, cosmic visions that seem to belong in one world appear in barely altered form in another. Felipe's horror of "the second opportunity" cannot prevent the cyclical repetitions of history. History mirrors fiction. Fiction reflects other fictions. The impulse to reintegrate these dispersed realities into a cohesive whole around a restored center is a major impetus in the novel.

Fuentes conceives of *Una familia lejana* as the concluding novel in a trilogy begun with *Aura* and *Cumpleaños*. It is and it isn't. The three do form a triad in that they share this theme of the potential for alternatives. Of the three, *Aura* is structurally the least complex, one of the elements that differentiates it from the more intricate *Cumpleaños* and *Una familia lejana*. In *Aura* possibilities are merely doubled, Aura is evoked by the old crone Consuelo and Felipe is the reincarnated General Llorente. But doubling is no longer an appropriate term to use in *Cumpleaños*, in which *all* female figures may be reduced to one, as all male figures, with the exception of a red-haired servant, are one consciousness whose most powerful representation is in the person of Siger de Brabant.

Una familia lejana is equally complicated in structure. The character of Branly is fairly simple; he is the Comte, and himself as a child. Though he is inextricably bound to the fortunes of the Heredias, it is the Heredias who can make no exclusive claim to their lives. The young Víctor Heredia is mirrored in the figure of the French Víctor Heredia, who is owner of the manor house at the Clos des Renards. This latter Heredia, who also appears mysteriously in scenes in Monterrey and Caracas, is later referred to as "Heredia," denying his claim to an authentic existence in the time and space of the narrative recounted by the Comte. There are various female figures: a silhouette glimpsed in a window of the Clos des Renards; the figure in a portrait (hands masking the face); the Mamasel of La Guaira; Lucie, the wife of Hugo Heredia; the new chatelaine to the Comte in the final pages; the woman the Comte had forgotten, but loved in the past. All are one.

But it is the figure of Hugo Heredia that ultimately is the most intricate, and the most fascinating. Although for a major portion of the novel Hugo Heredia is seemingly secondary both to the Comte and to his own son Víctor, we find that the structure of the novel underscores in several ways his preeminent role. The chapter dedicated to him, chapter twenty, is significantly longer than any other. Only three other chapters bear titles. The epigraph to Heredia's chapter consists of seven lines from the poem by Jules Supervielle that serves as a leitmotif throughout the book ("Branly recited a few lines from his favorite poem, the poem that for me was becoming the mysterious leit-motif of this story . . ." [p. 154]).

The long narrative, told in Hugo's voice, serves to clarify many of the puzzles in the novel: it explains his true relationship with his son and the abdication of his paternal responsibilities at the time of his son's disappearance in France; it reveals his strange pact with the French Víctor Heredia; and it at least partially accounts for the bond that unites Heredia and Branly: their shared rejection of the death of the past (". . . our shared rejection of the death of the past which is the present of our civilizations . . ." [p. 188]).

The proof of just how central Heredia is to *Una familia lejana* is ultimately found in the last pages when the Comte's friend returns to the club pool where Branly had nearly drowned during an unexplained disturbance of the water. There he sees the young Víctor and his French double André (son of the false Heredia) united. They float

in the pool like strangely-aged fetal Siamese twins, joined by an um-
bilicus, free forever from the tyranny of the past. But the voice he
hears identifies him, not them: "Heredia, you are Heredia" (p. 214).
The first-person recorder of the Comte de Branly's tale is engulfed by
the fiction. The fiction incarnates to absorb its narrator. One mask
is removed.

This Cervantine play with fictional reality, the attribution of
one's text to a more convincing or immediate author, and the layering of the narrative voices have been among Fuentes' most consistent hallmarks. His first novel, *La región más transparente*, is
marked by a Dos Passian ranging, shifting point of view. His second,
Las buenas conciencias, is his most traditional, his Balzac phase,
one might say. But the fact that this was intended as the first novel
of an uncompleted trilogy may indicate that from the very beginning
Fuentes was uncomfortable with the narrative mode of the nineteenth-century omniscient author. *La muerte de Artemio Cruz*
splinters the narrative voice into three: first, second, and third persons ("I," the personal or intimate "you," and "he"). In *Aura* Fuentes
elects the least conventional of these, the second person singular.
In the progression of his novelistic works, this is the most direct involvement of the reader to date. "You" are the actor, therefore you
are creator and narrator. *Zona sagrada* shifts between first- and
third-person voices, its narrative focus directed more toward the
creation of mythic space than the game of identification of voice.
But with *Cambio de piel* we see the first truly radical masking of the
narrator. An unidentifiable, floating narrative point of view mysti-
fies the reader until the last two words of the novel, written in the
form of a signature, Freddy Lambert, identify the narrator as a new
ingredient, a hitherto unknown participant in the narrative. Some
critics have seen this device as a trick. (It is, of course, no more un-
fair than the revelation of Melquíades' manuscript at the end of *Cien
años de soledad*.) But whatever the "fairness" of the device, it indicates an increasing obsession with masking the narrator. The very
title of the work underscores this layering, referring as it does to the
flayed god Xipe Tótec (who is to appear in both *Terra Nostra* and
Una familia lejana).

In *Cumpleaños*, which is the novel most closely related to *Una
familia lejana*, the dominant narrative voice, the "yo," is com-
paratively cohesive, but we have noted the complexity of the character. *Terra Nostra* is even more convoluted. The structure of this
novel has warranted a number of studies and numerous comments,
and is too baroque to disentangle here, but it is sufficient to say that
there has been no consensus among critics as to what narrator may

have written the *entire* novel, though attribution of individual sections is simple enough. It is interesting that in this era of self-conscious play with the narrative voice—and equally self-conscious critical voices—no one has simply attributed the novel to Carlos Fuentes.

The novel immediately preceding *Una familia lejana, La cabeza de la hidra*, was written as a spy-thriller in the manner of Raymond Chandler, and one would expect a reasonably straight-forward structure to underscore the nature of that genre. It is a further indication of Fuentes' compulsion to make the identity of his narrator as much an integral part of the mystery as the story line itself that again the narrator remains cloaked for a major portion of the novel.

Following this chronicle of steadily increasing preoccupation with the fiction of the author, one would expect—and is not disappointed—to find a similar masking in *Una familia lejana*. One wonders what new games, twists, confusions, he will encounter. We have seen that the friend lunching with the Comte de Branly in the Automobile Club de France, as the listener to the story, is its recorder. In this sense, he is the author. We have also seen that this first-person voice has been identified as a man whose phantom self is Heredia. But there is one more mask to be stripped away. Paradoxically, the revelation provides the ultimate mask. The listener/recorder/author/Heredia is Carlos Fuentes. *Fuentes*, he is addressed by the Comte during his last visit to the mansion on the Avenue de Saxe (p. 210). *Carlos*, he is called by Lucie (p. 204). This character is a palely disguised Fuentes whose youth was spent in Buenos Aires, not Mexico City, but whose career parallels that of the real Fuentes (at this point, may we speak of a "real" Fuentes?), born November 11, at twenty-five the author of a collection of short stories, and four years later, of his first novel, a figure described as "a Mexican creole with reddish skin, a black moustache, wavy hair and a studious and sad look behind horn-rimmed glasses" (p. 15).

So who is the true teller in *Una familia lejana*? This is an enigma that Fuentes poses to his reader, and though we must never lose sight of the fact that his characters are paper characters, that Fuentes does not subscribe to the theory of the autonomous character who "rises from the page" to appropriate the voice of the author, it is nevertheless true that the challenge is conscious. We note with interest that Branly proposes a toast to the variables in "Fuentes'" life, and then discusses the alternatives in fiction: "Just think that the same thing happens with all novels. There is another contiguous, parallel, invisible story of all we believe due to a unique text." Who, according to Branly, are the possible authors?

Hugo Heredia in the ruins of Xochicalco? The rustic proprietor of the Clos des Renards? I, who have told it to you? You, who some day will tell what I have told you? Someone else, unknown? And consider a different possibility: the novel was already written. It is the unpublished novel of phantoms, lying in a coffer buried beneath a garden urn, or behind loose bricks in the shaft of a dumbwaiter. Its author, it is superfluous to note, is Alexandre Dumas. (p. 205)

Is the reader the "desconocido," the last in this chain of potential narrators? We have heard the story told to Fuentes/Heredia by the Comte, the story written by any one of the proposed narrators, perhaps written even before it occurred. As every story is unfinished, new chapters remain to be written. Will the reader write them?

The allusions to author, narration, words, books, and fictions in the closing chapters of *Una familia lejana* are too numerous to reproduce here, but it is fair to say that from the time the two principal tellers, Branly and Fuentes, move to the locale of the club pool in chapter nineteen, this novel may be read as a discourse on the nature of fiction. A few examples will illustrate my point: "I did not want to be the one who receives, the one who knows and must spend the rest of his life searching for another victim to be the receiver, the knower. I did not want to be the narrator" (p. 190); "you know better than I where the fate of human destinies ends and the art of literary selection begins. . . . Can they be separated?" (p. 154); "I had never read, nor listened to, a story without accepting the pact my friend . . . was offering. But, was the same agreement possible between two friends in one another's company, as that between an irrevocably distanced author and reader?" (p. 157); "here we are, you and I, in one of the infinite possibilities in a life, or in literature. You are afraid to be the narrator of this novel about the Heredias . . ." (p. 204).

Una familia lejana is not only a novel that transmits a consciousness of its own fictionality, it is also permeated with allusions to other literary texts, supreme among them the poem "La chambre voisine," by Jules Supervielle. In the third chapter Branly explains to his friend, who, we know in retrospect, is Fuentes, that before retiring for the night he always reads this poem before the photograph of his father, who died as a young man. We recall that the poem is referred to within the text as a leitmotif, and with the exception of the two final lines it appears in its entirety in various quotations. Following the shift of scene in the Automobile Club de France, Branly and Fuentes continue their conversation in the solarium. They become involved in a discussion about courtesy—evoking two further literary references, the respective opinions of Erasmus and Lope de Vega. But to break the chain of their argument, Branly again refers to the poem. He claims that among many reasons, it is one of his favorites because it causes him to dream of "Lautréamont y Heredia y Supervielle," and because one of the lines, "Tournez le dos à cet homme, mais restez auprès de lui," led him to the true interpretation of his experiences at the Clos des Renards. He begins to recite the lines of the poem. His friend, in a strange correspondence between thought and spoken word, recognizes the words as those describing Branly's last dream at the Clos des Renards. And, strangely, he knows that the words had all been spoken before: "How strange that they had all been said before, by the poet, or by his reader, my friend Branly" (p. 124).

This is one way in which events coincide with the lines of the poem. A second application follows immediately in one of the most ingenious chapters of the novel. The poem, which surely must be considered the basic metaphor of the novel, is paraphrased, and the actions of the principal characters recounted in terms of the contents of the poem. In Branly's dream the Heredias' lives are joined. Branly is excluded, left standing alone in the Parc Monceau.

But proving the numerous possibilities for interpretation in a universal work, as well as the interrelatedness of all things ("all things are related, nothing is isolated" [p. 176]), I call attention to the fact that the structure of the novel recapitulates the structure of "La chambre voisine." The poem appears below, so that we may note the pertinent lines.

	La chambre voisine	The Adjoining Room
1	Tournez le dos à cet homme	Turn your back to that man
2	Mais restez auprès de lui,	But do not leave him, stay,
3	(Écartez votre regard,	(Avert your eyes from his gaze,
4	sa confuse barbarie),	His confused brutality),
5	Restez debout sans mot dire,	Unspeaking, stand close by
6	Voyez-vous pas qu'il sépare	Note how nearly he fails
7	Mal le jour d'avec la nuit,	To distinguish night from day,

8 Et les cieux les plus profonds	Similarly, farthest skies
9 Du coeur sans fond qui l'agite?	From depths of troubled heart.
10 Eteignez tous ces flambeaux	Extinguish every torch,
11 Regardez: ses veines luisent.	See his glistening veins
12 Quant il avance la main,	When he extends his hand
13 Un souffle de pierreries,	A breath of precious jewels
14 De la circulaire nuit	From the circular night
15 Jusqu'à ses longs doigts parvient.	To long fingers flows.
16 Laissez-le seul sur son lit,	Leave him alone, abed
17 Le temps le borde et le veille,	Time hovers near, keeps watch
18 En vue de ces hauts rochers	In view of high rock cliffs
19 Où gémit, toujours caché,	Where moans, forever concealed,
20 Le coeur des nuits sans sommeil.	The heart of insomniac nights.
21 Qu'on n'entre plus dans la chambre	Let no one enter again
22 D'où doit sortir un grand chien	The chamber from which will come
23 Ayant perdue la mémoire	An enormous dog that has lost
24 Et qui cherchera sur terre	All memory of the past
25 Comme le long de la mer	But will search the ends of the earth
26 L'homme qu'il laissa derrière	For the man it left behind,
27 Immobile, entre ses mains	Unmoving, in the care
28 Raides et définitives.	of strong, decisive hands.

Lines 1 through 20 are equal to the novelistic space of chapters 1 through 23. During this time the person addressed in the poem is given a number of admonitions: tournez, restez, écartez, voyez, éteignez, regardez, laissez. In line 21 there is a shift of address from "vous" to the impersonal "on," and a further shift which throws the focus onto a new entity, "un grand chien. . . ." This dog must search across the length and breadth of land and sea for "l'homme qu'il laissa derrière." (It should be noted that the last two lines, with the troublesome possessive pronoun "ses," are not quoted in the text, but appear in paraphrase in the dream, chapter 16.)

The person addressed in the poem, the "vous" of the reiterated injunctions, is most logically perceived as Heredia/Fuentes. Hence the opening lines are ironic, since it is Branly who turns away from Fuentes to look out over the Place de la Concorde as he begins to recount his story. And it is Branly for whom those lines illuminate his experiences at the Clos des Renards. Fuentes does, however, stay beside Branly (restez auprès de lui) without interruption until chapter twenty-two. The "barbarie" of lines 3 and 4 is the basis for a number of discussions on courtesy, aristocracy, and barbarism, as they apply to the Old and the New Worlds. Lines 6 and 7 remind us of Branly's often-mentioned vulnerability to light, as well as the French Heredia's custom of appearing only after the light of day has faded. Heredia's pronounced preference for the night hours leads Branly to question him specifically, "Are you a vampire?" (p. 77), as well as to a reference to him as the Nosferatu of Enghien-les-Bains (p. 94). Branly drifts in and out of dreams during the period of his recovery at the Clos des Renards, erasing the traditional boundaries between night and day (lines 6 and 7). Lines 8 and 9 recall the scene at the ruins of Xochicalco, the changing light and fleeting clouds that cause the heights of the distant volcanos and the depths of the abyss to seem interchangeable. The "flambeaux" (line 10) are recreated in the scene of the flickering vigil lights on All Saint's Eve, again at Xochicalco. Fuentes often calls attention to Branly's fine, long-fingered hands, translucent in their pallor, certainly a sign of his aristocracy, but also prefigured in the poem in "ses longs doigts" (line 15) and "ses veines luisent" (line 11).

When the Comte nearly drowns in the club pool he is accompanied to his home by Fuentes, who then abandons him ("Laissez-le seul sur son lit," line 16) to the charge of time ("Le temps le borde et le veille," line 17) and an insomniac night ("des nuits sans sommeil," line 20). This is Fuentes' last visit ("Qu'on n'entre plus dans la chambre," line 21). What then emerges in the poem is a dog—a monster?—without memory: Heredia to Fuentes: "You had a past and you do not remember it" (p. 189). This incomplete being must search "sur terre comme le long de la mer" (across two continents) for "l'homme qu'il laissa derrière": Lucie to Fuentes: "Do you know your phantom . . . ? You did not leave it behind" (p. 210). These lines, lines 22 to 26, contain the dire prophecy of the poem. They are the destiny of Fuentes in the novel.

A number of the literary allusions appear in two catalogues of authors. The first is of authors born in Latin America who then spent their literary lives in France (p. 120). Branly takes this occasion to remind Fuentes, who has earlier commented that "Buenos Aires and Montevideo are my lost cities" (p. 23), of the fact that he of all people, being from "over there," should understand what the New World meant to the Old in terms of forever destroying the potential for universality (p. 121). In the second instance, the author Fuentes specifically refers to "the titles of a number of books that have appeared in the course of this story" (p. 198), directing the reader's attention not to ignore the significance of these works to *his* text. Fuentes finds these books in the Comte's library: *La Duchesse de Langeais*, by Balzac; Lamartine's *Meditations*; the *Poesies* of Jules Supervielle, the source of the essential "La chambre voisine"; *Les chants de Maldoror* by Lautréamont; José María de Heredia's *Les trophées*; *L'imitation de Notre-Dame la lune* by Jules Laforgue; and the *Memoires* of Alexandre Dumas.

The important name in this list is the name Fuentes thought had not been mentioned previously, that of Alexandre Dumas. Then he remembers that Branly had overheard the two boys, Víctor and André, talking while they played of *The Count of Monte Cristo*, *The Three Musketeers*, and *The Man in the Iron Mask*. Spurred by idle curiosity he picks up the book and discovers a letter that unravels one of the mysteries of the plot. The letter reveals that in addition to being a date—for it has functioned as the date of the birth of the Comte's father, and until now has been assumed to be the date of construction of the Clos de Renards—the phrase 1870 A.D. inscribed in the molding above the door marks instead the date of a visit to Enghien by Alexandre Dumas. After exchanging a blond and handsome child for a black one, Dumas "sent a message by C. that in this manner he was settling all the old debts of honor, money, exploitation, and revenge" (p. 199). This letter, and Dumas' presence at the Clos des Renards, explains why Branly suggests that he is one of the possible "authors" of the novel.

In *Una familia lejana* there are none of the intertextual games involving characters that Fuentes often plays, no references to others of his own novels, nor does the reader find an identifiable character from another author's fiction (unless it be the spectre from "La chambre voisine"), though citations of authors and works abound. Fuentes recently commented about his *Terra Nostra* that it "should be read as an adventure novel." He added, "I believe the ideal novel is a mixture of Joyce's *Ulysses* and Dumas' *The Count of Monte Cristo*." [5] *Terra Nostra* was followed by the spy thriller *La cabeza de la hidra*. *Una familia lejana* makes clear that this prolific and innovative author has not modified his ideal.

To return for a moment to Borges' garden, we recall that Ts'ui Pên's labyrinth was not physical, but rather a labyrinth of symbols. And symbols abound in *Una familia lejana*. They may be literary, as we have seen, literature as metaphor, or they may take other forms. They may be objects: the gilt clock of Antoine-André Ravrio (parenthetically, the artist's first names are the same as those of sons of Hugo and Víctor Heredia); a gauzy Empire gown—or the shredded, tattered ruin of that gown; dead leaves in late summer; or an archeological treasure. They may be aural or visual experiences, the madrigal of the "claire fontaine," the light that wounds Branly's eyes. Or they may be metaphysical, the power failure that occurred just prior to young Víctor Heredia's arrival, signalling an interference in time; the scar that cuts across the rigorous order of the French garden of intelligence, that same "scar of creation" that appears in *Terra Nostra*. Windows serve as obstacles to passage, what is seen behind them belongs to a different time or space; pools of water and mirrors—or their absence—are symbols of doubling (they also hold images other than those of the persons who look into them).

Or individual words can assume a symbolism larger than their meaning: "the destiny that every word conceals, but also, like an oracle, announces" (p. 188). Certain words recur with mesmerizing insistency, *recordar, olvidar, memoria; soberanía, resentimiento, cortesía*. And a concordance would register an impressive number of entries for the noun *sueño*, and its related adjectival and verbal forms. Dream, dreaming, dreamers have invaded Fuentes' fiction. Consuelo dreams Aura. Artemio Cruz "dreams" as his mental processes degenerate into unpunctuated, uncontrolled stream of consciousness. The narrator of *Cumpleaños* dreams, and awakens to find sitting on the foot of his bed a young boy who is the projection of himself in a different time. In the Old World section of *Terra Nostra*, Pedro, Celestina, Simón, and Lucovico dream the future; in the Next World, reality is "a sick dream"; the three youths with six toes on each foot and flesh-red crosses on their backs dream one another, and if two cease to dream of one, he will die; the Pilgrim dreams a "circular dream" of recurring lives culminating in moments of death; and the Pilgrim lies down, dreams, and dies before awakening to his rendezvous with the girl with the tattooed lips. The obliteration of the line separating dream from reality, life from death, suggests an additional literary influence in *Una familia lejana*. In "The Garden of Forking Paths," the key to the puzzle is the one word that is not mentioned. The omission from the list of books Fuentes finds in the Comte's library of Calderon's *La vida es sueño* does not mean that a "phantom" reader would not find that book in Fuentes' library.

Earlier in these remarks I mentioned that *Una familia lejana* is in Fuentes' concept the concluding novel in a trilogy formed by it, *Aura* and *Cumpleaños*. I added, it is, and it isn't. It *is* related to those novels by content, the theme of Nietzsche's eternal return, the rejection of the Christian tenet that the soul is unique. The novels are also related in their irony, which may be seen even in the choice of titles. *Aura* is suggestive of aurora, the "dawn" of a new life. *Aura* may be a gentle breeze, or an aureole. But an *aura* is also a vulture. Aura, the beautiful green-eyed temptress, is redolent of carrion. The title *Cumpleaños* evokes a more subtle irony. Mother and Father sing "Happy Birthday, dear Georgie. . . ." But *when* is Georgie's day of birth? Even more harrowing, *who* is Georgie? But irony is at its most trenchant in *Una familia lejana*—the most cursory survey of the use of the word "friend" substantiates this view—and the play between the warm resonances of *familia* and the chilling undertones of *lejana* set the tone for a case study in irony.

But *Cumpleaños* and *Una familia lejana* differ significantly from *Aura* in their mode of narration. Though *Aura* is experimental technically, it is not characterized by the disguised narrative voice so integral a part of the structure of the other two novels. And still another quality, again a principal structural component in later novels, separates *Una familia lejana* from Fuentes' triadic grouping—the pull between the Old and the New Worlds. Though space, not place, is the setting for *Cumpleaños*, specific references to physical locales are from the Old World—Dalmatia, Paris, the Strand, and Covent Garden in London. *Aura*, in contrast, is set in the New World, indisputably Mexican. It is with *Cambio de piel* and *Zona sagrada* that Fuentes begins to play with the attraction and repulsion between the two cultures. This tension is the core of *Terra Nostra*, and in a different way is indispensable to *La cabeza de la hidra*. It is a motivating force in *Una familia lejana*. One of the narrator's disguises, one of the masks that prevent us from seeing him for who he is, is our belief that he is French. Branly, in a comment about Jules Supervielle, reminds the narrator that he, too, is from *that* world. "Fuentes" rejects such identity, claiming that Buenos Aires and Montevideo are his lost cities, whereas Paris, "the ultimate homeland for a Latin American," will never be lost to him. But he is denied the luxury of identification with the Old World, with its courtesy and magnanimity and aristocracy. It is Lucie, Lucie of the many guises, who states the devastating truth: "Carlos, you do not belong here, and you will never again be at home here." And referring to his phantom, that "other life" that accompanies every man and woman, she adds: "Have no illusions; you have not been able to lose it, no matter how hard you tried; you did not leave it behind in Mexico, in Buenos Aires, as you thought when you were a child" (p. 210).

"Fuentes'" phantom is always with him, not merely through one lifetime, but "yes, forever" (p. 207). In this novel Carlos Fuentes has told but one of "the infinite possibilities of life and of a narrative" (p. 204). All the others exist; all those "distant relations" are alive, in the garden of the forking paths.

Notes

1. Page numbers cited in my text to *Ficciones* (Buenos Aires: Emecé Editores, 1956).
2. All citations are to *Una familia lejana* (Mexico: Biblioteca Era, 1980); the English is my own, from my forthcoming translation of the novel as *Distant Relations*.
3. Page numbers from the 3rd edition (Mexico: Fondo de Cultura Económica, 1967).
4. Page numbers from the 5th edition (Mexico: Siglo XXI, 1969).
5. "Fuentes on His *Terra Nostra*," a note by R. G. M. (Robert G. Mead) in *Hispania*, 63, no. 2 (May 1980): 415.

Gloria Durán

Dolls and Puppets as Wish-Fulfillment Symbols in Carlos Fuentes

There are numerous psychological studies of the role of doll play in children. Dolls allow us to act out our fantasy worlds, to create worlds where we are in control. Doll play can also be a safety valve for pent-up aggressive behavior, and it then tends to duplicate the same aggressive tendencies that we feel in real-life situations. Novelists are grown-up children. They create literary characters which they use as word dolls, expressing both their desires and their feelings of aggression.

There have been relatively few novelists like Cervantes who almost seem to lose control of these creatures of their fantasy and permit them an independent existence. Fuentes is not one of these novelists. On the whole he keeps a fairly tight rein on his characters who, like puppets or dolls, docilely respond to the promptings of their master. As in the case of children's doll play, Fuentes' characters frequently express unconscious aspects of his personality. At other times they are recognizable reflections of the writer himself. When this happens, they, like him, must create new characters by producing dolls of their own. In the manner of Borges' dream-created characters in "The Circular Ruins," they must dream or fashion secondary characters in order to express the unconscious aspects of *their* personalities. Thus in Fuentes' works we are often two generations away from reality.

Frequently these secondary embodiments of the unconscious are feminine. Many show distinct features of the anima, which C. G. Jung identified as the woman in man and which he considered to be a principal archetype of the collective unconscious. Like all anima figures, Fuentes' dolls and puppets incarnate both positive and negative qualities. In this essay I shall consider the role of puppets and dolls in three of this author's works: "La muñeca reina" ("The Doll Queen"), a short story from *Cantar de ciegos*, published in 1964; *Zona sagrada*, his novel of 1967; and *Cambio de piel*, also published in the same year.[1]

"The Doll Queen," which to my knowledge has not yet been translated into English, seems to be told directly by Fuentes. The narrator (Carlos) recalls his idyllic relationship with a little girl of seven years, a relationship that dates back some fifteen years to a time when he was himself adolescent. The propellant of his reveries and also of the subsequent action is the child's faded note which accidentally falls into his hands. It is a note inviting him to her home and providing directions. Bored and lonely, Carlos impulsively decides to again seek out his old friend. Amilamia's directions lead him to a suburb of decaying buildings and a dilapidated house where he hears someone's breath on the other side of the front door but can gain no entry. Suspense is heightened by the narrator's sighting what appears to be his friend's apron still hanging on a rooftop clothesline.

In the next scene Carlos manages to enter the house by claiming to represent the landlord of the premises. But later he realizes that he has fallen into a trap of his own making. The aged couple who inhabit the place tell him that his supposed employer died long ago. Yet when he reveals the true nature of his sentimental visit, Carlos is rewarded by the couple with a visit to Amilamia's room. Here, in a windowless enclosure permeated by the odor of tropical flowers and burning wax candles, he encounters a lifesize image of Amilamia. Surrounded by all the worn-out toys and dolls of her childhood, the queen doll reclines inside a coffin on black satin sheets. The sunless room is the shrine that adoring parents have erected to a dead child. Once Carlos has seen this, they beg him never to return.

But as in most fairy tales, the hero does not heed the warning. Some time later he decides to go back in order to give the doll worshippers Amilamia's faded note. This time, however, it is not the parents who answer the doorbell but Amilamia herself. She is a woman of twenty-two, deformed and mentally retarded. Although at first delighted to see him, she reconsiders and asks him to leave. Her father screams obscenities at her and threatens another whipping. She has been forbidden contact with the outside world. In the last paragraph of the story we find the narrator still on the threshold, soaked by a heavy downpour but neither entering nor leaving.

Daniel de Guzmán has compared "The Doll Queen" to *Aura* in that both deal with man's attraction to a hideous woman, an attraction founded on illusion or hallucination.[2] I might also add that both touch on the theme of a death cult not very different from the worshipping of ancestral bones practiced by Teódula Moctezuma in *La región más transparente*. Compared to the cleanliness of real bones, however, a paste and cardboard doll represents a degenerate object of worship. The old couple incarnate the pathetic Mexican bourgeoisie, so frequently the object of Fuentes' attack. The Aztec death cult, which in Teódula's case was handed down intact, is here perverted into worship of a commercial object mounted on a junk heap of destroyed articles of consumption—toys, balloons, clothing, etc.

Unable to accept the reality of their daughter's crippling, the old couple have created a doll to make palpable their myth of her death as a beautiful child. Theirs is a denial of life and an affirmation of death which is tempting to contrast to the situation that prevails in Faulkner's "A Rose for Emily." In this a real corpse is kept locked in a room and treated as a lover by the heroine in her illusory denial of death. Or if we look for parallels rather than contrasts, a forerunner of "The Doll Queen" theme may be found in the movies (at least as powerful an influence on Fuentes as is Faulkner). The classic French film, *Les jeux interdits* (1952), which Fuentes must have seen when it played in Mexico, involves children's play at death rituals as an attempt to cope on the plane of make-believe with the terrible world of modern warfare. In Fuentes' story the parents become like children in their reversion to doll play and substitution of fantasy—even the fantasy of death—to escape a more intolerable reality.

This attraction of death and the use of death fantasies is common to much of Fuentes' fiction. According to a letter written to me by Fuentes, the fascination with death themes and ancient witches began when he was only seven. He relates:

But if I am totally frank, this obsession was born in me when I was seven years old and after visiting Chapultepec Castle and seeing the painting of the young Carlota of Belgium I found in the Casasola archives the photo of the same woman, now old, dead, lying inside her cushioned coffin, wearing the nightcap of a little girl: the Carlota who died, insane, in a castle the same year that I was born.[3]

This image of a little girl wearing her nightcap and lying inside her padded coffin is faithfully duplicated in "The Doll Queen." It is also implicit in two earlier tales, "Tlactocatzine, del Jardín de Flandes" from *Los días enmascarados* (1952) and of course *Aura* (1962).

Yet there is a fundamental difference between "The Doll Queen" and these other tales. In them the woman is more ghost than flesh. And predictably the hero falls victim to her in both cases; she is basically a creature of the writer's unconscious whom he has not yet dared to oppose. But in "The Doll Queen" the anima is seen from the viewpoint of reality rather than myth. Although fascinated by his memories of Amilamia as a child (just as the narrator of *Aura* is fascinated by the magical image of a young girl), Carlos is understandably uneasy about her metamorphosis into a repulsive young woman. He does not rush into her arms as Felipe Montero (the hero of *Aura*) would have done. In this story the death wish is not his, but that of the young woman's parents. We see him undecided at the end, wavering between entry and exit, exposed to natural elements in the real world. The doors to the dark house of the unconscious remain open, but he does not cross the threshold.

Another exceptional factor in "The Doll Queen" is that the doll symbol is used to express different needs by different characters in the story. There is not merely one queen doll but many dolls. The one representing Amilamia is surrounded by other less fortunate dolls, scalped and dismembered. These are the real child's dolls, and their sorry condition is testimony to the destruction that Amilamia wreaked on them in order to exorcise her aggressive feelings toward her parents. In this story Fuentes has used dolls in realistic fashion, demonstrated how they can serve as channels to express both desire and aggression. "The Doll Queen" does not portray the author's dream world, but rather that of his characters. He reports on observed fantasies from the vantage point of an author anchored in the conscious, everyday world.

On the other hand, in most of Fuentes' novels the element of make-believe may be ascribed directly to the author. Rather than merely reporting on doll play in the lives of his characters, Fuentes indulges in the fantasy himself. Characters become dolls and live in a doll house of Fuentes' creation. (Since all of these novels have been translated and are probably familiar to the reader, we shall dispense with the kind of summary provided for the short story.)

In *Cambio de piel*, which Fuentes has described as "total fiction,"[4] we have a single character, Herr Urs, who appears first as a real character—that is, a direct emanation of the author—and then as a puppet whose strings are apparently controlled by the novel's narrator. Yet this control is only illusory. The puppet is alive, walks and talks. He is not the supine, inanimate object that we found in "The Doll Queen," where the old couple were really in charge.

In *Cambio de piel* the puppet's role is infinitely more complex. Alternating between "real" character and puppet, he is never wholly dominated by the narrator, Freddy Lambert. Yet in the brief episode covering the puppet's removal from his trunk (pp. 434–445 of the Spanish edition), he appears at the narrator's summoning and represents an incarnation of wish fulfillment for Freddy on a far more complicated and precarious level than that exemplified by the death effigy from "The Doll Queen."

Like the ubiquitous anima, Herr Urs comes from the narrator's collective unconscious. Freddy resorts to him in order to combat its other emanations, the coven of witches known as "the monks." In other studies I have tried to demonstrate that Herr Urs is the embodiment of the wise old man, or the archetype of reason.[5] According to C. G. Jung, "if the name 'Lucifer' were not prejudicial, it would be a very suitable one for this archetype."[6] Again, like the anima, it is bipolar. Herr Urs is both good magician and evil dwarf. But when summoned as a puppet by Freddy in order to ward off the evil of the monks, the negative side of Herr Urs' being soon becomes apparent.

Furthermore, the complexity of the dwarf is further enhanced by his personal creation, when he was still a character (rather than a puppet), of puppets of his own. In an earlier episode we had seen the real Herr Urs as a corpse in a room full of hermaphroditic broken dolls which hung by wires attached to their necks. Although it is not clear whether Herr Urs himself mutilated these dolls or was in the act of repairing them, the former conclusion is the more likely since the bulk of paintings executed by the dwarf also reveal grotesque deformities, eschatological and obscene representations:

> The most traditional scenes . . . lay grouped beside horribly deformed canvasses, painted in sombre tones in which the wealth of furious brush strokes hardly allowed one to see hidden, the forms of open mouths and eyes captured by terror, hands of long fingernails, fecal matter, indecent copulation with animals, rotting snakes. . . . (p. 140)

An explanation for both paintings and dolls is also provided by Herr Urs in his final role of puppet: "I felt heroic, heroic and free as I repaired each doll and painted each painting. I was no longer poor and deformed and alone and was . . . was . . ." (p. 421).[7] (He finally confesses that he felt like a little god.) The dwarf, therefore, surrounded himself with a deformed world to cushion and assuage his own deformity. This is the simple psychological explanation for Herr Urs' artistic eccentricities. José Donoso utilizes and expands the same idea in the isolated world of monsters and dwarfs that he creates in *El obsceno pájaro de la noche.*

And yet we may suspect a substratum of aggression in the fact that the paintings are scenes of destruction and the dolls have been sexually deformed. Again, as in "The Doll Queen," Fuentes introduces a grotesque, misshapen character who releases pent-up aggressive feelings on his private society of defenseless scapegoats, his dolls.

However, given the metaphysical nature of the novel, any common psychological analysis of the characters will only scratch the surface. A much larger problem remains as to why Herr Urs chooses to deform his dolls by making them hermaphroditic. Does this truly represent aggression on his part or rather is it an expression of desire? Is hermaphroditism a positive or negative quality for Herr Urs? Perhaps no categorical answer can be given. Archetypal characters are always ambiguous. However, we have many clues with respect to Fuentes' own fascination with the idea of the hermaphrodite. Beginning with *Zona sagrada* we have real hermaphrodites and frustrated hermaphrodites in three major novels. (The other two are of course *Cambio de piel* and *Terra Nostra*.) To the extent that Fuentes is increasingly dealing with supernatural characters this development is not surprising.

Mircea Eliade, tracing the ancient history of the hermaphroditic deity, suggests its roots in prehistory and shows how it corresponds to a human need for completeness. He says that "the isolated individual feels incomplete in his limited maleness or femaleness, and visualizes his gods as perfect. . . ." He sees them as combining all opposites.[8]

It becomes apparent, therefore, that there is a natural human tendency toward fantasizing about hermaphroditic supernatural beings. This ideal in the case of someone like Herr Urs is particularly pronounced in that Urs is a creature of isolation and self-sufficiency. As puppet he remarks: "My freedom is my isolation. . . . Thanks to my isolation I exercise the power of a far-away infection. If I allowed myself to be touched by other spheres of life, those that intermingle and corrupt each other, I would cease to be who I am" (p. 422). Hermaphroditism, therefore, in that it incarnates completeness in a single being, is the obvious desire of those like Herr Urs who would isolate themselves from all others. This is perhaps reason enough to sustain the thesis that Urs' hermaphroditic dolls with their artificial phalluses are an incarnation of his desire rather than a desecration or simply a product of destructive impulses.

These dolls, in fact, only repeat on a plane even further removed from reality the hermaphroditic nature of all of the monks (whom the narrator sees as impregnating themselves) (pp. 416, 417), references that are summed up in the English translation as: "We are the androgynous pages . . . we are neither men nor women . . ." (p. 433).

All of Fuentes' archetypal characters who multiply by the end of the narrative are hermaphrodites with a puppetlike relationship to the narrator similar to that of the cardboard dwarf. And since they are all puppets of a narrator (Freddy) who is powerless to control them, they are all, ultimately, puppets of the master puppeteer, Carlos Fuentes. *Cambio de piel* is puppet theater within puppet theater.

The doll/puppet is self-generating throughout his work. Not only does the narrator evoke the puppet of Urs, but the hermaphroditic monks can also give birth to dolls. In the course of an orgy, White Rabbit gives birth to a tiny, male doll, apparently an effigy of Jacob Werner, another monk who is himself a mental projection of a concentration camp victim. This reproductive hallucination, this proliferation of increasingly unreal characters or what we might call the "dollification" of all characters in a self-contained world of make-believe, reaches its climax in *Terra Nostra*. This major work of Fuentes is far too complex to be dealt with within the confines of a brief study. However, we might simply observe that each of its triplets, the major protagonists, in fact become puppets, living according to the dreams of their fellow triplets who are again controlled by Fuentes, the puppetmaster.

And finally—in this study—*Zona sagrada*, which has been compared by many critics, including myself, to a womb or to the inner sanctuary of the hero's apartment, may just as easily be assimilated to a dollhouse. They are all enclosed, protected areas where outside reality is excluded. Fuentes himself explains the tale as based on the myth of Ulysses, not the Ulysses of Homer, but the less well known version of Robert Graves that appears in his *The Greek Myths*.[9]

But Graves' tale of the half brothers, Telemachus and Telegonus, who replace Ulysses as lovers of their father's mistress (Circe) and wife (Penelope) merely serves as intellectual background for the modern Mexican myth surrounding the movie star, María Félix, fictionally named Claudia Nervo. Claudia is really "the queen doll," but with the difference that here it is she who enslaves all who surround her and turns them into her personal puppets. She turns Bela, the Italian beauty whom Claudia "adopts," into a cloned version of herself. She not only controls all the hangers-on in her entourage, but she is also capable of projecting her being into them, of becoming them, whether they be men, women or animals. Claudia is the classic witch in twentieth-century attire. And like Herr Urs' dolls, she is also hermaphroditic. "Don't you find something very masculine about her?" asks one of the starlets.[10]

Like Urs' pictures and dolls, Claudia is also terrifying. As her son "Mito," remarks: "Celebrated for her beauty, the medusa also demands to be recognized for her horror."[11]

Yet even this super-powerful doll is not completely divorced from reality. As Lanin Gyurko points out: "Despite her vehement declaration of androgyny, Claudia is vulnerable to male influence. Her tragic flaw is her narcissism."[12] Claudia appears to be yet another version of Fuentes' anima, originally incarnate—as we have seen—in the Empress Carlota. Even the names show a certain similarity. Like Carlota, Claudia is also a queen—although of the cinema in this case. Also like her, she is old, but still seductive (the Consuelo-Aura syndrome), trapping her admirers, but in fact trapped by her own dependence on physical beauty or, in Gyurko's words, by her narcissism.

And if the queen doll is trapped, how much worse for the characters in her entourage, especially the twins Mito and Giancarlo, the Italian actor who comes to supplant Mito (myth) in his mother's affections. Claudia, at least, has the power to create living dolls, flesh and blood facsimiles of human beings. Circe-like, perhaps she creates them out of mice and other familiars whom we see her in the process of enchanting.

But Giancarlo must carve his dolls out of inanimate material, like wood. In the fashion of Herr Urs, he creates hermaphroditic effigies and, like the monks of *Cambio de piel*, he tries to recreate himself by the physical labor of giving birth. "You left the doll, rolled over, remained on your back, with your legs open, arched, supporting yourself on your elbows. And the birth was that of the being who returns each time that they forget him. . . . You sweat, you twist, slowly, beneath the gaze of the huge angels and the vampires, of the art that you inherited and the art that you created. . . ."[13]

All these Fuentian characters who attempt miraculous childbirths seem to be striving for an identity with their creator, a creator whom we may identify as God or merely as Fuentes. The attempt of Giancarlo to produce a child is hardly different in essence from the later attempt in *Terra Nostra* of Isabel to create a royal lover from portions of royal corpses. They are both magic doll play, the manipulation of things to replace human beings or in fact to create a human being. So many of Fuentes' characters are alchemists at heart, revolutionaries who attempt to usurp the divine monopoly on magic and creation. *Zona sagrada*, therefore, is naturally saturated with incest, hermaphroditism, homosexuality, all those elements in literature which Northrop Frye classifies as "demonic."[14] They belong to a stage in literary development which he considers not creative, but in fact destructive, characteristic of a highly troubled society.

Mito, for example, does not desire a normal sexual relationship with Bela, the starlet, but rather a means of penetrating the mother, Claudia, whose creature Bela has become. Like Claudia, he too is arrested at a narcissistic stage of development where things, make-believe, are more important than people. Mito plays with Bela as with a doll, uses Bela for his own magic designs—his desire to in fact become Claudia.

Mito's collection of dogs, gifts from Claudia, are also part of the doll play. He refers to them as his *"corte,"* decides which shall live and which shall be sacrificed by being tossed into the path of speeding cars. (Mother Claudia, too, we may remember, also practiced animal sacrifice, her rug being covered by the dismembered portions of animal bodies: birds, pumas, falcons, hummingbirds, monkeys.)[15]

Such loathsome details, however, are not simply gothic trimmings. As discussed in my *The Archetypes of Carlos Fuentes: From Witch to Androgyne* (see n. 3), magical power has often been thought to derive not only from sacrifice but from anarchy. Carnival and unbridled license produce the energy for the new creation. But Mito, in spite of his dog-dolls, his dressing in Claudia's clothes, his dollification of Bela, and his apartment-dollhouse, becomes the victim of Claudia's own doll play and is turned into a dog.

Mito's twin Giancarlo is hardly any better off. Giancarlo too has his own dollhouse in an inner chamber, velvet-lined (a symbolic uterus), of an Italian palazzo. Here, as we have already observed, he performs magic rites and sexual aberrations with life-sized dolls, all pregnant, dolls he also has created. A hermaphrodite in desire if not in fact, Giancarlo, like Mito, plays at the role of a woman about to give birth: "I want to endure; I am seeking the only way I know."[16] Giancarlo in his doll play also seeks to become his own mother, to again give birth to himself. His preliminary courtship and rape of the self-created dolls is part of a symbolic ritual. Again, this is a cosmic game, and its physical setting repeats many of the elements in Herr Urs' eschatological paintings. In Giancarlo's "sacred zone" there is a carousel of beheaded statues and rag dolls, cancerous mouldings, a rotation of lunar objects, of hogs' heads and rooster crests, etc. Again and again Fuentes tries to show that the idea of human birth is founded on a precondition of anarchy or entropy, a common leveling of disparate objects in states of decay. In less philosophical and more instinctive form, we met the same idea in *La región más transparente* and *La muerte de Artemio Cruz* where the death of others is often a precondition for the birth of sons (or the death of the son, e.g. Manuel Zamacona in *La región más transparente*, for the spiritual rebirth of the father). On either the intuitive or intellectual level, violence and sacrifice are the keys to creation. Again Mircea Eliade documents this idea repeatedly in his *Mephistopheles and the Androgyne*.

But in the case of Fuentes' characters, the attempt at rebirth and immortality is not a social enterprise (as described by Eliade), but an individual one, as we see in the attempts of Herr Urs, Giancarlo, Mito, or the Emperor Felipe of *Terra Nostra*. Thus the original catastrophe from which the world was formed and which must be duplicated in social rituals (Eliade's thesis) is scaled down to the confines of a single battle (for Felipe), or the depravities that can be contained in a single room. Individuals, moreover, unless they are kings, cannot play with human beings, so the necessary sacrifices must be animals or dolls.

For this reason dolls serve Fuentes' characters in much the same way that these characters serve Fuentes. Both create a private, magical world only faintly duplicating the one outside, with the profound difference that in the private world the individual is in complete control. Everyone outside the magic circle of the dollhouse is brought in tamed, objectified, obedient to our slightest wish. They can satisfy a craving for love which is divorced from reality (as in "The Doll Queen"); they can substitute for the real object of our desire (as Bela does in *Zona sagrada*); they can serve the sadomasochistic feelings of the relatively powerless (as was the case of Herr Urs or of Mito and Giancarlo). They can also be sacrificed and tortured with impunity, as the "real" Amilamia vented her rage on her own play dolls or as the characters in *Zona sagrada* treat both living beings and objects or animals under their control.

In brief, since Fuentes is both a playful and an intellectual writer, creating his own literary world of "total fictionality," it is natural that he also grant his characters the freedom of action provided by a solipsistic environment. But to do this, he must surround them too with creatures of *their* imaginations, creatures who in Borgean fashion reflect and reproduce themselves in an inverted or introspective world of puppets or dolls.

Notes

1.   *Cantar de ciegos* (Mexico: Joaquín Mortiz, 1964); *Zona sagrada* (Mexico: Siglo XXI Editores, 1967); *Cambio de piel* (Mexico: Joaquín Mortiz,

1967). All citations to *Cambio de piel* are to this edition, with my own translations.

2. Daniel de Guzmán, *Carlos Fuentes* (New York: Twayne Publishers, 1972), p. 85.

3. Reproduced in my appendix to *The Archetypes of Carlos Fuentes: From Witch to Androgyne* (Hamden, Conn.: Shoestring Press, 1980).

4. Andrés Avellaneda, "Función de la complejidad en *Cambio de piel* de Carlos Fuentes," *Norte*, 10, no. 2 (March–April 1969), p. 27.

5. Gloria Durán, *La magia y las brujas en la obra de Carlos Fuentes* (Mexico: UNAM Press, 1976); Durán, *The Archetypes of Carlos Fuentes*, see index.

6. C. G. Jung, *Archetypes and the Collective Unconscious* (New York: Pantheon, 1959), p. 37.

7. Here, the reader will note that, although in the dwarf's words he was "repairing" the dolls, it is evident that the verb should not be understood in the sense of "making normal," but rather of creating an ideal, which in Herr Urs' case was a doll with hermaphroditic characteristics.

8. Mircea Eliade, *Mephistopheles and the Androgyne* (New York: Sheed and Ward, 1965), pp. 103–111.

9. C. Fuentes, "La situación del escritor en América Latina," *Mundo Nuevo*, 1 (July 1966): 15.

10. *Zona sagrada*, p. 124.

11. Ibid., p. 153.

12. Lanin Gyurko, "The Pseudo-liberated Woman in Fuentes' *Zona sagrada*," *Journal of Spanish Studies: Twentieth Century*, 3 (1975): 40.

13. *Zona sagrada*, p. 103.

14. Northrop Frye, *Anatomy of Criticism* (New York: Atheneum, 1969), p. 149.

15. *Zona sagrada*, p. 122.

16. Ibid., p. 103.

Merlin H. Forster

Carlos Fuentes as Dramatist

The contribution of Carlos Fuentes to the development of a "new" prose fiction in Spanish America is unquestioned. Other essays in this volume deal with the steady succession of novels and short stories which began with *Los días enmascarados* (1954) and *La región más transparente* (1958), a production which is enhanced by several volumes of critical essays on the "new novel" and other literary topics. Given the centrality of prose fiction in Fuentes' creative and critical work, the appearance in 1970 of two plays raises some interesting questions. Why should Fuentes choose to experiment with the drama after long and successful use of the narrative? Are there some dimensions of dramatic form, for example, which serve his purposes at times better than narration? How well do his two plays function as plays, keeping in mind the peculiar nature of drama? In short, what conclusions can be drawn about Carlos Fuentes as dramatist?

Todos los gatos son pardos (Mexico: Siglo XXI, 1970), accompanied by an author's prologue, has gone through at least six printings in the same editorial house. A somewhat changed version of the play, with an expanded prologue, is included in *Los reinos originarios: Teatro hispanomexicano* (Barcelona: Barral Editores, 1971). To the best of my information, the play has never been staged, but it has attracted critical attention, particularly for its historical and mythological contexts.[1] The other piece is *El tuerto es rey* (Mexico: Joaquín Mortiz, 1970), which also has an author's prologue and is included with the same prologue and virtually unchanged text in *Los reinos originarios*. This second play has had little critical commentary,[2] but in contrast to *Todos los gatos son pardos* it has been presented on stage at least once. The premiere performance was in Vienna on May 25, 1970, in French and with the title *Le Bourne est roi*.[3]

Todos los gatos son pardos is dedicated in the Siglo XXI editions to Arthur Miller and his wife, and Fuentes indicates in his prologue that Miller's interest in the conflict between Montezuma, a man with everything, and Hernán Cortés, a man with nothing, gave initial impetus for the writing of the play. The prologue makes clear that the play attempts to verbalize and reduce to three essential characters the historical process of the conquest: "Power and the word. Montezuma or the power of fate; Cortés or the power of the will. Spanning the two banks of power, a bridge: the interpreter, Marina, who through words converts the history of both powers into destiny" (p. 6).[4] In the Barral version of the play, Fuentes extends his prologue to deal more completely with the myths and figures of the Aztec pantheon, and then suggests that the post-conquest history of Mexico is a continued search for a problematic identity, "a newly-extended search between necessity and liberty: more than concepts, living signs of a destiny which at once was resolved in the meeting of pure fate and pure chance. Fateful for the Indian. Uncertain for the Spaniard" (p. 15).

Fuentes carries these ideas into the action of the play by pitting forces against each other in such a way that the three primary figures are portrayed in depth against a background of secondary figures and events which give a sense of time and place. The play is constructed in nine scenes, the first eight of which oscillate between Montezuma's court and Cortés' forces, with Marina as a bridge between two opposing worlds. The ninth scene portrays each of the major figures in turn, and is used to express, in sharp relief, a final relationship between them. Events and circumstances are chosen for their impact on the central figures rather than for their historical veracity or importance. In short, as Usigli did at an earlier time, Fuentes expresses a dramatic rendering of historical events by a selection of detail and a focusing of conflict and tension.

The central conflict of the play is summarized in the principal figures. Montezuma, for example, is portrayed as a troubled and insecure king, who is beset by apocalyptic visions of an end to his reign and who is pulled in many directions by contradictory divine and human counsel. In the Siglo XXI version of the play, Fuentes surrounds Montezuma with choruses of soothsayers and counselors, while in the Barral version much of that is omitted and the monarch's sense of decline seems much more obsessive and elliptical. In both versions, Montezuma is pressured by circumstances which he cannot fully comprehend, and he reaches the end of his life, in chains and about to be stoned by his own people in Tenochtitlán, still questioning his own actions: "Gods, gods, why did you abandon me? . . . I tried to serve the two divine principles: Huizilopochtli, by sacrificing; Quetzalcoatl, by honoring his prophesied return. Gods:

do not the obsidian knife nor the copal smoke satisfy you now? Gods, gods, did I by chance betray you? By chance did I not understand what you told me?" (p. 162).

Hernán Cortés is portrayed at the opposite end of the spectrum from Montezuma. He is decisive, active, and able to impose his will on others around him. Fuentes puts in the character of Cortés a clear vision of the New World as a place of unlimited opportunity:

> Now, we have a goal on earth: the New World. This is our heaven and at times our hell also. This is our place beyond. Here we can be lords. Here there is no limit to our imagination, will, and fortune. We have found a very real and tangible paradise, which before was only a distant illusion. This is the truth, Father, and if you deny it you have not understood the men whose souls you claim to care for. (pp. 105–106)

In the final scene of the play, however, we see Cortés stripped of all of his rights in the conquered territory, and while waiting for another audience in the royal court in Madrid he reflects ironically on his own fallen state: "Cortés, victim of two forces: the defeated and the victorious. Marina . . . Marina . . . I lost your land . . . and I didn't win my own. . . . Cortés, the god who came from the east, as Montezuma's predictions announced . . . Montezuma, my blind twin . . . Montezuma, all-powerful lord, look at your conqueror, look at him . . ." (p. 185).

Marina serves as a linguistic, cultural, and physical link between the two opposing worlds in which she lives, and in Fuentes' presentation is the only one of the three principal characters who really senses the importance of the events in which they are all taking part. Marina is at first only the object of Cortés' sexual desire, but after a time they develop genuine affection for each other. Marina also grows in her understanding of Cortés and his possibilities for effecting change, and in one impassioned speech asks him to try to understand the world which he is bent on destroying: "Oh, sir, try to understand us, give us a chance, don't blot out our dreams from the earth with your sword, don't destroy our fragile identity. Take what has been built here and build at our side; let us learn from your world, you learn from ours!" (p. 153). In the ninth scene of the play she gives birth to Cortés' child and in a long monologue reflects on the impossibility of the understanding that she had once sought and recognizes that this child of mixed ancestry is the beginning point of a changed world: ". . . you should be the plumed serpent, the land with wings, the bird of clay, the bastard and bastardized son of Mex-

ico and Spain. You are my only inheritance, the inheritance of Ma-
lintzin, the goddess, of Marina, the whore, of Malinche, the mother
. . ." (p. 175).

The sense of transformation across extended time is very much
apparent in the ninth scene of the Siglo XXI version of the play,
which in its three circles enclosing Montezuma, Marina, and Cortés
can be seen as a microcosm of the entire play. After Cortés' final
speech the stage is filled again by the principals and the supporting
actors, who now take recognizable roles from contemporary life:
workers, police and soldiers, businessmen, generals, beggars, etc.
Montezuma appears in a black suit wearing the presidential sash,
Cortés is dressed as a general in the United States Army, Marina is a
cabaret hatcheck girl. All begin to take final bows when the youth
who was sacrificed earlier in a ceremony at Cholula, now a university student, runs on stage and is shot by the police and the soldiers.
Marina leans down to comfort the dying youth, and at that instant
multiple spotlights focus on a point in the audience where Quetzalcoatl has appeared. On stage there is a rain of dead *zopilotes*, which
was one of the signs in which Montezuma read his own decline and
fall.

The Barral version extends this scene somewhat. In a reversal of
the popular tradition in which characters unmask themselves to
make a final speech, each character puts on a new mask, represented
not only by a change of costume but by the wearing of dark glasses
as well, and makes a final ironic comment. Cihuacoatl, one of Montezuma's attendants, now in the costume of a blind beggar, observes
the following: "And remember that in the evening all cats look
grey." The entire modernized cast then responds: "Don't look me in
the eyes, because the sun is very strong in America" (p. 126). This
final scene, particularly in its extended version, makes clear Fuentes' desire to apply the lessons of this play to modern-day exploitation and repression.

What additional comments can be made on the possibilities of
Todos los gatos son pardos as theater? In the first place, I feel that
this work is more powerful in dramatic form than it would be as a
novel. Fuentes as playwright is able to focus our attention more
sharply on a central conflict and on individual personalities who are
instrumental in developing that conflict. Moreover, he uses to advantage the on-stage present time and the visual impact of theatrical
technique to underscore dimensions of character. For example, in
the final scene Cortés keeps his back to the audience as attention is
focused first on Montezuma and Marina, and only when the light
falls on him and he turns to speak do we see him as an old man,

removed from Mexico and in perpetual waiting before the king for a further hearing of his case. Such a situation could be described in a novel, but it would be difficult to communicate the character's changed circumstance with the same impact. On the negative side, the large number of characters and the extension of some of the scenes, particularly the battle scenes, would be difficult to handle in conventional staging. The massacre in the temple of Cholula, for example, could probably not be done in the ·matter-of-fact way in which Fuentes gives stage directions: "The captains brand the women, the stage is an inferno of blood, screams, cries, screeches, bodies, destruction . . ." (p. 151). If the play were actually being staged, I suspect that some kind of multimedia presentation of sound and projected image would be needed to supplement the on-stage action. The same would be true, I am sure, for the portion of scene 9 where the playwright asks that the Aztec and Spanish forces engage in hand-to-hand combat, as a symbolic representation of the battle for Tenochtitlán: "a pitiless battle, man to man, in the aisles, ramps, orchestra seats, etc." (p. 164). Perhaps Fuentes was thinking more of cinematographic technique in some of the rather grandiose demands he would place on theatrical space. Also the hand of the novelist seems evident in the more than occasional use of extremely long soliloquies or monologues, particularly for the principal characters. Especially in the Siglo XXI version of the play these are often interrupted by a series of pauses, indicated as such in the stage directions, which might or might not have corresponding dramatic effect for the audience. Much would depend on the capacity of the individual actor and his or her capacity to maintain interest in a sustained monologue presentation.

Let us turn now to Fuentes' other text, *El tuerto es rey*. This piece presents a number of interesting contrasts with *Todos los gatos son pardos*. Rather than moving across historical time with clearly defined characters, *El tuerto es rey* is confined in space and time and uses two characters who in turn are doubled or multiplied in their roles and relationships. The play is organized in two acts and is set in a room furnished with what was at one time rather elegant period furniture, now somewhat the worse for wear. Donata and Duque, both apparently blind but without realizing the limitation of the other person, wait for the expected return of the Señor, who has been away from home for almost a week on a business or perhaps even a gambling trip. Donata is the Señora and Duque is the servant of the house, but from the very beginning of the play there is an insistent suggestion of games and the playing of roles:

DONATA: It's useless, Duque. We'll never be able to agree. Be-
      sides, I'm tired now.
DUQUE: My lady is ignorant of the roots.
DONATA: The house is too long and time is too short to play
      the tower game.

(*The Duque doubts, begs the audience.*)

DUQUE: Shall we play at taking care of each other?
DONATA: That's another unending argument. And you're a
      cheat. (p. 21)

As the play progresses, the relationship shifts and each character
takes on different roles: brother, sister, lover, spouse, and at times
even animals, moving on all fours to consume food and drink from
dishes placed on the floor. There is constant reference to the absent
husband and to Marina (a possible connection to *Todos los gatos son
pardos?*), with whom Duque has maintained an intimate relationship. The metamorphoses and multiplicity of levels within the characters are such that one begins to wonder if the blindness of Donata
and Duque, expressed in actions on stage and ultimately in the text
itself, is simply one more of the various roles that the characters
play in an endless series of puzzling games. One case in point is a
scene in the second act in which Donata sits down with a stack of
newspapers and begins to clip articles from them, reading to Duque
as she goes along with no limitation from her supposed blindness.
The final change of roles comes when the Señor returns, on Sunday
as he had indicated, and we realize that he is Duque in a different
guise. He comes in in a rush, calling for Duque and Marina and com-
plaining about the disorder of the room. At that point he is accosted
by a group of Guerrillas who enter suddenly from both the audience
and off stage and is shot when he is unable to justify his presence in
his own house.

As a counterpoint to the constant metamorphoses of Donata
and Duque, which result in the violent death on stage of Duque-
Señor, there is a parallel metamorphosis on a strictly animal level
which becomes part of the often confusing mechanisms of the play.
At several points in the early sequences the howling of a wolf is
heard, along with repeated rattlesnake sounds. Later, Duque matter-
of-factly takes a dead wolf out of the wardrobe and begins to eviscer-
ate it with a kitchen knife. Even later in the action whinings and
howlings and rattlesnake sounds are again heard. The final detail in
the sequence, which is also connected with the final metamorphosis

of Duque, is to be found in the stage directions for the entry of the Guerrillas:

> *From the rear of the theater, from the sides and the ward-robe, and through the door, five bearded Guerrillas come toward the Duque, armed with machine guns, wearing camouflaged campaign uniforms, similar to snakeskin. The commander of the group is also wrapped in a wolf skin. They surround the Duque.* (p. 126)

There are several other real or imagined objects which because of their frequent appearance are important for characterization in the play. For example, early in the play imaginary letters are opened and referred to, and the rustle of the supposed envelope and letter is made part of the sound effects at certain moments. Newspapers are used effectively as a part of the physical setting, are wadded up and burned in one scene of the play, and become the means of the communicative exchange between Donata and Duque already mentioned. The items extracted from the newspapers by Donata, however, turn out to be articles written at the time of Maximilian and Carlota and raise the possibility of still other roles for the central characters. All mirrors in the house have been destroyed at Donata's insistence, but at one point Duque produces a stone which has the qualities of a mirror and in which he sees the essence of Donata:

> DUQUE: My lady doesn't recognize her image . . . and yet it is the most certain of all . . . it is the image of open stone . . . the agate mirror . . . the opaque mirror . . . pink and blue . . . gray and violet . . . the indestructible mirror, because its quicksilver is the dead water embedded in the heart of the stone. (p. 79)

In general, props, lighting, and stage effects are well handled. Most effective, I think, is the use of street noises to support several scenes, and, in particular, one in which Donata threatens to abandon Duque in the midst of a terrifying press of city traffic. The one exception is one of the final scenes in which the playwright gives stage directions for a masculine figure outlined in dust to appear on the bed in the room, apparently as a symbol of the fragility of human form. Duque says, as it appears: "Don't touch it, my lady. Your breath alone is enough to return this total fragility to the air and the earth from which it came" (p. 122). I can see the symbolic possibilities of this figure in the literary sense, but I am not at all certain how such a thing would be carried off in a stage presentation. The playwright's directions ask for Donata to hold the "brazo de polvo" in her open hands, and Duque is to take the other "brazo" in one hand and find his way off stage. The sudden appearance of this phantasmagoric figure and its dismemberment by the two characters could be handled perhaps if one had the variety of angles and close-up capability of cinema technique, but in a stage production some additional device would be necessary to convey in visual terms the dimensionality of the image.

As quoted by Fuentes in his prologue, Octavio Paz sees in *El tuerto es rey* an over-arching theological unity: "Donata and the servant are projections, children of the Lord, making it possible to view the totality . . . as a new version of the Fall" (p. 9). I do not find sufficient internal logic in the play to make that idea convincing, and would prefer to view it as an only partially successful illustration of the devices and the studied pointlessness of absurdist theater.

To come back explicitly to the questions posed at the beginning of this discussion, I would conclude that Carlos Fuentes is not a dramatist-novelist to the same extent as is Vicente Leñero, to suggest a contemporary Mexican comparison, nor does he achieve the substantial interconnections between the two genres which one can see in writers such as Thornton Wilder or Jean Giraudoux. Fuentes' two plays, now ten years old, reveal an awareness of the unique possibilities of dramatic form and considerable skill in taking advantage of them, but at the same time they represent a brief experimentation which was not sustained and which was only partially subjected to the ultimate test of production. As far as the plays themselves are concerned I arrive at a curious conclusion: the play which has never been staged is better theater, I think, than the one which has been produced.

Notes

An earlier version of this article was read as a paper at the Kentucky Foreign Language Conference, April 25, 1980, at the University of Kentucky.

1. James Stais, "*Todos los gatos son pardos*: un acto de rebelión en nueve escenas," in *Homenaje a Carlos Fuentes*, ed. Helmy F. Giacomán (New York: Las Américas, 1971), pp. 465–471; Gary Brower, "Fuentes de Fuentes: Paz y las raíces de *Todos los gatos son pardos*," *Latin American Theatre Review*, 5, no. 1 (Fall 1971): 59–68; Joseph A. Chrzanowski, "Consideraciones temáticas-estéticas en torno a *Todos los gatos son pardos*," *Latin American Theatre Review*, 9, no. 1 (Fall 1975): 11–17; Lanin A. Gyurko, "Vindication of La Malinche in Fuentes'

Todos los gatos son pardos," *Ibero-Americanisches Archiv,* 3 (1977): 233–266; Eduardo Peñuela Cañizal, "Myth and Language in a Play by Carlos Fuentes," *Latin American Theatre Review,* 13, no. 1 (Fall 1979): 15–27.

2. The only criticism I have been able to find is Louis H. Quackenbush's commentary on the connections between the play and the scriptural Adam and Eve account, set out in his short article "La desavenencia religiosa: una clave a *El tuerto es rey* de Carlos Fuentes," *Explicación de Textos Literarios,* 4 (1975–76): 83–86.

3. Brief information on this initial performance, together with a series of related photographs, can be found on p. 17 and between p. 82 and p. 83 of the 1970 Joaquín Mortiz edition. Mario Serenellini also includes an interview with Fuentes on the European premiere in his article "Il teatro latinoamericano," *Sipiario* (Milan, Italy), 292–293 (August–September 1970): 32–45.

4. Page references for citations from the plays and their prologues will be indicated in the text.

Manuel Durán

Carlos Fuentes as an Art Critic

How does a writer become interested in art? The reasons may be varied and complex. In the case of Fuentes I believe it was a case of avocation (as an adolescent he toyed for a while with the idea of becoming a cartoonist) and the influences of time and place. Mexico has been for many centuries a land where the visual arts have been honored and cultivated extensively. During his formative years Fuentes grew up in a Mexico where painting, architecture, and the cinema were more active, important, and celebrated than literature: they were the years when newspapers discussed continually the latest accomplishment, or the latest polemic, involving Diego Rivera, José Clemente Orozco, David Alfaro Siqueiros, and a dozen other prominent Mexican artists. Pablo Neruda has remarked in his *Memoirs* that at the beginning of the forties Mexico's intellectual life was dominated by painting.[1] Moreover, Fuentes was possibly—probably is a better word—influenced by the example of his friend and mentor, Octavio Paz, who has devoted many hours and numerous written pages to the study of art, whether the art of ancient and modern India, Mexican art, or the art of the Surrealist movement. Such powerful siren calls could not be long resisted by a writer whose imagination is primarily visual.

From painting to poetry—or rather to short story and novel—is a road often travelled by our author: as has been noted by Gloria Durán,

> the source of inspiration, as well as the expression of it, seems to be frequently related to the visual arts. We are told by Emir Rodríguez-Monegal that it was Alberto Gironella's parodic painting of the Spanish Hapsburg court, a caricature of Velázquez, that helped generate the historic setting for *Terra Nostra*. Another painting, the version by José Luis Cuevas of Van

Eyck's "Marriage of the Arnolfini," may also have inspired the more metaphysical aspect of the novel. In his discussion of this work, Fuentes foreshadows his approach to *Terra Nostra* by observing: "Times and spaces of characters and spectators penetrate each other; so do identities." This interaction between painting and viewer becomes a prominent motif in *Terra Nostra*, where the painting from Orvieto almost takes on the role of a character (much like the photo in Julio Cortázar's "Las babas del diablo"), shaping the action and in turn being shaped by it.[2]

Obviously the attraction of art, the charm of the visual approach, has become for Fuentes so strong that occasionally he is bound to rebel against it, looking for an antidote elsewhere, without fully succeeding in finding it but at least stating consciously the need for a balancing counterweight.[3] Thus in his short story "Fortuna lo que ha querido," part of *Cantar de ciegos*, a painter who is not unlike Cuevas states,

> For six centuries now we have been using our eyes to paint. Everything is optics. Do you realize what a limitation that is? Line, color, shaping, perspective, shade. Or else geometry, impression, form. Everything visual. As if we did not have other organs. I am furious at myself, I swear. It took me eleven years to find out. From Giotto to Mondrian, they are all fucked-up: they all try to use their eyes. Painting is no more than a seeing-eye dog. And Oedipus only understood when he became blind, is it not so? With his eyes wide open he did not understand anything.[4]

The same short story offers a capsule about art history, aesthetics, and finally the creation, both problematical and promising, of a new art school, a new trend, "pop art." Everything happens with dazzling speed. First the theory and the historic insights: the painter talks and paints at the same time:

> The painting was crowded with night lights: a forest of advertisements over the dark buildings—I know it doesn't work, don't look at me like that. Wait. First one must conceal what will be revealed at the end. How long did it take people to realize that Cézanne's cones and spheres were actually pears and apples? How long did it take to realize that Suerat's dots were a beach and Monet's lights a railroad station? I have to

paint it first like this in order to get rid of all these false glories later: memories, time, premonitions. I must get rid of all that. . . . In my earliest paintings I tried to say that among us a sacred art was still possible. All my figures were the representation of our dark side, of the hidden and sacramental essences that were still a facet of our being. . . . But it was a lie. . . . Art can be sacred only when Nature is dangerous. It needs a Heaven and a Hell, an extreme option outside this earth. . . . But neither our earth nor man are sacred any longer. *This* is sacred: this final profanation . . . the negation of sacredness. What *they* consume. Alejandro pointed towards the finished painting. It was the perfect reproduction of a jar of instant coffee. A glass jar with its cover and a red label and the letters NESTLÉ INSTANT COFFEE WITHOUT CAFFEINE, MADE IN OCOTLÁN, JAL. TRADE MARK REG.[5]

A few pages later in the story, Fuentes gives us a lesson in art history and art criticism when he compares two painters, a modern French artist, Delaunay, and a great classic, Rembrandt. The lesson is so concise and condensed that the reader may not understand it. Fuentes writes: "Alejandro leafed through the pages of the Delaunay book and concluded that it was pure light, no subject: the end period of Rembrandt."[6] The reader will, in all probability, miss the connection. Robert Delaunay (1885–1941) is a minor French painter who bridges the gap between the primitive Rousseau and the first Cubists; in his better-known canvasses light plays an essential role, not the light of the Impressionists but the light of exploding Cubist planes. How can Fuentes link him with Rembrandt?

The answer is simple. In many of the last paintings by Rembrandt the light seems to come from within the figures, almost supernaturally illuminating their faces and garments. This is "the end period of Rembrandt," and as for Delaunay, the transition between the primitivism of Rousseau and the new techniques of Cubism (let us not forget the influence of Fauvism and their worship of pure color) creates a somewhat similar effect: planes, pure color, exploding surfaces, absence of shadow, all tend to produce the overall impression that light has taken over; subjects no longer matter except as a pretext to produce lighted surfaces. It can be argued, of course, that Rembrandt's psychological and spiritual insights were impossible to duplicate in Delaunay's time. The fact is that Fuentes has given us an original and powerful insight and has established a continuity in art history that no academic art historian can match.

A comparison between a contemporary painter and a great master of the Baroque period is also the main subject of the pages devoted to the Mexican artist Alberto Gironella in *Tiempo mexicano*. The framework for these pages is an approach to past and present Spanish culture; myth and reality, art and history, are fused in Fuentes' analysis, his capsule version of Spanish history:

> Poor, worn out Spain: a rocket of incense and silver flying across the skies, it gave its light to the whole world and fell down, burned out, on a barren plateau, an age-old garden devastated by the mystical guilt of a king who loved death. Don Quixote locked himself up in the Escorial and was devoured there by pus and worms. And Don Juan, finally tamed, posed with his wife and his moronic children for the portrait which Goya painted: Charles IV and his family. Power without greatness. "What does this old decrepit ghost want?"[7]

Let us point out that the last sentence in this quotation comes straight from Goya; it is a caption Goya wrote for one of his *Caprichos*. It should also be obvious that the whole quotation is close to being a "dress rehearsal" for *Terra Nostra*, with its mixture of history and fantasy, fake history, X-ray history, invented footnotes to historic facts, and factual characters who become symbols. After this paragraph Fuentes is in the proper frame of mind to discuss the art of Alberto Gironella, and more specifically the series of canvasses in which Gironella both imitates and degrades the great canvasses by Velázquez. Fuentes' imagination is swift, biting, almost too quick to understand and savor as we go on reading. First we see Gironella walking along the Castellana and entering the Prado Museum. Right after this Fuentes tells us that Gironella's Velázquez is also Ortega y Gasset's Velázquez, the first painter to liberate painting from the influence of sculpture and to try to paint pure light. Immediately afterwards he adds that Gironella's Velázquez is also Velázquez as interpreted by Foucault, a structuralist Velázquez who is assumed by Foucault (at the very beginning of *Les Mots et les choses*) to be endowed with a *royal outlook*, since we see the whole painting of the *Ladies in Waiting* from the very viewpoint, the same angle of vision, of the King and Queen, whose spectral profiles are reflected in a mirror in the background of Velázquez's canvas. (Here readers cannot enjoy fully Fuentes' analysis unless they have also read the brilliant pages in which Foucault compares Velázquez and Cervantes; the constant transposition of visual images and abstract ideas which is Foucault's trademark is also a technique employed by Fuentes time and time again.)

The second cultural allusion follows fast on the tracks of the first; Fuentes points out that Gironella's interpretation of Velázquez reminds him of Buñuel's films: "a Buñuel-like Velázquez, who has as much to say about the model posing for him as about the character which the model is supposed to represent."[8] (Here, of course, the reader will not enjoy Fuentes' capsule interpretation and description unless he or she has read Ortega's celebrated essay, "Tres cuadros del vino," published first as a newspaper article and later included in his *El Espectador*, and has also seen one of Buñuel's most important films, *Viridiana*, in which a group of beggars around a table suddenly appear to organize their bodies and their expressions much like the Apostles and Jesus in Leonardo da Vinci's *Last Supper*.)

Buñuel's film sequence is above all grotesque, bordering on the obscene. (A "snapshot" supposed to "freeze" the actors in the da Vinci positions is provided by an actress lifting her skirt.) The elements of the grotesque, the obscene, and the satanic are constants in Fuentes' novels and short stories. Yet the main thrust of his interpretation of Gironella's paintings is neither grotesque nor sublime; rather Fuentes tries to establish a link between different interpretations of "the real world." He pointed out that in the great canvasses which Velázquez painted, everybody is playing a role in which they are themselves and at the same time someone else—all the world is a stage. Vulcan, Mars, the Virgin, are at the same time a common blacksmith, a stable boy, a kitchen maid. This is something that Velázquez makes clear in his art. His dwarfs and court jesters are treated by Velázquez with the same respect deserved by his king: the same costumes and attitudes, because the artist is underlining the essential impotence of power. Yet Velázquez is still too close to Titian and the idealization of Renaissance art for his message to be crystal-clear; it takes a modern artist, Gironella, to reveal the weakness and corruption beneath the polished masks of courtly fashion. Velázquez does it in too subtle a way: by paying as much attention, Fuentes points out, to the dwarfs and the morons. They are not idle ornaments of the Hapsburg court, they are basically interchangeable with the monarchs, as the future (the reigns of Charles II, the sickly moronic Hapsburg, and Charles IV, the cuckolded, weak-willed Bourbon) will clearly show. By using Buñuel and Gironella to probe into Velázquez's canvasses, Fuentes underlines that beneath the beauty and polish artistically enhancing Velázquez's court portraits there is a negative undertow, the ebb of Spanish glory, that Velázquez has deftly incorporated into his royal portraits. Gironella is no longer, as most of us thought, intent upon creating the negative grotesque equivalent of Velázquez; he is simply letting us know what

Velázquez intended to show us, but could only hint at in an indirect way. Once more the parallel between two artists far away from each other in time and space yields unexpected rewards.

There are, of course, many other insights into the world of art scattered through the pages of Fuentes' essays and novels. In "Radiografía de una década (1953–1963)" he points out that during that period the so-called Mexican School of Painting—Orozco, Rivera, and Siqueiros—goes bankrupt because its followers are chauvinist copycats incapable of going one step beyond the message of their elders; only Rufino Tamayo in art, and Paz, Yáñez, and Rulfo in literature, can become a bridge to the future.[9] What is essential, what I want to emphasize, is that the literary vision of Fuentes includes three kinds of images. There are the murky, mysterious images of the subconscious: the world as seen through a "third eye." There are also brightly colored images of Fuentes' moral insight: a clarion call to battle. There is, however, another vision: the clear, aesthetic eye, the focus on beauty, order, symmetry, and on the powers of darkness inasmuch as they are needed to balance the forces of light and order. Fuentes needs every angle, every lens: the moral approach, the aesthetic vision, the dark lenses of the unconscious. Only when all images are put together, superimposed by our eye (the reader's vision, the only one that can compete with the author's presentation) will the whole panorama become meaningful.

Notes

1. See Pablo Neruda, *Memoirs*, trans. Hardie St. Martin (New York: Farrar, Strauss & Giroux, 1977), chap. 7, "Mexico, Blossoming and Thorny," esp. pp. 153 ff.

2. Gloria Durán, *The Archetypes of Carlos Fuentes: From Witch to Androgyne* (Hamden, Conn.: Shoestring Press, 1980), p. 181. It is a well-known fact that the friendship between Fuentes and Cuevas has been a mutual influence. Cuevas has become more and more "literary" in his paintings; Fuentes as a writer has become increasingly sensitive to visual values.

3. This observation is also based upon the previously quoted study. Fuentes is the most Hegelian of our modern writers, since he is always looking for a synthesis (the radical thought plus the aesthetic vision) that seems to elude him—and us.

4. Carlos Fuentes, "Fortuna lo que ha querido," *Cantar de ciegos* (Mexico: Joaquín Mortiz, 1964), p. 59. It is my opinion that Fuentes is a better writer of short stories and essays than a creator of novels. Given the lowly status accorded to the short story in our publishing world, and the limited audience for the essay as a literary genre, it seems obvious that

on the whole Fuentes will go on being discussed primarily as a novelist. Only future generations may change this viewpoint.

5. Ibid., pp. 61–62. The tension between the sacred and the profane elements in history and in everyday life is perhaps the only constant in the works of Fuentes. Even when the sacred elements are absent we feel their absence as a void, as a wound.

6. Ibid., p. 56. It is a curious fact that Fuentes, who is fond of long descriptions, is very brief when dealing with artistic or intellectual definitions, so much so that the reader is sometimes at a loss to interpret his message.

7. Carlos Fuentes, *Tiempo mexicano* (Mexico: Joaquín Mortiz, 1971), p. 52. This is perhaps the best book of Fuentes' essays so far, and his ideas about Mexican history in its pages clearly sketch *Terra Nostra*. In other words, it should be required reading for *aficionados* of *Terra Nostra*.

8. Ibid., p. 83.

9. Ibid., p. 84.

George Gordon Wing

Some Remarks on the Literary Criticism of Carlos Fuentes

This study begins with some observations on the state of contemporary literary criticism in general. Then, more specifically, in order to place the literary criticism of Carlos Fuentes in its proper perspective, I have attempted to describe some features of the dominant trend of criticism in the United States—a trend that belies an apparent heterogeneity—for this description will throw into sharp relief the basic differences between this type of criticism and that of Fuentes. I have also addressed the problem of Fuentes' ambivalence—certain discrepancies between his theoretical speculations on the novel, on the one hand, and his novelistic practice, on the other, discrepancies that give a peculiar direction to his critical work. Finally, I have examined in some detail Fuentes' provocative analysis of *Moby Dick*, a critical piece of work that is not only typical of his best efforts but also typical of the tradition that nourishes him.

The question of whether or not the creative writer is capable of first-rate literary criticism—an issue that has provoked some heated debate in the United States[1]—has not yet arisen in Spanish America. If we are to believe the complaints of its writers, this is because serious and organized criticism scarcely exists in Spanish America.[2] This situation, however, does encourage the creative writer to try his hand at criticism without the defensive attitude that characterizes so many of his counterparts in the United States. On the other hand, these same writers, Fuentes included, admire and even envy *our* critical establishment, and since they already have, in my opinion, one foot in this promised land, a word or two is in order about what Randall Jarrell has called our "Age of Criticism,"[3] for it may well represent the image of Spanish America's immediate future. Imagine, if you can, a vast and ramifying institution shored up by the academicians, the professionals, of whom Stanley Edgar Hyman has boasted, "He [the critic] is alone, on the authority of his own knowledge, taste and intelligence, the sole guardian of art and its magic portals."[4] Naturally enough, it is the creative writers themselves who have challenged this pretension to absolute critical authority. In fact, it was Randall Jarrell who coined the term "Age of Criticism" as a protest against what he took to be a dehumanized scientism, going so far as to claim that the creative writer, since he is the only one who really knows what a work of literature really is, can be the only competent judge of literary value. As for those critics who argue irrationally for and practice elegantly the absolute autonomy of criticism—Northrop Frye is an excellent example—the most devastating denunciations of this fallacy have been made, not by creative writers, but rather by traditional critics such as René Wellek.[5] Finally, the academic establishment as a whole has come under attack from within, by the younger critics of the so-called "dissenting academy," political leftists for the most part, who object to a criticism without any real social relevance, although the influence of this group seems to have melted away with the passing of the 1960s.[6] Actually, this movement represented, on the one hand, a last-ditch defense against a dehumanizing scientism in literary criticism, and on the other, a protest against an anti-ideological stance in politics they recognized as an ideological justification of the status quo. Since developments in contemporary criticism and politics are closely related, I shall return to this question later when I discuss what has come to be known as the "anti-ideology debate."

In spite of internal bickering, however, most establishment critics display an inordinate sensitivity when they believe imaginative critics to be poaching on their preserves. In their disparagement of the writer as critic, moreover, they have found allies where least expected. W. H. Auden, for instance, himself a brilliant literary essayist as well as a poet, has affirmed that "critical opinions of a writer should always be taken with a large grain of salt. For the most part they are manifestations of his debate with himself as to what he should do and what he should avoid."[7] Auden's point of view, common enough among creative writers, has far-reaching implications. It rests on the assumption that the subjectiveness, bias, passion, and self-interest of the writer—his defense of his own work—necessarily dispose him to judgments which, because they are supposedly nonobjective and partial, are incorrect. It also assumes the existence of a hierarchy of professional critics, who, possessing none of these so-called "defects," systematically grind out "correct" and "definitive" readings of literary texts.[8] The truth is, of course, that among full-time critics there are competent men, and even a few who are brilliant. At any rate, there does not exist, nor will there ever, a single universally accepted critical method. As R. P. Blackmur has put

it, "Any rational approach is valid to literature and may be properly
called critical which fastens at any point upon the work itself."[9]

Since this paper deals with Fuentes' criticism of fiction, my
point is that there are novelists who not only speak with authority
on the theory and practice of fiction, but who also provide us with
both acute and subtle analyses of particular works and trends. Carlos Fuentes, however, might seem to agree at times with Auden that
the creative writer can at best be an amateur critic. In a fairly recent
interview, at least, he has declared somewhat modestly that "it is
very difficult for me to talk about technique because I am not conscious of it. If I were . . . , I'd be a literary critic."[10] Nevertheless, in
spite of this disclaimer, Fuentes has produced a large body of provocative critical essays which, if rarely criticism in the academic sense,
do contain some extremely perceptive readings of both classics and
contemporaries. A representative sampling of these essays is to be
found in two collections published as *La nueva novela hispanoamericana* (1969) and *Casa con dos puertas* (1970).[11]

Rather than do a systematic analysis of this criticism, which
ranges from Jane Austen through William Styron, I have chosen to
comment on Fuentes' evaluations of other novelists as a by-product,
in part at least, of his own novelistic theory and practice. Although
in his criticism Fuentes frequently pays lip service to exponents of a
great many recent critical theories, in practice he more often than
not uses his own version of a Marxist historical and sociological approach that at times shades off into the sort of philosophical criticism we usually associate with Sartre.[12] That this approach has the
defects of its virtues goes without saying, but surely the reverse is
true. And even though, from an academic point of view, the "charge"
that might be leveled against him is that he continually uses literary
criticism as a springboard for social and political commentary, if
there did exist in Spanish an anthology analogous to that published
by Miriam Allott, *Novelists on the Novel*,[13] Fuentes would certainly
figure prominently in it. What I mean is that Fuentes' commentaries
on the nature and craft of fiction would indeed, as Allott has said of
the discussions by the novelists she has anthologized, "contribute to
a recognized 'working' aesthetic of the novel." This is especially true
of Fuentes' observations on the problems of the contemporary novel
in general and of the Spanish American novel in particular. In short,
if, as Allott claims, "Only the practitioner can speak with the final
authority about the problems of his art," then we need only take
"his" to refer to an individual novelist to realize that her statement
is a useful truism.[14] Furthermore, as W. J. Harvey has reminded us,
"it is obviously true that the critical remarks of James, Conrad, E. M.

Forster, D. H. Lawrence, Edith Wharton, Virginia Woolf and many others must have had an immense influence on modern critical attitudes to the novel."[15]

As for Fuentes, he has always tended to see the problems of the Spanish American novelist, even the formal and technical ones, against the background of deeper problems stemming from "the situation of the novelist in Spanish America."[16] As early as 1962, Fuentes had set down in broad outline what he saw as the principal task of the novelists of his generation (not only Spanish American novelists)—how to go beyond the realistic or naturalistic thesis novel, which for him no longer had any validity, while at the same time resisting the undeniable attractions of art for art's sake. It seems to me, however, that Fuentes in practice has been unwilling to abandon "realism," for his principal concern as a novelist has always been the representation of reality. At any rate, in 1966, we find him couching the problem of "what to do?" in terms that are essentially those of a "realist." We Latin American novelists, he says,

> live in countries where everything remains to be said, but also where the way to say all of this has to be discovered. The immediate reality of Latin America offers us the themes that Balzac and Dreiser have dealt with, but our problem is how to take up those themes again in order to draw a parallel between them (*paralelizarlos*), let us say, to give them their present-day relevance, their national relevance for our readers, for our community, and at the same time, to lay bare that deeper background (*trasfondo*), that second reality, or to create that parallel reality that might give them their universal meaning.[17]

By the time the foregoing was published Fuentes had already coined a term, "symbolic realism," to which he keeps returning in order to define his own novelistic practice. One of the points he wants to make is that the central task of discovering the profound or latent reality behind the world of appearances can only be carried out by the invention of new and adequate techniques. Fuentes defined a symbol, which he sharply contrasted with allegory, as "a reference to something that is in doubt, something that must be sought out actively. It is an attempt to tell the truth."[18] Admittedly, the concept of "symbolic realism" is much too imprecise to do more than serve as a signpost for an extended journey through Fuentes' novelistic production. Nevertheless, we might think of it as a kind of crude compass by means of which he tries to chart a course between his own private Scylla and Charybdis, allegory and photographic real-

ism, both of which seem, strangely enough, to hold for him an attraction inversely proportionate to his vehement rejection of them
as valid novelistic forms in our time.

What I should like to stress, however, is the central importance
of this concept, "symbolic realism," for Fuentes the *critic*. Modified,
expanded, and adapted to meet his needs for the discussion of any
particular work, "symbolic realism" has become the touchstone for
Fuentes' evaluation and explication of the novels of others. It must
be emphasized, however, that "symbolic realism" is not to be understood abstractly, since for Fuentes the problem of the novel is obviously the problem of man in relation to history and society. It
would not be too much to say that Fuentes would agree with the David Daiches who once affirmed

> dogmatically that that critical approach is most useful which
> involves relating the art of fiction at any given time to the civi-
> lization of which it is a part, and endeavoring to see all other
> questions of form, technique, style, and subject matter against
> the background of this relationship, while remaining aware
> that this may not appear a self-evident truth to all and that to
> those to whom it does not so appear it would be impossible to
> prove.[19]

Furthermore, it requires little or no imagination to see that
Daiches' position expressed here could serve, with little or no
change in content, as a general working program for most "committed" novelists, among whom Fuentes has always counted himself. I should like, then, to elaborate somewhat on my observation
that Fuentes' criticism bears a strong resemblance to that of Sartre,
who is not only a committed writer and critic *par excellence*, but
who is more than anyone else responsible for the wide dissemina-
tion of the concept "commitment" (*engagement*). It will be instruc-
tive, first of all, to look at the well known dictum of Sartre which
appears in his essay on Faulkner's *The Sound and the Fury*: "A fictional technique always relates back to the novelist's metaphysics,
and the critic's task is to define the latter before evaluating the former."[20] My point is that in this essay, as in so much of his critical
writing, Sartre comes up with a definition of the author's "metaphysics" in which philosophy becomes indistinguishable from or
subordinate to social and political "ideology." A good example in
Fuentes of this sort of criticism appears in his "Cortázar: la caja de
Pandora," in *La nueva novela hispanoamericana*, an essay which he
begins with the affirmation that *Rayuela* is a Latin American novel

precisely because "it participates in a magical atmosphere of an in-complete pilgrimage."[21] Although Fuentes does explore the general metaphysical significance of the pilgrimage or unending quest, in the course of his essay philosophical commentary cannot be di-vorced from the historical (already present in the statement just quoted), social, psychological, and moral dimensions of the novel—all of these elements, of course, related to what he considers pri-marily aesthetic.

There are, in fact, a great many similarities between Fuentes' *La nueva novela hispanoamericana* and Sartre's *What Is Literature?*, not the least of which is a broad-ranging eclecticism and a readiness to transform political and social partisanship into literary judg-ments. I should like to stress, however, the fact that Sartre's work is unquestionably a masterpiece of rhetoric (persuasion), a political as well as a literary polemic in the best sense of the word.[22] And so too is *La nueva novela* of Fuentes, although one could scarcely claim for it the same degree of influence as *What Is Literature?*. The point I should like to make, however, is that Sartre's book bears witness to the fact that in France, however technical literary criticism might be, individual practitioners of the different schools engage willingly in public debate on a level that is more philosophical and political than strictly literary—that is, underlying assumptions are laid bare and argued often more heatedly than the literary and critical ap-proaches seen as deriving from them.[23]

In the United States, on the other hand, critics have increasingly come to isolate and focus upon technique and structure to the ex-clusion of their social origins and function. Perhaps it is a truism to say that you may banish history and politics from literary criticism, but history and politics have a way of going on behind our backs, whether we will or not. As Kenneth Rexroth has put it, "literature generally, but literary criticism in particular, has always been an area in which social forces assume symbolic guise, and work out—or at least exemplify—conflicts taking place in the contemporary, or rather, usually, the just-past wider areas of society."[24] The crux of the matter has to do with the different nature of left-wing and right-wing ideologies. David Caute's statement, for example, that "right-wing ideology tends to be implicit, masked, and refracted when it is conservative" is particularly appropriate when applied to present-day literary criticism in the United States.[25] It should be obvious, in the first place, that criticism here, even that produced by men who outwardly proclaim themselves political liberals, has been moving steadily toward the right. Not only does this movement parallel closely the drift of American society at large, but it may also be taken as a kind of literary equivalent of a type of right-wing politics whose mask of neutrality or pretense at apoliticality is even more insidious than the position of an expressed reactionary. Perhaps the best example of this new conservatism is to be found in the so-called "end-of-ideology" debate that took place in the sixties and early seventies.

To put it as briefly as possible, the right-wing position (including the self-proclaimed liberal one) in the end-of-ideology debate involves two basic premises. The first states that modern industrial society (or to use the term that seems to be so much in vogue, "post-industrial" society) is characterized by the absence of ideological politics and that contemporary crises are due merely to underplanning. The second premise is a positive value judgment: "We've reached, or at least are well on our way to reaching 'the good society,' and ideology can only serve to hinder the progress we are making."[26] One would have to be particularly obtuse not to realize that this anti-ideological stance is itself an ideology. The new concept of "planning" in politics and economics, according to this way of thought, would necessarily be limited to dealing pragmatically and in a piecemeal fashion with problems (naturally, always partial) as they arise. This approach to the problems of society exalts the role of the expert, the engineer, the technocrat—bureaucrats of the soul whose antiintellectual practicality and apoliticality are in essence a defense of the status quo. The dominant trend in American literary criticism, too, is an analogous neopositivism in which "professionalism," generally involving the fetishistic loyalty of the individual critic to his own "scientific" method, is now the rule.[27] This type of criticism, too, goes hand in hand, implicitly or explicitly, with a defense of the political status quo, and as for the critical exercises themselves, more often than not they come to resemble impersonal treatises on engineering that have the decided effect of dehumanizing the literary works being analyzed.

I refer as a case in point to the enthusiastic and often uncritical reception of French structuralism by American critics, scholars, and graduate students of literature during the past few decades. Leaving aside for the moment the question of the intrinsic value of some of the original models, what seems to attract their imitators is the aura of science or pseudoscience that envelops these imported products. It is no accident, then, that we are now confronted with an enormous quantity of mediocre literary analyses that depend on the mechanical application of methods which reveal structures (real or imaginary) in the works being examined, and which often leave out what is most important to an understanding of their specific literary values and techniques, not to mention their social function. One of the American scholars most bedazzled by structuralism, Robert Scholes, whose *Structuralism in Literature* is in some ways a valuable introduction to the subject despite his obvious biases, reveals clearly and frankly attitudes that many other American structuralists hold unconsciously. To begin with, Scholes states not quite accurately that the major French structuralists have insisted that structuralism is an activity or a method, not an ideology. Scholes, however, unlike most American structuralists, insists that any method implies an ideology and that "it is precisely the ideology of structuralism that we need most desperately today." Although reasons of space prevent me from examining all of his conclusions concerning the role of structuralism as a panacea for the ills of modern man, let me say that the banality, superficiality, and ingenuousness of these conclusions are unsurpassed. But when Scholes states specifically what he believes to be the political importance of structuralism, the cat is out of the bag. "The great failures of our government in recent years," he claims, "have been failures of imagination. What we need in all areas of life is more sensitive and vigorous feedback." [28] From whom to whom? This particular defense of the status quo, of course, is nothing more than a revival of the fallacy that the government is actually, or should be, left to the managers and technocrats whose decisions would necessarily be, since they are "scientific," for the good of all. The belief that the problems of a capitalistic society can be solved without taking into account class and property relations as they shape and are shaped by history is quite simply unrealistic. This is the sort of thought that produces in both literary criticism and "ideology" what Hegel once called "a ballet of bloodless categories."

Scholes belongs to a generation of American critics for whom "the leftist squabbles of the past were pointless and immature." [29] Fuentes, on the other hand, belongs to a generation of Spanish American writers for whom Marxism provides the very climate of intellectual discussion. Fuentes himself, a prolific essayist, has produced a sizable body of work that is essentially a Marxist interpretation of the most varied social and political phenomena. Most of this work, widely scattered in magazines, reviews, and newspaper supplements, is still uncollected. Some of his best essays dealing with contemporary Mexico, however, have been published as *Tiempo mexicano* (1971), a book that deservedly became a best-seller.[30] By reason of his militant Marxism alone, Fuentes the literary critic would certainly be considered by those critics in the dominant American tradition as an interesting "essayist" at best, or at worst as an anachronistic amateur.

I have already suggested that Fuentes' debate with himself as a practicing novelist has, on the one hand, centered around his struggle against the temptations of allegory and naïve realism. On another level, the debate springs from his attempts to reconcile the ideal of the autonomy of art with his recognition of the necessity of the writer's commitment. Although it is Marxism, naturally enough, that provides the touchstone for the elements of this quarrel with himself, in what follows I shall not be concerned with delineating what is specifically Marxist. To begin with, then, Fuentes the theorist of the novel has of late been insisting that the novel is nothing but a verbal construct, or that "the novel *is* myth, language, and structure."[31] His emphasis on the novel as verbal structure may, of course, be a healthy reaction against the anachronistic language of a great deal of Spanish American literature of the immediate past. It may also involve an attempt by the novelist to reverse the trend that has resulted in the universal debasement of language in our time. But when Fuentes stridently proclaims the present impossibility of realism itself, is he merely echoing the death-of-the-novel dirge that others have been chanting for so long, or is he guilty of a failure of nerve? Is it true, as he would have it, that the exploration of personal and social relations—the traditional matter of the novel—has now been completely usurped by the social sciences and the visual mass media? It frequently sounds as if Fuentes were formulating a theory of the novel as an almost completely self-reflexive form. But this attitude must somehow be made to square with his statement that the problem of the novelist today consists of finding a way to construct a new "literary reality" that will project a true image of our technological society, a feat that, according to him, depends on the capacity of the novelist to express the myths and prophecies of an age about which men are yet radically ignorant.[32]

To discuss the theoretical ramifications of the apparent radical skepticism of Fuentes would take me beyond the scope of this paper. Nevertheless, what needs emphasizing is that Fuentes' notion of the novelist as mythmaker and prophet leaves the door open for the infiltration into his fictional world of all of the elements he has theoretically banished—psychology, sociology, and ideology. In a world characterized by the bankruptcy of all traditional values, moreover, the introduction into the novel of conventional methods of interpretation and representation may be used to accentuate the very inadequacy of these methods. Fuentes, at least, believes that he has

invited them to the banquet, not to wine and dine them, but rather
to poison them off. He has admitted, for example, of *Cambio de piel*
(1967) that

> all the traditional psychological elements are in the novel, but
> they are there to be destroyed. I've had so many fucking, god-
> damned Mexican and Latin American readers say, "The novel
> was very good until this point—when you had a magnificently
> traditional novel and suddenly you destroyed yourself." I say
> this is the whole point of the novel.[33]

One might read Fuentes' observations on *Cambio de piel* as the
expression of what seems to be the plight of the committed writer in
our time. Apparently, in order to subvert the established order, it is
no longer sufficient or even possible to mirror reality directly. As
Michel Zéraffa has said of the great novelists of the twentieth century, by which he means those who have condemned social reality
as fatal to man himself, their "protest would have remained a dead
letter if these novelists had not expressed this offense against society by means of forms themselves offensive to the established order and official culture."[34] This line of reasoning underlies Fuentes'
admiration for contemporary North American novelists, for he believes that both he and they exemplify the characteristics extolled
by Zéraffa, and as we shall see, this admiration has influenced his
criticism. What Irving Howe considers, then, in a sense, as the de-
fect of the recent American novel, Fuentes would, with reservations,
see as its principal virtue. According to Howe,

> these novels have in common a certain obliqueness of ap-
> proach. They do not represent directly the postwar American
> experience, yet refer to it constantly. They tell us little about
> the surface tone, the manners, the social patterns of recent
> American life, yet are constantly projecting moral criticism of
> its essential quality. They approach that experience on the sly,
> yet are colored and shaped by it throughout. And they gain
> from it their true subject: the recurrent search—in America,
> almost a national obsession—for personal identity and free-
> dom. In their distance from fixed categories and their concern
> with the metaphysical implications of that distance these nov-
> els constitute what I would call "post-modern" fiction.[35]

Anyone acquainted with the most important novels of Fuentes' first
period, *La región más transparente* (1958), *La muerte de Artemio*

Cruz (1962), and *Cambio de piel* (1967), is aware that he *has combined* the obliqueness of approach described by Howe with the direct representation of the surface tone, the manners and morals of postwar Mexico. And this obliqueness of approach in the novels of Fuentes has always involved the mythification of real elements of modern life.

Now, of the three primary elements that, according to Fuentes, make up today's novel—myth, language, and structure—it is undoubtedly myth, together with prophecy, which is *de facto* the most important for his criticism. While myth and prophecy are indeed formal elements in a novel, they may also be considered part of the "content" in a way that language and structure are not, and "content," as David Caute has said, "always refers to the world (material, mental, associative or whatever) *outside* the work of art mediated and reshaped by form."[36] At any rate, in Fuentes' criticism the use of myth and prophecy is one of his principal devices for relating the form of the novel to the social context in which it is produced and received.

Since, for reasons of space, I have opted to close this essay with the consideration of a single piece of Fuentes' criticism, it is perhaps fitting that it should be "La novela como símbolo: Herman Melville."[37] It is a brilliant analysis of *Moby Dick* in terms of its profound meanings, and it is typical enough to give us a good idea of Fuentes' general approach to both classics and contemporaries. To begin with, Fuentes takes great pains to show that Melville's novel is not an allegory but rather a symbolic epic. It is, he says, an open work of art with a plurality of meanings that are inexhaustible— hence its radical modernity. The plurality of meanings (*significados*) coexist in a single signifier, the novel itself, and the symbol is the link between the unity of the work itself and the truth of the outside world it seeks to capture.

Fuentes asks himself, then, what is *Moby Dick*? If some of his answers are necessarily commonplaces, others, on which he elaborates in the essay, are based on highly original insights. The novel is a great sea adventure, a great factual account of the whaling industry, and a great hymn to nature and to the dignity of man. But, as Fuentes says, it is also an epic of democracy and at the same time a theology of the diabolic. Above all, the novel is prophecy that time itself has borne out. The prophecy and the myth are based on Melville's deep probings into the spiritual and political texture of the United States. Melville stripped off the mask of innocence and complacent optimism to disclose overweening pride, evil, and transgression. *Moby Dick* is a dialectical narrative of the demands of fraternity at war with the demands of self-reliance.

Although Fuentes examines all of the major characters, it is Ahab, of course, to whom he devotes most of his attention. As a Puritan, Ahab feels compelled to carry on the work of God; and as a Manichean, he feels compelled either to redeem or destroy all of the nonelect—the others. And since he is a romantic, he puts forth a subjective ideal as a universal value. His gnosticism convinces him that he is right. Furthermore, as a Puritan, he has come into the world with a strong sense of sin. Therefore, he must either assume his guilt, thereby affirming a sense of solidarity with his fellow men, or he must rationalize innocence by denying his guilt. Isolated by his pride that makes of him a solipsist, in his messianic pursuit of the white whale, he is able to enlist others under his banner by contaminating them with his terrible desire for vengeance. They pursue an illusion, however, for the target of Ahab's wrath, the white whale, is merely the projection of his self-hatred on "the other." *Hubris*, a perverted extreme of self-reliance, leads him and his followers to destruction. Pride and self-righteousness are solipsism's twins, and since the others do not exist except as creations of his mind, he has the right to dispose of their lives and deaths.

As I have indicated, Fuentes gives us a Melville who is not only a subverter of the established order but also a prophet whose prognostications gain validity in our own time. Melville could not accept the idea of the United States held by his fellow countrymen—God's chosen people, a nation that had never experienced defeat and felt itself heir to the future. Melville had a vision, Fuentes says, of the excesses to which all of these certainties could lead: to the imposition of false ends and private fetishes; to the sacrifice of the collective good on the altar of an abstract freedom of the individual; to the simplistic division of history into a Manichean struggle between the good—the United States—and the evil—those who oppose the United States; to manifest destiny; to "the lonely crowd," inorganic atomism; to the confusion between private opinion and general truth; to the radical lack of comprehension of the truth of others whenever it does not correspond to the particular vision of things held by a North American: as a consequence, the truth of others is suspect and must be destroyed. Indeed, Fuentes concludes, in our time, Captain Ahab still lives, and his name is MacArthur and Dulles, Joe McCarthy and Johnson; the white whale is in Cuba, in China, in Vietnam, in Santo Domingo, in a film, in a book. . . .

I have said that Fuentes deals with the major characters of the novel, all of whom are presented, too, as embodying specific traits of American society and of the human condition as well. In his discussion of Peleg and Bildad, for example, Fuentes makes some shrewd comments on the pernicious absurdities of a proselytizing Puritanism that has persisted on many levels of contemporary American life. As for Starbuck, Fuentes draws attention to him as an example of the insufficiency of goodness when it must rely on a pragmatism lacking all organic content. Lest it be thought, however, that Fuentes ignores all but the dark side of American life as it appears in *Moby Dick*, let me conclude with his judgment on the social role of Ishmael and with a few related matters. For Fuentes, Ishmael embodies, above all, the dignity of man in his work. He willingly accepts his destiny (that of a common sailor) and his dignity resides in his free choice of a destiny that is, paradoxically, determined. Conscious at the same time of his material alienation and his spiritual freedom, Ishmael finds a solution to his problem in human solidarity. Fuentes, furthermore, asserts that Melville has written a prose epic, which unlike its classical counterparts, does not exalt martial, ethical, or political virtues. Since it is an industrial epic, naturally it celebrates the domination of nature by technology or technique (*la técnica*). In this new world, nobility (*areté*) is not the birthright of a social hierarchy, but rather it has its origins in the fraternity of men and races of diverse origins. According to Fuentes, Melville implies that nobility is also a quality that is bestowed automatically on captains of industry, explorers, hunters, and other exemplary men of action. Finally, though, Fuentes reminds us that, in spite of Melville's praise of democracy, the novel makes us acutely aware of the fact that Captain Ahab is surrounded and accompanied by a "democratic" world, a microcosm of society at large. For all of its virtues, however, Melville seems to be saying, it can't stand up to Ahab, and its members allow themselves to be led to destruction.

In this essay, I have of necessity treated a complex subject in a somewhat fragmentary and incomplete fashion. Nevertheless, I hope to have awakened some interest in pursuing further any of the topics I have deliberately left truncated. I trust, too, that I have demonstrated Fuentes' strength as a critic—not only a sharpened sensitivity to literary values as such, but also an imagination that never flags in the task of relating these values in a meaningful way to man and society. Fuentes, a voracious reader, is a person who loves and lives the great works of literature with an intensity that breaks down the walls of contemporary specialization and "professionalism."[38]

Notes

1. See, for example, an excellent discussion of the problem by René Wellek, "The Poet as Critic, the Critic as Poet, the Poet Critic," *Discriminations: Further Concepts of Criticism* (New Haven and London: Yale University Press, 1971), pp. 253–274.

2. Octavio Paz, "Sobre la crítica," *Corriente alterna* (Mexico: Siglo XXI Editores, 1967), pp. 39–44. This is a clear if impassioned analysis of a deplorable situation which ideally should be a symbiotic one between imaginative writers and critics.

3. Randall Jarrell, "The Age of Criticism," *Poetry and the Age* (New York: Vintage Books, 1959), pp. 63–86.

4. Stanley Edgar Hyman, *The Armed Vision: A Study in the Methods of Modern Literary Criticism* (New York: Knopf, 1948), p. 407.

5. Wellek, "The Poet as Critic," pp. 257–258.

6. Theodore Roszak, ed., *The Dissenting Academy* (New York: Vintage Books, 1968). See also Frederick Crews, *Out of My System: Psychoanalysis, Ideology, and Critical Method* (New York: Oxford University Press, 1975).

7. W. H. Auden, *The Dyer's Hand and Other Essays* (New York: Vintage Books, 1968), pp. 9–10.

8. Walter J. Ong, "The Knowledge Explosion in the Humanities," *In the Human Grain: Further Explorations of Contemporary Culture* (New York: Macmillan, 1967), pp. 41–51. Ong realizes that the growth of "knowledge" in the humanities is not without its drawbacks.

9. R. P. Blackmur, "A Critic's Job of Work," *Form and Value in Modern Poetry* (Garden City, N.Y.: Doubleday Anchor Books, 1957), p. 346.

10. Carlos Fuentes in Herman P. Doezema, "An Interview with Carlos Fuentes," *Modern Fiction Studies*, 18, no. 4 (Winter 1972/73): 494.

11. Carlos Fuentes, *La nueva novela hispanoamericana* (Mexico: Joaquín Mortiz, 1969) and *Casa con dos puertas* (Mexico: Joaquín Mortiz, 1970).

12. A very valuable bibliography of Fuentes' own work and of the criticism of it by others is Richard Reeve's "An Annotated Bibliography on Carlos Fuentes: 1949–1969," *Hispania*, 53 (October 1970): 595–652.

13. Miriam Allott, *Novelists on the Novel* (New York: Columbia University Press, 1966).

14. Ibid., p. xv.

15. W. J. Harvey, *Character and the Novel* (Ithaca, N.Y.: Cornell University Press, 1968), p. 195.

16. See, for example, Carlos Fuentes, "Situación del escritor en América Latina," *Mundo Nuevo*, no. 1 (July 1966): 5–21. This is an interview or dialogue with Emir Rodríguez Monegal.

17. Ibid., p. 17.

18. Fuentes elaborates on this and other aspects of his work in interviews with Carballo: Emmanuel Carballo, *El cuento mexicano del siglo XX* (Mexico: Empresas Editoriales, 1964), pp. 78–79; and Emmanuel Car-

ballo, *Diecinueve protagonistas de la literatura mexicana del siglo XX* (Mexico: Empresas Editoriales, 1965), pp. 429–430.

19. David Daiches, *The Novel and the Modern World* (Chicago: University of Chicago Press, 1939), p. 211.

20. Jean Paul Sartre, "On *The Sound and the Fury*," *Literary Essays*, trans. Annette Michelson (New York: Philosophical Library, 1957), pp. 79–87.

21. Fuentes, *Nueva novela*, p. 67.

22. Jean Paul Sartre, *What Is Literature?*, trans. Bernard Frechtman (New York: Philosophical Library, 1949).

23. Although not strictly literary, I mention the running debate between Sartre and Lévi-Strauss as an excellent example of the importance attached to philosophy and ideology as well as to its implications for literary criticism.

24. Kenneth Rexroth, "Disengagement: The Art of the Beat Generation," *New World Writing*, no. 11 (New York: Mentor Books, 1957): 28.

25. David Caute, *The Illusion: An Essay on Politics, Theatre and the Novel* (New York: Harper Colophon Books, 1972), p. 53.

26. Chaim I. Waxman, ed., *The End of Ideology Debate* (New York: Clarion Books, 1969), p. 5.

27. See Erich Kahler, *The Tower and the Abyss: An Inquiry into the Transformation of Modern Man* (New York: Compass Books, 1967). Kahler calls attention to the fact that we now have a huge corpus of institutionalized knowledge in all of the sciences which no single scientist can grasp. "It is a truism," says Kahler, "that many scientists do not even know what goes on in their neighboring field." Kahler calls this huge corpus a "collective consciousness." Knowledge is there, all right, but no one individual or small group is capable of either understanding or using it, even though it is rational. It seems to me that not only the humanities in general but also literary criticism are now faced with the same situation.

28. Robert Scholes, *Structuralism in Literature: An Introduction* (New Haven and London: Yale University Press, 1974), pp. 197–200.

29. Crews, *Out of My System*, p. 116.

30. Carlos Fuentes, *Tiempo mexicano* (Mexico: Joaquín Mortiz, 1972).

31. See, for example, *Nueva novela*, p. 20.

32. See, for example, *Nueva novela*, "Situación del escritor," and much of his novelistic criticism in *Casa con dos puertas*.

33. Doezema, "An Interview," p. 497.

34. Michel Zéraffa, *Roman et société* (Paris: Presses Universitaires de France, 1971), p. 33.

35. Irving Howe, "Mass Society and Post-Modern Fiction," in *The American Novel since World War II*, ed. Marcus Klein (New York: Fawcett Premier Book, 1969). Howe's article has been reprinted numerous times.

36. Caute, *The Illusion*, p. 151.

37. Fuentes, *Casa con dos puertas*, pp. 34–51.

38. I need only mention in closing a work of Fuentes the title of which might mislead the reader into believing that it is a work of literary criticism, *Cervantes o la crítica de la lectura* (Mexico: Joaquín Mortiz, 1976). At the risk of oversimplification, I should merely say that it is an interesting exercise in cultural history.

Chronology

1928	Born in Mexico City on November 11.
1933–1946	Residence and early education in Washington, D.C., Santiago de Chile, Río de Janeiro, Buenos Aires, Montevideo, Quito, and Mexico City.
1950–1951	Studied international law at Institut des Hautes Etudes Internationales in Geneva, after having earned a Bachelor of Law degree at the Universidad Nacional Autónoma de México.
1950–1952	Member of Mexican delegation to the International Labor Organization, Geneva. Secretary of Mexican Delegation to International Law Commission of United Nations. Cultural attaché to Mexican Embassy in Switzerland.
1954	Assistant Head of Press Section, Ministry of Foreign Affairs, Mexico. Publication of first book, *Los días enmascarados* (stories).
1955	Co-founded (with Emmanuel Carballo) the *Revista Mexicana de Literatura*. Editor until 1958.
1955–1956	Assistant Director of Cultural Dissemination, Universidad Nacional Autónoma de México.
1957–1959	Head of Department of Cultural Relations, Ministry of Foreign Affairs, Mexico.
1958	Publication of first novel, *La región más transparente*.
1959	Publication of *Las buenas conciencias* (novel).
1959–1961	Co-editor of *El Espectador*.
1960	Editor of *Siempre*. Editor of *Política*.
1962	Publication of *La muerte de Artemio Cruz* (novel). Publication of *Aura* (novel).
1964	Publication of *Cantar de ciegos* (stories).

1967	Publication of *Zona sagrada* (novel). Publication of *Cambio de piel* (novel).
1968	Publication of *París: la revolución de mayo* (essay).
1969	Publication of *La nueva novela hispanoamericana* (criticism). Publication of *Cumpleaños* (novel).
1970	Publication of *El tuerto es rey* (drama). Publication of *Todos los gatos son pardos* (drama). Publication of *Casa con dos puertas* (essays).
1971	Publication of *Tiempo mexicano* (essays).
1974	Fellow at Woodrow Wilson International Center for Scholars, Washington, D.C.
1975	Publication of *Terra Nostra* (novel).
1975–1977	Ambassador to France.
1976	Publication of *Cervantes o la crítica de la lectura* (essay).
1977	Norman Maccoll Lecturer, Cambridge University. Virginia Gildersleeve Professor, Barnard College.
1978	Henry L. Tinker Lecturer, Columbia University. Adjunct Professor of English, University of Pennsylvania. Publication of *La cabeza de la hidra* (novel).
1980	Visiting Professor at Princeton University. Publication of *Una familia lejana* (novel).
1981	Visiting Professor at Dartmouth College. Publication of *Agua quemada* (stories).

Notes on Contributors

Jaime Alazraki is Professor of Hispanic American Literature at Harvard University. He is the author of books on Pablo Neruda and on Jorge Luis Borges, as well as numerous articles and reviews on varied topics.

John S. Brushwood is Roberts Professor of Latin American Literature at the University of Kansas and the author of numerous studies of fiction in Latin America and of Mexican literature in general. His best known books are *Mexico in Its Novel* and *The Spanish American Novel: A Twentieth Century Survey*. A new book experimenting with different critical approaches to the nineteenth-century novel, *Genteel Barbarism*, appeared recently.

Frank Dauster has taught at Wesleyan and Rutgers, where he is presently Professor of Spanish. He is the author of *Breve historia de la poesía mexicana*; *Ensayos sobre poesía mexicana*; *Historia del teatro hispanoamericano, siglos XIX–XX*; *Xavier Villaurrutia*; and *Ensayos sobre teatro hispanoamericano*; and he has co-edited five anthologies.

Mary E. Davis is Assistant Dean of the College of Arts and Sciences and Associate Professor of Modern Languages at the University of Oklahoma. Her most recent research treats Fuentes' use of mythic and movie analogues in *The Hydra Head*, and she is investigating the presence of William Faulkner in the prose of Mario Vargas Llosa.

Gloria Durán teaches at the University of Connecticut in Waterbury. She has published two books on Carlos Fuentes, including *The Archetypes of Carlos Fuentes: From Witch to Androgyne*.

Manuel Durán is Professor of Spanish and Chairman of the Department of Spanish and Portuguese at Yale University. He has published several books and many articles dealing with Mexican literature.

More than one third of his book of essays, *Tríptico mexicano*, is devoted to Fuentes.

Malva E. Filer is Associate Professor at Brooklyn College of the City University of New York. She is the author of *Los mundos de Julio Cortázar*, and has published articles on Mallea, Cortázar, Vargas Llosa, Di Benedetto, and other Spanish American writers.

Merlin H. Forster is Professor of Spanish and Portuguese and departmental chair at the University of Texas at Austin. He formerly taught at the University of Illinois, Urbana-Champaign. His research interests include twentieth-century Latin American poetry and drama, and the history of avant-garde literature in Latin America.

Roberto González Echevarría, Professor of Spanish at Yale University, has published *Calderón y la crítica: historia y antología*, *Alejo Carpentier: The Pilgrim at Home*, and *Relecturas: ensayos de literatura cubana*, as well as many articles and reviews on Spanish Golden Age literature and contemporary Latin American literature. He is a member of the editorial boards of *Diacritics* and *Revista Iberoamericana*.

Lanin A. Gyurko is Professor of Spanish at the University of Arizona. He has published essays on Fuentes, Rulfo, Sainz, Borges, and Cortázar in such journals as *Hispania*, *Hispanic Review*, *Kentucky Romance Quarterly*, *Revista Hispánica Moderna*, *Romanic Review*, *Symposium*, *Texas Studies in Literature and Language*, and many others. He is currently writing a book-length study on the narrative art of Carlos Fuentes.

Luis Leal, who was born in Mexico, retired in 1976 from the University of Illinois and since then has been Visiting Professor at the University of California in Santa Barbara. He has published several books, among them *Mariano Azuela: vida y obra*, *Historia del cuento hispanoamericano*, and *Breve historia de la literatura hispanoamericana*.

Margaret Sayers Peden is Middlebush Professor of Romance Languages at the University of Missouri, Columbia, and a former chairman of that department. Author of *Emilio Carballido*, she is translator of works by Carlos Fuentes, Pablo Neruda, Octavio Paz, Horacio Quiroga, Emilio Carballido, Egon Wolff, and others. She has published numerous critical articles on the Spanish American theater, novel, and short story. She serves on the editorial board of the *Latin*

American Theatre Review, the advisory board of *Translation Review*, and the advisory board of the American Literary Translator's Association.

Richard M. Reeve is Professor of Spanish at U.C.L.A. His research focuses mainly on Mexican fiction, but he has also published (in collaboration with Gerardo Luzuriaga) *Los clásicos del teatro hispanoamericano*. He has served on the editorial boards of numerous journals and encyclopedias. An up-dated hardcover version of his annotated bibliography of Carlos Fuentes is forthcoming.

George Gordon Wing, presently Associate Professor of Spanish at the University of Texas at Austin, has taught previously at the University of California at Berkeley. He has written on Octavio Paz, César Vallejo, and on varied topics treating Hispanic literature, particularly Mexican literature.